DEFEATING THE BROTHERHOOD OF DEATH

DAVID J. DIONISI

TEACH PEACE FOUNDATION

U.S.A • Canada • Japan • Korea • UK

The pages that follow unveil closely guarded secrets of the mystery of iniquity. A key message of this book is a supernatural solution to defeat the kingdom of Satan exists. This book explains the Fatima peace solution. I wish to thank the many courageous people who helped the world know the Fatima truth.

The front and back cover is a drawing of Christ returning and defeating Satan and his kingdom. On the front cover, the ground battle is fought by the faithful. A key leader in raising awareness of Our Lady's solution for victory, Fr. Nicholas Gruner, is shown leading an Army of Fatima warriors. Fr. Gruner had read this book and shared with the author that he was impressed and wanted to meet him. The author traveled from California to Massachusetts on April 29, 2015 to meet Fr. Gruner. Unfortunately, the meeting never occurred because Fr. Gruner died of a heart attack on April 29, 2015.

Defeating the Brotherhood of Death is the product of research in Belgium, Canada, Egypt, England, Ethiopia, France, Gaza, Germany, Ghana, Indonesia, Israel, Italy, Japan, Kazakhstan, Liberia, Luxembourg, Qatar, Philippines, Russia, Singapore, South Korea, Switzerland, the United Arab Emirates, and the United States. Concepts in this book are further explained in the five Vigilant Christian books which expose various dimensions of the Brotherhood of Death.[1]

Order this book online at http://www.teachpeacefoundation.org or call 1 530 554 7061 (USA & Canada).

www.teachpeace.com
North America & International
contact@teachpeace.com

Dedicated

to

Our Lord Jesus Christ

King of the World

and

of every Nation and State.

Contents

1

UNIVERSAL DECEIT

"In a time of universal deceit - telling the truth is a revolutionary act."[2] Eric Arthur Blair

The information in this book will be difficult for many people to believe because we live in a time of universal deceit. God tells us not to hate the speaker of the truth.[3] If we are the person being attacked with lies, God says to rejoice when persecuted for the reward in heaven is great.[4]

Mysterious forces in the service of Satan are planning to cap the Great Pyramid of Giza.[5]

Many people are deceived to think Satan does not exist. The kingdom of Satan is at war with Christ and His people. This book offers proof of this and solutions to defeat evil.[6]

Satan's Guaranteed Defeat

Thank God for the Fatima message. Satan knows that when the requests of the Blessed Virgin are fulfilled, his kingdom on earth will be defeated. God knew Satan would do everything in his power to influence people to suppress the Fatima message. While the world would be a better place if people knew the truth, the suppression helps us see what Pope Paul VI called the "smoke of Satan."[7] Specifically, the suppression of the Fatima message has provided the faithful with a trail of evidence proving the smoke of Satan is in the Vatican.[8]

People deceived to think Pope Paul VI was only speaking of the 20th century are reminded of the last warning to the current Pope's electors.[9] On March 13, 2013, the conclave that selected Pope Francis was warned of the Brotherhood of Death danger explained in this book, using its ancient name of the *Mystery of Iniquity*.[10] The warning came from the 87-year-old Augustinian Maltese Prosper Grech. In a section of the meditation titled "Smoke of Satan in the Church" he said "the evil spirit of the world, the mysterium iniquitatis, constantly strives to infiltrate the Church."[11]

Jesus said "Amen, amen I say to thee, unless a man be born again, he cannot see the kingdom of God." [12] Being born again is necessary to see the truth. Christians are encouraged to remember what we pray for when we say the "Our Father." The words in the prayer "Thy kingdom come" are asking for God's kingdom to arrive. We literally pray asking God for the Fatima world changing event.[13] This point is important, as doom and gloom should not be confused with the Christian teaching to cherish each day and look to the future with joy, hope, and anticipation.

Greatest 20th Century Miracle

What we know and do not know is often the result of media reports and information taught in schools. For this reason many people are unaware of the greatest miracle in modern times. People who are aware of the 1917 Fatima miracle are sometimes unable to fully understand it because they fail to realize members of the same secret society helped create both Capitalism and Communism.

Francisco Marto, Lúcia Santos and Jacinta Marto with their mothers in 1917.[14]

Prophecy is intended to change our behavior to conform to the will of God. The Fatima miracle is officially endorsed by the Catholic Church and accurately predicted multiple important events in the 20th and 21st century. The essence of the Fatima message is that the Vatican comes under the control of Satan, the demonic forces of Satan run rampant on earth, many souls go to hell, and an Exodus cleansing event occurs.[15] The good news is Satan and his forces for evil are defeated.[16]

This book will help people deepen their understanding of the Bible. The Fatima miracle and message is for everyone. The part of Fatima message that Satan wants most to hide from us is a supernatural solution to defeat his kingdom of death is within our reach.

Every Soul is a Calvary

God clearly tells us what we should do and what happens when we fail to follow His commands. In the time of Noah people thought they were good enough and did not need to worry about the flood or hell.[17] The Fatima message highlights most people are good but not good enough to enter heaven.[18] We become good enough when we love as Jesus taught us.

A view of the Dome of the Rock through the Dominus Flevit chapel window.[19]

World events reveal that we are witnessing a reenactment of Calvary across the globe.[20] Our world has not yet been crucified but acts of evil around the globe "flog" the body of Christ. As in the days of the early Christian community, the faithful are scattered and followers are persecuted. A modern day example of persecution is religious leaders once universally respected are now often disrespected due to the enemy infiltrating their ranks with pedophiles.

The "flogging current state" is also illustrated by the evaporating Christian community. One of the great benefits of the Church established by Jesus was community. People prayed together, helped the poor together, and helped each other. In the 21st century, organizations teaching good family values and offering community benefits are often spiritually corrupting.[21] Events bringing people together ranging from the Superbowl to the Olympics are routinely littered with occult rituals and symbols. The offense to God is increasing daily and is a sign that the world is starting to ascend the heights of Calvary.

In the tenth station of the Cross Jesus was stripped of His clothing. With no material possessions as a person from Galilee, He saved the world as a universal poor man. As we approach the time of tribulation, we should expect to be stripped of wealth and possessions. Revelation 18 explains a time will come when "all fat and goodly things are perished from thee" and "in one hour are so great riches come to nought."[22]

2

MIRACLE OF FATIMA

"We would be mistaken to think that Fatima's prophetic message is complete." Pope Benedict XVI at Fatima in May 2010

On September 25, 1888, Pope Leo XIII experienced a vision of demonic forces that traumatized him to the point of physical collapse.[23] He foresaw the Vatican becoming the throne of Satan with the "iniquitous design that when the Pastor (the true Pope) has been struck, the sheep may be scattered."[24] The short version of Pope Leo XIII's prayer to St. Michael is below and was said after the Catholic Church Low Mass from 1888 to 1964.[25]

> Blessed Michael the Archangel, defend us in the hour of conflict. Be our safeguard against the wickedness and snares of the Devil. May God restrain him we humbly pray; and do thou, O Prince of the heavenly hosts, by the power of God, thrust, down to hell, Satan, and with him all the other wicked spirits who wander through the world for the ruin of souls. Amen

The April 20, 1884 encyclical of Pope Leo XIII explains secret societies serving the kingdom of Satan seek to infiltrate and destroy the Catholic Church.[26] This is noteworthy because on August 1, 1884, the world leader of Freemasonry issued his response to Pope Leo XIII's encyclical letter. In his reply, Masonic Pope Albert Pike acknowledged a state of war with the Catholic Church existed.[27]

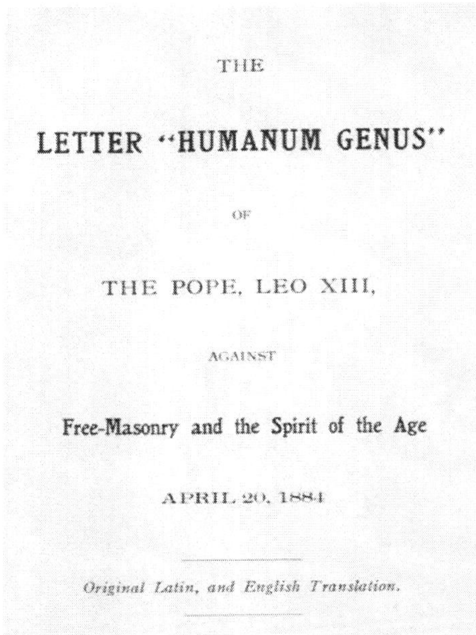

THE

LETTER "HUMANUM GENUS"

OF

THE POPE, LEO XIII,

AGAINST

Free-Masonry and the Spirit of the Age

APRIL 20, 1884

Original Latin, and English Translation.

The 1884 encyclical of Pope Leo XIII.[28]

The Brotherhood of Death or Satan's partisans for a New World Order, has existed even before the United States was created. If you open your mind, even one percent, to the possibility that a powerful one-world government organization exists, this book can change your understanding of the world that you live in.

The Ark of the Covenant

Understanding the special relationship that the Blessed Virgin has with Jesus is necessary to understand the Fatima miracle.

Mary, while not God, has special powers as the woman who bore the Divine Person, Jesus. Mary is the Queen of Heaven. Revelation 11:19 and 12:1 are among dozens of examples in the Bible that explain Mary is the Queen of Heaven.[29] The prophecy of Jeremiah explained the Ark would be replaced by the Lord's presence.[30] Mary is the Ark of the New Testament. The Tabernacle and Ark represents God's plan to intervene in human history to fix a broken creation.

An illustration of the Ark.[31]

The New Testament magnifies and clarifies the Old Testament. The following are a few examples from Luke in the New Testament that clarify the Old Testament.

New Testament	Old Testament
Luke 1:35 explains the Holy Spirit overshadowed Mary and her womb became the dwelling place of God.	Exodus 40:34-35 explains the Holy Spirit overshadowed the Ark and became the dwelling place of the presence of God.
Luke 1:35 explains the Blessed Virgin Mary contained the living Word of God, the living bread from heaven, the Branch that came back to life.	Deuteronomy 10:3-5 and Hebrews 9:4 explain the Ark contained the Commandments, a pot of manna, and Aaron's rod that came back to life.
Luke 1:39 explains Mary traveled to the hill country of Judah to rest in the house of Elizabeth.	2 Samuel 6:10-11 explains the Ark traveled to the hill country of Judah to rest in the house of Obededom.
Luke 1:41 explains John the Baptist leapt for joy in Elizabeth's womb when she heard the salutation of Mary.	2 Samuel 6:14 explains that King David danced with joy when he approached the Ark.

In the Old Testament, the Ark of the Covenant was a sacred chest which contained the stone tablets of the Ten Commandments. The Ark containing the Word of God was the holiest thing on Earth.

People often forget or do not know that the Ark could move and the poles were used both to carry and be carried. Men holding the Ark poles were led where God wanted them to go. When King Solomon offended God, the Ark of the Covenant created during Moses' lifetime left the temple. Where it went is debated.[32] To replace the missing Ark, King Solomon rebuilt an almost identical new Ark as explained by Rabbi Abraham Stone.[33]

> "The gates gave honor to the holy Ark. For, when King Solomon made the Ark, he made it 10 cubits long, and the entrance gates of the Temple Sanctuary were 10 cubits wide."[34]

When an idol, most likely gold in appearance, is put on top of a counterfeit holy of holies, this abomination of desolation event angers God, triggering a time when His patience ends.[35] The Brotherhood of Death Ark was unveiled on September 9, 2001. Earth Charter Commissioner and Chair of the Earth Charter Drafting Committee, Steven Rockefeller, helped unveil the "Ark of Hope" at Shelburne Farms, Vermont.[36]

The Ark of Hope is a 49" x 32" x 32" wooden chest created to contain the Brotherhood's Earth Charter.[37]

The King Solomon Ark and Brotherhood's Ark of Hope are counterfeits.[38] The Blessed Virgin Mary is the greater fulfillment of the Ark of the Covenant because she contained the Word of God. Mary gave birth to the Word of God as flesh.[39]

The Power of Intercession

The intercession of a king's mother is shown in the Bible to be incredibly powerful. Jesus performed His first miracle before His appointed time, turning water into wine, because of the intercession of his mother.[40] Understanding the special devotion Catholics have to Mary, not as divine but as the mother of God, is necessary to understand the Fatima miracle.

One Old Testament example of a person who understood the power of the Queen Mother is Adonias. He knew King Solomon would deny his request to marry Abisag unless Solomon's Mother interceded.[41] The influence of the Queen Mother on King Solomon was so great that Adonias observed "he cannot deny thee anything."[42] This is why King Solomon "bowed himself to her and caused a throne to be set up for her next to him."[43]

Both the Ark of the Old Covenant and Ark of the New Covenant have awesome power over Satan.[44] This miraculous or supernatural power, communicated from heaven in 1917, is a solution to defeat the Brotherhood of Death.[45]

The Events of 1915 to 1917

The Fatima miracle begins in 1915 and continues with three children in Portugal seeing the Blessed Virgin between May 13, 1917 and October 13, 1917.[46] Mary, also known as Our Lady, appeared to the children a total of six times.[47] On July 13, August 19 and September 13, the children were told that a miracle would occur at midday on October 13th "so that all may believe."[48]

Until 1917 at Fatima never in world history has a dancing of the sun event previously occurred. Only the miracle of Joshua where the sun and moon did not move for an entire day is remotely close.[49]

Thousands of people witnessing the Fatima miracle.[50]

The dialogue between the Blessed Virgin and the children is in Appendix D. A detailed listing of related key Fatima events is in Appendix E.

Jacinta Marto, Lucia dos Santos and Francisco Marto.[51]

Many people believed the children and witnessed the Fatima Miracle of the Sun on October 13, 1917.[52] Dr. Joseph Garrett, professor of natural sciences at the University of Coimbra, was present and estimated approximately 100,000 people witnessed the miracle. While the exact number of people witnessing the miracle may be closer to 70,000, the key point is many people witnessed the miracle which lasted approximately ten minutes.

People witnessing the Fatima miracle. [53]

Thousands of people reported that after a period of rain, the dark clouds broke and the sun appeared as a spinning disc in the sky. The sun danced in the sky and previously wet clothes became completely dry. The muddy ground that had been previously soaked was suddenly dry. The Blessed Virgin told the three children that millions of souls would be saved by the solemn public Consecration of Russia to Her Immaculate Heart by the Pope and all the Catholic bishops of the world. The Blessed Virgin also instructed the people to practice a new devotion on the first Saturday of five consecutive months.[54]

O MILAGRE DE FÁTIMA

Newspaper report with pictures showing people looking at the Sun during the October 13, 1917 apparitions.[55]

The Message Parts

The Fatima message is often called the "Secret" or "solution for global peace." Since 1930 the Catholic Church has officially endorsed the Fatima message as a vital prophecy. The message is incorporated into the life of the Catholic Church with May 13th as the Feast of Our Lady of Fatima.

Parts of the prophecy are published. Details of the secret part have been shared, but the exact text is not published. For this reason the unpublished portion is called the Third Secret or the

Fourth Secret.[56] The reason both of these names are used is in 2006 the general public learned that in 2000 the Vatican did not fully publish the complete Third Secret.[57]

The first part of the Fatima message is a horrifying vision of hell and contained an urgent plea for people to be faithful to God.[58] The Blessed Virgin said in 1917 that Russia would spread its errors across the earth, fomenting wars, annihilating nations and persecuting people. The second part accurately prophesied the outbreak of World War II and predicts the inevitable conversion of Russia to the Catholic faith.[59] The third part of the secret is partially revealed. The partially revealed text had been kept secret from July 13, 1917 to June 26, 2000.

Bishop Da Silva was entrusted from 1944 to 1957 with keeping the Third Secret of Fatima.[60]

The Vatican Announcement

The full Third Secret was to be read no later than immediately after Lucia's death or in 1960. On June 26, 2000, the Vatican announced it published the Third Secret.[61] With information previously confirmed as in the Third Secret still not disclosed, the question of a major deception surfaced. Mother Angelica speaking to her *Eternal Word Television Network* audience on May 16, 2001 said: "As for the Secret, I happen to be one of those individuals who thinks we didn't get the whole thing … Because I think it's scary."

For purposes of making what happened in June 2000 easier to understand, the Vatican announced secret is referred to as 3a. The part not revealed by the Vatican is 3b. The 3a part is unsigned, is 62 lines long, and is on four sheets of paper.

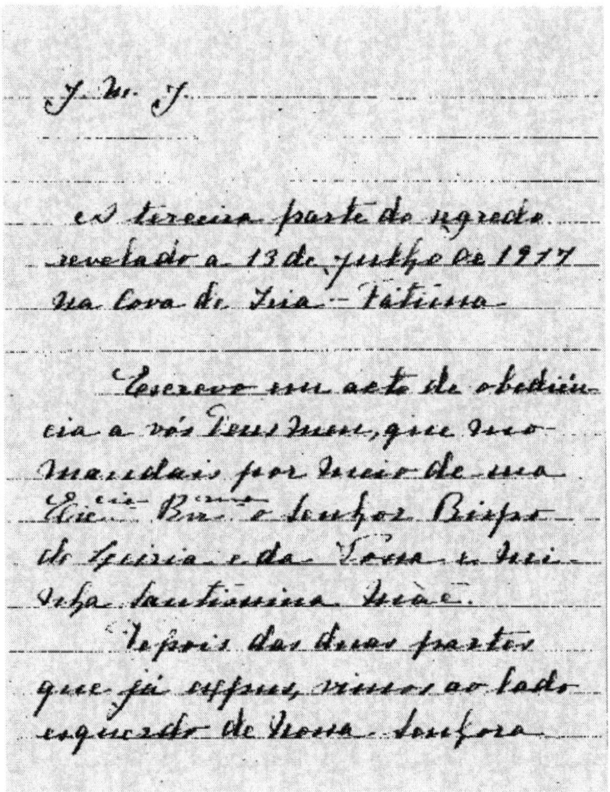

J. M. J.

A terceira parte do segredo
revelado a 13 de julho de 1917
na Cova de Iria - Fátima.

Escrevo em acto de obediên-
cia a Vós Deus meu, que mo
mandais por meio de sua
Ex.cia Rev.ma o Senhor Bispo
de Leiria e da Vossa e mi-
nha Santíssima Mãe.
Depois das duas partes
que já expus, vimos ao lado
esquerdo de Nossa Senhora

The first sheet and 12 lines of the 3a Third Secret text.[62]

Unlike the 3a part, the 3b part was signed by Sister Lucia and written on a single sheet of paper.[63] The 3a text released by the

Vatican was proven to not be the entire text.[64] The 3a text that the Vatican released is as follows:

> "After the two parts which I have already explained, at the left of Our Lady and a little above, we saw an Angel with a flaming sword in his left hand; flashing, it gave out flames that looked as though they would set the world on fire; but they died out in contact with the splendour that Our Lady radiated towards him from her right hand: pointing to the earth with his right hand, the Angel cried out in a loud voice: 'Penance, Penance, Penance!'. And we saw in an immense light that is God: 'something similar to how people appear in a mirror when they pass in front of it' a Bishop dressed in White 'we had the impression that it was the Holy Father'. Other Bishops, Priests, men and women Religious going up a steep mountain, at the top of which there was a big Cross of rough-hewn trunks as of a cork-tree with the bark; before reaching there the Holy Father passed through a big city half in ruins and half trembling with halting step, afflicted with pain and sorrow, he prayed for the souls of the corpses he met on his way; having reached the top of the mountain, on his knees at the foot of the big Cross he was killed by a group of soldiers who fired bullets and arrows at him, and in the same way there died one after another the other Bishops, Priests, men and women Religious, and various lay people of different ranks and positions. Beneath the two arms of the Cross there were two Angels, each with a crystal aspersorium in his hand, in which they gathered up the blood of the Martyrs and with it sprinkled the souls that were making their way to God."

The Secret Still Suppressed

The Part 3b of the Third Secret, also called the Fourth Secret, has not been released by the Vatican.[65] The following 3b text is compiled from information provided by people who read the Portuguese language secret.[66]

> In Portugal the dogma of the Faith will always be preserved.
> If people do not repent and better themselves, the Father will

inflict a terrible punishment on all humanity. A great war in the Twenty-First Century launched by Satan's partisans in the East will come. Those surviving will envy the dead. Death will briefly reign, raised to triumph by the brothers of death, who seek to be masters of the earth.

A time of very severe trial is coming for the Church. All the world be will thrown into great confusion. Each day recite the prayer of the Rosary and pray for the Pope, bishops and priests. Satan will reign over the highest places and succeed in infiltrating to the top of the Church. The Church will be obscured. One-third of the clergy will serve Satan. Entire nations will lose the faith and almost everyone on earth condemned to hell. Cardinals will oppose Cardinals and Bishops will oppose Bishops. Rotten changes in Rome must not be retained.

Fire and smoke will fall from heaven and waters from the ocean will turn to steam throwing their foam to the sky. Millions of people will die by the minute. The only arms which will remain for you will be the Rosary and Sign left by my Son.

At last, those who survive these events will repent and become true followers of Jesus Christ, and serve Him like before, when the world was not so corrupted. In the end, My Immaculate Heart will triumph. The Holy Father will consecrate Russia to Me, and she will be converted, and a period of peace will be granted to the world.

The "Sign left by my Son" is the Holy Eucharist. The 3b text is repeated on the next page, approximately matching the paper size and margins as observed by Bishop João Pereira Venâncio.[67]

In Portugal the dogma of the Faith will always be preserved. If people do not repent and better themselves, the Father will inflict a terrible punishment on all humanity. A great war in the Twenty-First Century launched by Satan's partisans in the East will come. Those surviving will envy the dead. Death will briefly reign, raised to triumph by the brothers of death, who seek to be masters of the earth.

A time of very severe trial is coming for the Church. All the world be will thrown into great confusion. Each day recite the prayer of the Rosary and pray for the Pope, bishops and priests. Satan will reign over the highest places and succeed in infiltrating to the top of the Church. The Church will be obscured. One-third of the clergy will serve Satan. Entire nations will lose the faith and almost everyone on earth condemned to hell. Cardinals will oppose Cardinals and Bishops will oppose Bishops. Rotten changes in Rome must not be retained.

Fire and smoke will fall from heaven and waters from the ocean will turn to steam throwing their foam to the sky. Millions of people will die by the minute. The only arms which will remain for you will be the Rosary and Sign left by my Son.

At last, those who survive these events will repent and become true followers of Jesus Christ, and serve Him like before, when the world was not so corrupted. In the end, My Immaculate Heart will triumph. The Holy Father will consecrate Russia to Me, and she will be converted, and a period of peace will be granted to the world.

The part of the 3b that is worse than an entire nation being annihilated is the deception of Satan is so masterful that almost everyone has been led astray. The 3b secret communicates demonic forces at work and nature turning against itself. Earthquakes, typhoons, comets or meteors, pandemics and wars appear to play some role.[68] A fabricated alien threat using genetically altered humans posing as a threat is a possibility.[69] A rain of fire and three days of darkness are expected.[70] The elect are not to leave their homes, look at or talk to anyone outside their home.[71]

In 1994 and 1995 the Brotherhood of Death commissioned four nightmarish murals by Leo Tanguma and had them displayed at the Denver International Airport.[72] The murals communicate the Fatima 3b secret from the perspective of the Brotherhood of Death.

This Denver International Airport mural shows a ghostly demon soldier awakening to slaughter humanity.[73]

Mothers in a long line hold their dead children in their arms. A dead child holds her teddy bear. A rainbow at the top of the picture transforms into deadly gas and the soldier of death wears a gas mask. He holds a machine gun in his left hand and a scimitar or large curved sword in his right hand. He is trying to kill the dove of peace with the scimitar, a Masonic symbol and traditional Muslim sword.

The following Denver International Airport mural shows nature turning against itself and a holocaust striking the earth.

This mural shows the destruction of the world, a "Global Hiroshima," and the preservation of some life.[74]

The Global Hiroshima mural shows the 3b prophecy with a green plague or gas over a city, forests burning out of control, animals becoming extinct, plants dying, children crying, and the death of three girls in open-caskets. The three girls represent the death of many Africans, the death of many Native Americans, and the death of Jews and Christians. The girl in the open-casket on the right is wearing a "Juden" star. She has a rose and a Bible under her hand representing a key Brotherhood objective, to secretly eliminate the Word of God. One child holds the Mayan tablet communicating the end of an era.

What has terrorized Popes beyond World War III, is the question Jesus posed in the Gospel of Saint Luke: "But yet the Son of man, when he cometh, shall he find, think you, faith on earth?"[75] The 3b Third Secret tells us almost everyone is deceived.[76] This seems impossible but consider how many people were deceived and applauded Osama bin Laden's death. A man who had nothing to do with the September 11, 2001 terrorism.[77]

Again, the Denver International Airport murals communicate what has terrorized multiple Popes, the loss of faith which is worse than a global Hiroshima.[78]

This mural is officially titled "Peace and Harmony with Nature" but should be titled "Christ Rejected."[79]

The "Christ Rejected" mural shows the Antichrist holding a plant symbolizing rebirth. People are happy and seeking to be with the Antichrist. The global population adheres to the Brotherhood of Death Ten Commandments.[80] The people in the mural are at an altar, and instead of celebrating the Eucharist, they are mesmerized by a genetically modified plant. Nowhere in the "Christ Rejected" picture is anyone with a Christian symbol found.

The people in the mural appear to react joyfully following the elimination of billions of people. Animals are mixed with humans to create alien species. This abomination is revealed with human faces on the baby tigers. All animals and people in the mural focus their attention on a the Antichrist and genetically modified plant. The genetically modified plant is important because total control is achieved with poisoned or weakened food and withholding food from people who refuse to worship the Antichrist. The people in the mural welcome the Brotherhood religion that promotes the individual becoming god.

Expert Testimonies and Analysis

The compiled 3b Third Secret, while not the exact text, is in compliance with expert testimonies.

> "I cannot reveal anything of what I have learned at Fatima concerning the Third Secret, but I can say that it has two parts: one [part 3a] concerns the Pope; the other [part 3b] logically (although I must say nothing) would have to be the continuation of the words: "In Portugal, the dogma of the Faith will always be preserved."[81] Fr. Joseph Schweigl

> "The Message of Fatima is a call to conversion, alerting humanity to have nothing to do with the dragon whose tail swept down a third of the stars of heaven, and cast them to earth."[82] Pope Paul II

> "In the Third Secret it is foretold, among other things, that the great apostasy in the Church will begin at the top."[83] Cardinal Mario Luigi Ciappi

> "I consider it [the Fatima revelation] to be the key event in the declining fortune of the Roman Catholic organization and the defining event for the near future of the Church in the next millennium, the third millennium."[84] Fr. Malachi Martin

Fr. Martin was the personal secretary to Cardinal Bea in Rome when he was given the 3b secret to read in February 1960.[85] The 3b "Satan will succeed in infiltrating to the top of the Church" was confirmed by Fr. Martin when he was asked to respond yes or no to text given to Art Bell. Bell read the sentence: "The last Pope would be under the control of Satan."[86] Fr. Malachi Martin responded: "Yes, it sounds as if they were reading or being told the text of the Third Secret. Sounds like it but it is sufficiently vague to make one hesitate."[87]

Additional expert testimonies confirm that nations disappear, the faith of billions of people is lost, apostasy occurs in the Church, and the Immaculate Heart of Mary triumphs.

> "Tell them, Father, that many times, the most Holy Virgin told my cousins Francisco and Jacinta, as well as myself, that many nations will disappear from the face of the earth." [88] Sister Lucia conversation with Fr. Augustin Fuentes

> "The loss of faith of a continent [in the Third Secret] is worse than the annihilation of a nation; and it is true that faith is continually diminishing in Europe."[89] Bishop Alberto Cosme do Amaral

> "The Blessed Virgin was alerting us against apostasy in the Church."[90] Cardinal Silvio Oddi

> "In the period preceding the great triumph of the Immaculate Heart of Mary, terrible things are to happen. These form the content of the third part of the Secret. What are they? If 'in Portugal the dogma of the Faith will always be preserved,'... it can be clearly deduced from this that in other parts of the Church these dogmas are going to become obscure or even lost altogether."[91] Fr. Joaquin Alonso

Frère Michel de la Sainte Trinité, an important Fatima expert, reported Sister Lucia said of the secret: "It's in the Gospel and in the Apocalypse, read them!" Sister Lucia specifically identified Apocalypse Chapters 8 through 13.

Frère Michel de la Sainte Trinité's analysis supports the 3a and compiled 3b parts of the Third Secret. He wrote:

> "Having reached the end of our inquiry, we are able to discern, with near certainty, the essential elements of Our Lady's final secret: While 'in Portugal, the dogma of the Faith will always

be preserved,' in many nations, perhaps in almost the entire world, the Faith will be lost. The pastors of the Church will fail gravely in the duties of their office. Through their fault, consecrated souls and the Faithful in great number will let themselves be seduced by pernicious errors spread everywhere. This will be the time of the decisive battle between the Blessed Virgin and the devil. A wave of diabolical disorientation will be hurled over the world. Satan will introduce himself even to the highest summit of the Church. He will blind the minds and harden the hearts of pastors. And God will deliver them to themselves as a chastisement for their refusal to obey the requests of the Immaculate Heart of Mary. This will be the great apostasy predicted for the 'last times'; 'the False Lamb' and 'False Prophet' will betray the Church to the profit of 'the Beast,' according to the prophecy of the Apocalypse."

The Blessed Virgin Akita Message

Mary communicated with Sister Agnes Katsuko Sasagawa in Akita, Japan on July 6, 1973, August 3, 1973 and October 13, 1973.[92] In the final communication the Blessed Virgin warned that there would be a worldwide chastisement for sins in which a great part of humanity would be killed and that those who survive would envy the dead.

Prior to the first communication by the Blessed Virgin, on June 12, 13 and 14 in 1973, Sister Agnes Sasagawa saw brilliant mysterious rays emanate from the tabernacle. She also received the stigmata on her left hand and a statue of the Blessed Virgin Mary began to bleed from a wound in the statue's right hand on June 28, 1973. The blood flowed from the wound in the statue's hand until September 29, 1973. On that day, the wound disappeared and "sweat" appeared on the forehead and neck.

Sister Agnes Sasagawa in 2015.[93]

On September 15, 1981, after weeping 101 times over a period of six years and eight months, the weeping stops. On September 28, 1981, an angel instructs Sister Agnes to read Genesis 3:15 to understand the meaning of 101 tears. Genesis 3:15 is the first mention in the Bible of a Savior from a woman for mankind. Sister Agnes is told:

> "There is meaning to the figure one hundred and one. This signifies that sin came into the world by a woman and it is also from a woman that salvation should come. The "zero" between the two signifies the Eternal God who is from all eternity until eternity. The first "one" represents Eve and the last "one" the Virgin Mary."

Understanding the message to Sister Agnes can be further advanced by understanding a pronoun change the Latin Vulgate version of the Bible. Specifically, the 1899 Douay-Rheims American Edition changes the word He to she and it is important to note that scripture is very clear that it is Jesus who will return and destroy Satan. Genesis 3:15 takes on a clearer meaning when we understand the word He versus she.[94] The earlier versions of the Bible were more precise and by stating "He" and referring more directly to Jesus who is God who came from Mary, it was clear that Jesus upon his return shall crush thy head which means to destroy Satan.

Often people are misinformed and do not know the Catholic position is "He" is the correct translation. The translation "she" of the Vulgate is interpretative; it originated after the fourth century, and cannot be defended critically. The conqueror from the seed of the woman, who should crush the serpent's head, is Christ; the woman at enmity with the serpent is Mary.[95]

The Akita message is a continuation and reminder of the Fatima message. The former Philippine ambassador to the Vatican, Howard Dee, said that "Bishop John Shojiro Ito was certain Akita was an extension of Fatima, and Cardinal Ratzinger personally confirmed to me that these two messages, of Fatima and Akita, are essentially the same."[96]

With the parts of the Fatima message that have been confirmed as still withheld by the Vatican are known, it becomes apparent that the Blessed Virgin's October 13, 1973 message to Sister Agnes reveals the hidden part of the Fatima message. The Third Message of Akita follows.[97]

> "My dear daughter, listen well to what I have to say to you. You will inform your superior.
>
> As I told you, if men do not repent and better themselves, the Father will inflict a terrible punishment on all humanity. It will be a punishment greater than the deluge, such as one will never seen before. Fire will fall from the sky and will wipe out a great part of humanity, the good as well as the bad, sparing neither priests nor faithful. The survivors will find themselves so desolate that they will envy the dead. The only arms which will remain for you will be the Rosary and the Sign left by My Son. Each day recite the prayers of the Rosary. With the Rosary, pray for the Pope, the bishops and priests.

The work of the devil will infiltrate even into the Church in such a way that one will see cardinals opposing cardinals, bishops against bishops. The priests who venerate me will be scorned and opposed by their confreres...churches and altars sacked; the Church will be full of those who accept compromises and the demon will press many priests and consecrated souls to leave the service of the Lord.

The demon will be especially implacable against souls consecrated to God. The thought of the loss of so many souls is the cause of my sadness. If sins increase in number and gravity, there will be no longer pardon for them.

With courage, speak to your superior. He will know how to encourage each one of you to pray and to accomplish works of reparation.

It is Bishop Ito, who directs your community.

You have still something to ask? Today is the last time that I will speak to you in living voice. From now on you will obey the one sent to you and your superior.

Pray very much the prayers of the Rosary. I alone am able still to save you from the calamities which approach. Those who place their confidence in me will be saved."[98]

The solution communicated at Akita, the Fatima solution, is further explained in the final chapter of this book.

3

MANY MASKS

"My people have been silent, because they had no knowledge..."[99] Hosea 4:6

Many people know that the Organization of the Petroleum Exporting Countries (OPEC) is real, and that this cartel influences the price of oil.[100] Why, then, is it that a far more powerful cartel is often unknown? This more powerful cartel is the behind-the-scenes power for OPEC, the global drug cartel, the international bank cartel and many secret societies.

The Masonic temple near the White House. [101]

Cartels and secret societies have existed for thousands of years and have been influencing governments long before the creation of the United States or even the oldest European countries. In an effort to remain hidden, the names of blood oath secret societies often changed. The external names that are used are often a variation of an internal name. Fortunately, today people are increasingly waking up to realize that there is a secret plan to establish a one world government. Knowledge of this secret plan for a so called "new age of reason" is necessary to prevent global totalitarian rule.

The cartel that spawned the atomic bomb is the same secret group that Pope Leo XIII warned the world about in his 1884 encyclical.[102] This group had been plotting and scheming for many years to destroy the Catholic Church. By the nineteenth century the tentacles of this cartel reached every corner of the globe. In the twentieth century their influence over the western world's economies and governments was so great that they often played a major role in initiating major conflicts.

Many Names - Same Secret Purpose

The cartel wants people to be confused so the name or mask is periodically changed. Some front terms and affiliated labels used by the cartel include:

All-Seeing Eye
Alta Vendita
Abaddon
Apollyon
Antichrist
Arcanum Arcanorum [103]
Aquarian
Atlantean
Babylon
Black Hand
Black Nobility
Bilderberg
Brotherhood of Death
Club of Rome

Mafia
Money Trust
Moriah
Mystery Forces
Mystery of Iniquity
Mystery Religion
New World Order
Olympian
One World
Open Conspiracy
Order of the Snake
Organized Atheism
Pharaoh
Prometheus

Committee of 300	Pythagoras
Communist	Rhodes
Council on Foreign Relations	Rothschild
Dragon	Round Table
Egyptian Mystery	Royal Secret
Enoch	Sanat Kumara
Frankist	Satanic [104]
Freemasonry	Shadow Government
Globalist	Shekinah[105]
Global Drug	Skull and Bones
Great Work	Technocratic
Illuminati	Templar
International Bank	Trilateral
Internationalist	Whirlwind
Luciferian	White Club
Magnum Opus	Windsor
Mephistopheles	World Government
Merovingian	World Federalist
Metratron	World Revolutionary
Military Industrial Complex	World State

Behind the Mask - The Brotherhood of Death

The cartel uses blood oath secret societies that recognize no borders, laws or rules other than their own and require the death of members who violate secrecy rules. This is one reason why blood oath secret society insiders sometimes refer to themselves as "a brotherhood of death." Brotherhood blood oath secret societies often require people to participate in a "death" ritual before they can become a member.[106]

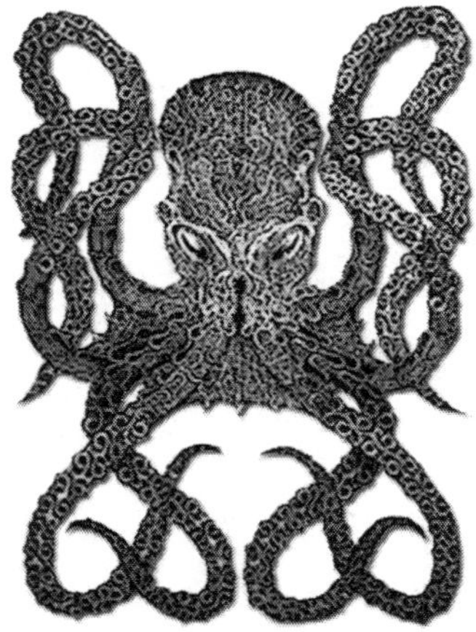

The octopus structure behind the mask with many tentacles. [107]

The tentacles of this blood oath collection of secret societies effectively control key people in governments around the world. While the top leaders of the cartel that seeks to rule the world are actively involved in an ancient mystery religion, the vast majority of supporting members unknowingly serve as helpers to bring about a one-world religion. Secret society members, who are not told the real purpose, create camouflage for organized evil to grow like an undetected cancer.

For the remainder of this book, the name "Brotherhood of Death" is used for this cartel because after over a decade of research, the author has concluded this name best encompasses all of the names or masks and reflects the true purpose of the cartel.[108]

Financial cartels and groups seeking global domination have existed in prior times. Controlling money leads to controlling governments, and controlling values and beliefs. The agenda of the Brotherhood of Death does not stop with a battle for money but is ultimately a war for souls. This dimension regarding the religious beliefs of some of the most powerful people in the world is extremely hard to accept.

The Brotherhood of Death agenda can be summarized with four points.

1. End national sovereignty with a one world government.
2. Control the issuance of money and thereby control everything money is needed to buy.
3. Abolish family life, end the institution of marriage, and eliminate the primary influence of parents in raising their children.
4. Destroy Christianity and convert humanity to a global Luciferian religion also known as Illuminism.

Brotherhood of Death marble sphinx in Washington, D.C. [109]

All major intelligence services are controlled by the Brotherhood of Death. To create terrorism in the Muslim world in the 20th century, the Brotherhood created the Society of Muslim Brothers or Muslim Brotherhood. The organization was founded in 1928 by Hassan al-Banna with the slogan: "The Koran is our constitution." Using the smokescreen of restoring the purity of Islam, the hidden purpose surfaced in 1930.[110] At that time the Secret Apparatus was established as a Brotherhood of Death intelligence and terrorist unit. In the 1950s until his death in 1995, a top Brotherhood of Death's Muslim Brotherhood terrorist was CIA agent Said Ramadan.[111]

ISIS is also a Brotherhood of Death creation to intensify the fear of Christians and maintain support for military deployments. ISIS is the abbreviation for the Islamic State of Iraq and Syria or Islamic State of Iraq and al-Sham.[112] The accurate description of ISIS is a Brotherhood of Death fueled organization to replace al Qaeda's role as an enemy. With Osama bin Laden no longer alive and numerous reports confirming no al Qaeda involvement in acts of violence, a new enemy was needed. The official story is the group was closely linked to al Qaeda until February 2014 when al Qaeda cut all ties with ISIS.

The Brotherhood of Death strategy is anytime support for militarism or a distraction from exposure of the New World Order is needed, instructions are sent to behead a captured individual. The individuals targeted for capture and execution are often journalists who have discovered ISIS is funded by the Brotherhood of Death. If a greater than normal distraction is needed, the individual is tortured and killed with horrific methods greater than beheading. To maximize public anger, videos of the person suffering and being killed are distributed by Brotherhood of Death controlled media outlets.

In June 2014, Christof Lehmann reported the ISIS headquarters was the U.S. Embassy in Ankara, Turkey.[113] On September 20, 2014, *The New York Times* published the article "Suspicions Run Deep in Iraq That C.I.A. and the Islamic State are United."[114] Shiite cleric Moktada al-Sadr publicly blamed the C.I.A. for creating the ISIS to justify redeploying ground troops in Iraq.[115] Omar al-Jabouri, a Sunni Muslim living in Iraq, said: "It is obvious to everyone that the Islamic State is a creation of the United States and Israel."[116]

The fact that ISIS is secretly directed by the Brotherhood of Death via intelligence services was also disclosed by former U.S. National Security Agency employee Edward Snowden. Documents he made available show the Mossad, CIA and British intelligence worked together to create ISIS.[117]

On February 27, 2015, the Iraqi Parliament National Security and Defense Committee reported two British planes carrying weapons for ISIS were shot down.[118] Iraqi Minister of Parliament Al-Zameli said ammunition from Israel, the U.S. and some European countries was recovered.[119] ISIS continues to be used because the deception is working to fool most U.S. tax payers to support the Brotherhood of Death agenda. *Vigilant Christian II: Preventing an American Hiroshima* provides additional information explaining ISIS, al Qaeda and other Brotherhood of Death's terrorist creations.[120]

Truth Sets Us Free

The Brotherhood of Death is actively promoting a false version of history because they know the truth helps us love and serve God. The Brotherhood produces a vast amount of disinformation. Churches and other organized peacemaking groups are targeted for infiltration and perversion. Fortunately, getting beyond the false information is possible by understanding the many layers of this cartel, especially their monetary control and religious beliefs.

Never conclude that a person does not love God or seeks to hurt other people just because of his or her membership in a secret society. Secret society membership routinely offers business and networking opportunities. Good people are intentionally deceived to join secret societies.

Although the Brotherhood of Death uses many secret societies as fronts to advance their agenda, the inner workings of its most famous front, Freemasonry, are explained in the next chapter. Freemasonry is selected because it is one of the oldest and largest Brotherhood of Death fronts and its long history provides centuries of authenticated official documents as evidence.[121] Confirmation that the documents are authentic includes first-hand testimonies of former Freemasons.

4

LARGEST BROTHERHOOD SECRET SOCIETY

"As a whole [it] was, is and will always be the struggle against the Church and the Christian religion, and the struggle of those who have not against those who have... All secret societies have almost analogous initiations, from the Egyptian to the Illuminati, and most of them form a chain and give rise to others."[122] Count Jean-Emmanuel Le Couteulx de Canteleu

Freemasonry is one of the oldest and largest Brotherhood of Death fronts.[123] Freemasonry's long history provides centuries of authenticated official documents as evidence. Confirmation that the documents are authentic includes first-hand testimonies of people who have renounced Freemasonry. As a result, Freemasonry is the most visible octopus tentacle or Brotherhood of Death front organization.

This chapter explains Freemasons teach that the secret society existed before the "first Lodge" of 1717 in London. Masonic authors claim Tubalcain was the first Freemason and King Solomon was also an early Mason.[124] Sir John A. Cockburn said:

> "No unprejudiced observer can fail to perceive that Freemasonry is the legitimate inheritor of a secret doctrine which has been transmitted from the earliest ages through successive repositories of the Ancient and Mediaeval Mysteries... It is no idle boast to maintain, as does the ritual, that it has existed from time immemorial."[125]

Despite assertions from Freemasons who claim the secret society is not a religion, Freemasonry is a religion. The secrets of Freemasonry are explained, not because what Masons believe is accurate, but because elite members serve the Brotherhood of Death. Although the Brotherhood uses many secret societies to advance their agenda, Freemasonry is selected in this chapter to explain the Brotherhood's real purpose.

The outer Masonic doctrine is extremely clever as it enables most members to believe Freemasonry is a charitable organization. The deception is advanced with symbols that have multiple misleading meanings crafted to give currency to Freemasonry as a charitable organization.

Modern Freemasonry, called "Speculative Science," has few members who are builders. Speculative Science is a name Freemasons have selected to conceal the Masonic religion. When a Freemason says he is participating in a Speculative Science ritual he is participating in a Masonic religious ritual.

Craftsmen working with stone in the Middle Ages are "Operative Art" Masons. To conceal the secret work to destroy Christianity, Operative Art Masonry was hijacked by Luciferians and Satanists in the 18th century. Operative Masons were selected because this group used secret codes to communicate their level of building knowledge in order to be accepted and free to work in a city. The secret handshakes and passwords served a commercial purpose during a period of history when people often did not know how to read or write.

Understanding that Operative Art Masonry was hijacked helps explain why Masonic leaders claim Speculative Science Freemasonry started in London in 1717 and also claim their secret society predates ancient Babylon.

Masonic Government Influence

The influence of Freemasonry on the United States was verified by the 110th Congress House Resolution number 33. The resolution recognized "the thousands of Freemasons in every State," and notes the majority of the Founding Fathers and signers of the Constitution were Freemasons.[126] The Resolution also confirms that Freemasonry's "long lineage extends back to before the nation's founding."[127]

Almost all U.S. Presidents have been a member of Freemasonry or another Brotherhood-affiliated secret society. Presidents officially acknowledged as Freemasons include George Washington, James Monroe, Andrew Jackson, James Polk, James Buchanan, Andrew Johnson, James Garfield, William McKinley, Theodore Roosevelt, William Howard Taft, Warren Harding, Franklin Roosevelt, Harry Truman, Lyndon Johnson, and Gerald Ford.[128] The list of presidents closely affiliated with Freemasonry is longer. For example, on February 11, 1988, Ronald Reagan became an Honorary Scottish Rite Mason by the Grand Lodge of Washington, D.C.[129]

President Harry Truman[130]

Presidents who have been members of other secret societies often communicated their support of Freemasonry by taking their oath of office using a Bible owned by the St. John's Masonic Lodge in New York City. This is the Bible used for the oath ceremony on April 30, 1789 by George Washington. Non-Masons who have shown their support of Freemasonry by using the St. John's Masonic Lodge Bible include: George H. W. Bush (1989), Jimmy Carter (1977), and Dwight D. Eisenhower (1953).[131] The following picture is of a painting of George Washington wearing Masonic regalia.[132]

President George Washington

Blood Oaths

Every Freemason is required to make a blood oath, called Solemn Obligations, to protect the organization's secrets. If secret societies were pursuing the truth, there would be no need for secrecy. Contrasting Masonic secrecy, Jesus' teachings are to be shared openly with everyone.[133]

Any family member of a Mason who doubts the organization is anti-Christian need only consider the blood oath that is taken. In the very first blood oath, the candidate for initiation agrees to protect the secrets of Freemasonry "under no less penalty, on the violation of any of them, than that of having my throat cut across, my tongue torn out by the root, and buried in the sand of the sea at low water mark."[134]

Masonic blood oaths violate God's direction that we are never to give permission for our bodies to be tortured or killed. The candidate initiation blood oath includes language that binds the candidate to the Brotherhood for eternity. Freemasons, spouses, and family members are encouraged to remember that oaths sworn on false pretenses are null and void.

As Freemasons ascend to higher levels, the methods in which they agree to be tortured, killed, and kill others increases. Blood oaths are one reason why Freemasonry and Christianity are diametrically opposed. To stress this point, in the very first initiation a candidate for Freemasonry renounces baptism. Upon becoming a Freemason, an individual has rejected Christ and promised to serve a god that is not the God of Abraham. Later in this chapter, in the section *Freemasonry and Christianity*, additional reasons are explained to expand on why Freemasonry and Christianity are incompatible.

Secret Publications

Freemasons who take home sensitive documents sometimes fail to return them. Family members of deceased Freemasons are often unaware of the blood oath. As a result, official Masonic books occasionally appear at estate sales.

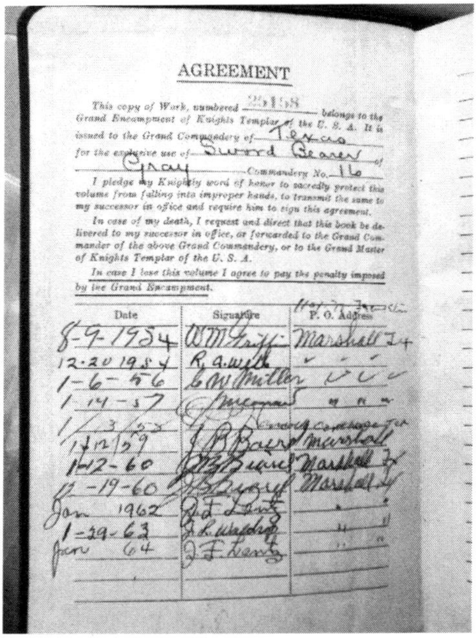

AGREEMENT

This copy of Work, numbered _____ belongs to the Grand Encampment of Knights Templar of the U. S. A. It is issued to the Grand Commandery of _____ for the exclusive use of _____ of _____ Commandery No. _____

I pledge my Knightly word of honor to sacredly protect this volume from falling into improper hands, to transmit the same to my successor in office and require him to sign this agreement.

In case of my death, I request and direct that this book be delivered to my successor in office, or forwarded to the Grand Commander of the above Grand Commandery, or to the Grand Master of Knights Templar of the U. S. A.

In case I lose this volume I agree to pay the penalty imposed by the Grand Encampment.

Date	Signature	P. O. Address

Masonic death penalty agreement.[135]

The death penalty warning in Masonic books is sometimes cloaked with innocuous words and symbols. The previous picture is from a carefully guarded Freemasonry book, and shows how the non-initiated can easily miss the death penalty warning. The words underlined "In case I lose this volume I agree to pay the penalty imposed" literally mean that the person confirms he may suffer the death penalty if he misplaces the book. The books Freemasons want most to keep out of the hands of the general public are books classified for an inner group of elite Freemasons who have fulfilled a 15-year probationary period.

The most tightly controlled secret society documents use gematria, which is a system of assigning numerical values to words. Secret societies interchange letters containing special names, phrases, and passages with their numerical equivalent. Super-sensitive Masonic documents are protected from most Freemasons and outsiders using gematria code with the languages of Hebrew, Greek, Latin, Arabic, and the modern European languages, including English. In the years before the computer existed, secret society leaders failed to realize that the gematria code would easily be deciphered and shared.[136]

Freemasonry is now easily exposed due in part to deciphered codes and access to their original works. It is important to understand that the name Jesus Christ is not allowed to be spoken or written in a Masonic Lodge. If spoken or written, Orpheus which in Greek is ΟΡΦΕΥΣ, is one name that could be used in lieu of Jesus Christ. To equate Jesus to Orpheus is blasphemous, which is a key Masonic objective. Elite Freemasons would then use the Agrippa gematria code, of which the number 1275 or ΟΡΦΕΥΣ communicates a false meaning of Orpheus and a correct meaning of Jesus Christ.[137] The following coding diagram is one of Freemasonry's gematria codes. 'Jesus Christ' is equated with the number 1275 or 600 + 5 + 90 + 200 + 90 + 3 + 8 + 80 + 9 + 90 + 100.[138]

A 1	B 2	C 3	D 4	E 5	F 6	G 7	H 8	I 9
K 10	L 20	M 30	N 40	O 50	P 60	Q 70	R 80	S 90
T 100	U 200	X 300	Y 400	Z 500	J 600	V 700	Hi 800	W 900

Freemasons place special emphasis on numbers in their belief system. Freemasons believe each number and even categories of numbers have layers of meaning. For example, odd numbers symbolize male exclusivity. Two examples of odd number exclusivity include the Brotherhood's selected date for the Osama bin Laden execution on May 1, 2011 and the date for the September 11, 2001 terrorism. The occult significance of these specific dates is explained in *Vigilant Christian III: The Occult Religion of the 9/11 Attackers*.

The most sensitive documents and books, by using gematria, deny even Freemasons with full access to Masonic libraries the ability to decipher secrets. Gematria allows Freemasons to find a very different message in a Masonic Bible than what is taught in Bible-based churches. The following photograph is of a Masonic Cabala or Kabbalah book on the left and a Masonic Bible on the right.

Photograph of a Masonic Cabala or Kabbalah book on the left and a Masonic Bible on the right.[139]

The next two pictures show the inside front cover and title page of the Cabala book. The warning to safeguard the book or pay the death penalty is communicated on the inside cover through Hebrew letters and secret society symbols.

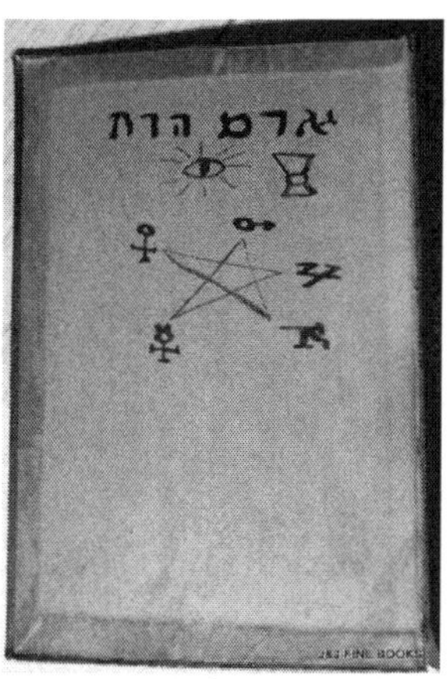

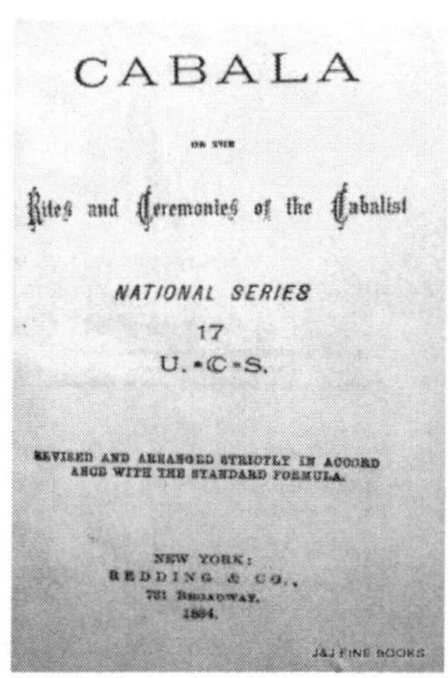

Cabala inside front cover and title page.[140]

Freemasons have published books where the death penalty warning is easy to understand without knowing the meaning of symbols. One example is *Morals and Dogma*, a book that includes the death penalty warning "ESOTERIC BOOK, FOR SCOTTISH RITE USE ONLY: TO BE RETURNED UPON WITHDRAWAL OR DEATH OF RECIPIENT." The warning, shown opposite Albert Pike's picture, is deadly serious.[141]

Morals and Dogma death penalty warning.[142]

Albert Pike

Albert Pike was one of the founders of the Ancient Accepted Scottish Rite of Freemasonry. He was the Grand Commander of North American Freemasonry from 1859 to 1891. Pike was appointed Brigadier General and Indian Commissioner for the Confederacy on November 22, 1861. During the March 6-8, 1862 Battle of Pea Ridge in Arkansas, Indian troops under his command scalped Union soldiers before murdering them.[143] The scalping and murder of American soldiers shocked people both in the North and South. Pike's executions of Union soldiers embarrassed the

Confederate leadership, and he resigned his commission on November 19, 1862.

After the Civil War, Pike continued to terrorize Americans as the chief judicial officer of the Ku Klux Klan or KKK.[144] He served as a KKK leader while simultaneously serving as the Southern Jurisdiction Sovereign Grand Commander of the Scottish Rite of Masonry.[145]

The power of the Freemasons in the U.S. is so great that the statue of Albert Pike, a confirmed murderer of Americans, still stands at Judiciary Square in Washington, D.C. Pike's eleven-foot bronze statue, erected in 1901, is amazing because he is the only Confederate officer to be honored with a monument in the U.S. Capitol.[146] Below his statue is a bronze lady in a Greek dress holding the Scottish Rite banner.

Albert Pike statue in Judiciary Square.[147]

Pike is holding in his left hand his book *Morals and Dogma.*[148] His monument bears the inscription: Author, Poet,

Scholar, Soldier, Philanthropist, Philosopher, Jurist, and Orator. The monument also has the text "Vixit Laborum Ejus Super Stites Sunt Fructus" meaning: "He has lived. The fruits of his labors live after him." The fruits of Albert Pike's labors include: murdering U.S. soldiers, helping start the Ku Klux Klan, creating the 33 Masonic degree system, and planning three world wars.[149]

Pike's secret publications are often now in the public domain. His writings are deemed authentic by Freemasons and highly valued by secret societies. Secrets revealed by Pike include Freemasonry is the continuation of a secret society that has worked for centuries to advance a one-world religion enforced by a one-world government. He wrote:[150]

> "My Brother, you desire to unite yourself to an Order which has laboured in silence and secrecy for more than five hundred years with a single end, in which it has as yet only partially succeeded, and to which, if you join us, you must devote yourself. You have been partially prepared for this in some of the degrees that you have already taken."[151]

Determining Authenticity

Freemasons use a combination of titles, signatures, photographs, symbols, and special words to convey that a book is both authorized and accurate. One example is shown in the picture of Albert Pike's *Morals and Dogma* book. The text is "Prepared for the Supreme Council of the thirty-third degree for the Southern Jurisdiction of the United States and published by its authority."[152] Often, a well-known high ranking Mason is listed by the author in order to signal that the book is authentic.

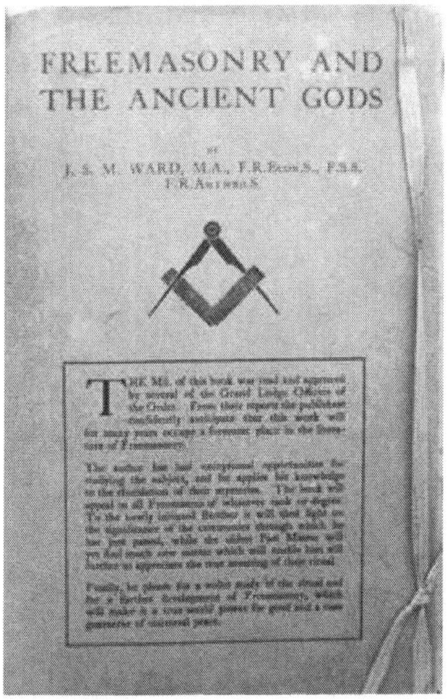

A testament of accuracy is shown on the cover of some books available to lower level Masons.

An example of a lightly safeguarded book is shown on the book cover of *Freemasonry and the Ancient Gods*. A photograph of the cover shows the text: "The MS. [manuscript] of this book was read and approved by several of the Grand Lodge Officers of the Order. From their reports the publishers confidently anticipate that this work will for many years occupy a foremost place in the literature of Freemasonry."[153]

The author's credentials in *Freemasonry and the Ancient Gods* disclose:

> "Member of the Royal Asiatic Society; Former scholar and prizeman of Trinity Hall, Cambridge; Master Mason; Mark Master Mason; Royal Ark Mariner; Royal Arch; Most Excellent Master; Royal Master; Select Master; Super-Excellent Master; Knight Templar; Knight of Malta; Brother of St. Lawrence; Knight of Constantinople; Knight of the Red Cross of Babylon; Grand Tyler of K.S. 18o; Grand High

Priest; Royal Order of Scotland; Secret Monitor; Red Cross of Constantine; Knight of St. John and the Holy Sepulchre; P.M., P.Z., P.M.W.S., Etc."[154]

The above titles mean little to outsiders, but Freemasons know that this information communicates that the author is an elite member of the secret society.

Freemasonry may be served when lower level secrets are published. The secret society is served if a book helps recruit new members, retain existing members, or serves to conceal higher level secrets.

Sometimes it serves Freemasonry and other secret societies to have information published by someone who appears to be an objective outsider. Authors claiming not to be secret society members may actually be in the service of a secret society even if non-members. One example is David Ovason's *The Secret Architecture of Our Nation's Capital.*[155] Well-known Freemason C. Fred Kleinknecht endorsed Ovason's book by writing the Foreword. For eighteen years including the time Kleinknecht wrote the Foreword, he was the Sovereign Grand Commander of the Supreme Council, 33°, of the Southern Jurisdiction, U.S.A., Mother Council of the World.[156] Kleinknecht's endorsement means the information made available to the public somehow serves Freemasons.

Death Penalty Enforced

Freemasons have ritually executed members for violating their blood oath and outsiders for revealing their secrets; three of the better known examples are Roberto Calvi, Captain William Morgan, and Gracia Moreno.

Freemason and Italian banker Roberto Calvi was murdered on June 17, 1982 for stealing at least $1.3 billion from Freemasonry.[157] He was found the following day with a Masonic cable tow around his neck and masonry bricks in his pockets which served as a warning to other Freemasons.[158] Calvi was hung in a ritual manner at the Blackfriar's Bridge in London, also known as the P-2 Masonic Lodge. The location is significant because Calvi's Masonic blood oath was made at Frati Neri, which is Italian for the Black Friars.

Calvi was Chairman of Banco Ambrosiano, which went bankrupt in 1982. The media called Calvi "God's Banker" because of his close association with both the Rothschild family and the Vatican.[159] He laundered money for the Brotherhood of Death by channeling Mafia money through Vatican Bank accounts.[160] Author John Daniel wrote: "In his multi-million-dollar transfers of money, he would use the Rothschild banks in Zurich, Switzerland, and in Guernsey, England, as well as the National Bank of Paris in Panama through P-2 shell corporations, such as Bellatrix in Panama."[161]

The day before his murder, his secretary Graziella Corrocher died after falling from the Banco Ambrosiano's fifth floor window. Both Calvi and Corrocher were at the intersection of a battle between English and French Freemasonry.[162] While Calvi was working to undermine the Catholic Church, he was also stealing from British Freemasonry on behalf of Grand Orient or French Freemasonry. The competing and sometimes conflicting interests of Masons is further explained in the three volume book series titled *Scarlet and the Beast: A History of the War between English and French Freemasonry*.[163]

Another carefully documented enforcement of the Masonic blood oath was the 1826 murder of Captain William Morgan. Morgan was a Royal Arch Mason who violated his blood oath.[164] Morgan was sentenced to death by his brother Freemasons for publishing Masonic secrets.[165] Former Mason Charles Finney is one of many who have confirmed that Morgan's publication accurately communicated Masonic blood oaths and rituals.[166] When asked if Morgan's book was a true revelation of

Freemasonry, he wrote: "it was a verbatim revelation of the first three degrees as I had myself taken them."[167]

Front cover of Morgan's publication.[168]

Henry L. Valance explained to Dr. John L. Emery in his 1848 deathbed confession how he was assigned to help capture and murder Morgan because Morgan violated his blood oath. Emery wrote:

> "Morgan, on being informed of their proceedings against him, demanded by what authority they had condemned him, and who were his judges. 'He commenced wringing his hands, and talking of his wife and children, the recollections of whom, in that awful hour, terribly affected him. His wife, he said, was young and inexperienced, and his children were but infants; what would become of them were he cut off; and they even ignorant of his fate?' What husband and father would not be 'terribly affected' under such circumstances--to be cut off from among the living in this inhuman manner?"[169]

Freemasons Nicholas Chesebro, Loton Lawon, and Edward Sawyer were convicted of the kidnapping of Morgan. Eight people were involved in killing Morgan. Emery wrote:

> "It was resolved in a council of eight, that he must die: must be consigned to a 'confinement from which there is no possibility of escape--THE GRAVE.' Three of their number were to be selected by ballot to execute the deed. 'Eight pieces of paper were procured, five of which were to remain blank, while the letter D was written on the others. These pieces of paper were placed in a large box, from which each man was to draw one at the same moment. After drawing we were all to separate, without looking at the paper that each held in his hand. So soon as we have arrived at certain distances from the place of rendezvous, the tickets were to be examined, and those who held blanks were to return instantly to their homes; and those who should hold marked tickets were to proceed to the fort at midnight, and there put Morgan to death, in such a manner as should seem to themselves most fitting.' Mr. Valance was one of the three who drew ballots on which was the signal letter. He returned to the fort, where he was joined by his two companions, who had drawn the death tickets. Arrangements were made immediately for executing the sentence passed upon their prisoner, which was to sink him in the river with weights; in hope, says Mr. Valance, 'that he and our crime alike would thus be buried beneath the waves.'"[170]

Valance's 1848 deathbed confession confirms he was the Freemason who pushed Morgan out of the boat and into the Niagara River.[171] Valance said:

> "A short time, brought us to the boat and we all entered it--Morgan being placed in the bow with myself, along side of him. My comrades took the oars, and the boat was rapidly forced out into the river. The night was pitch dark, we could scarcely see a yard before us, and therefore was the time admirably adapted to our hellish purpose."[172]

> "This cord, I took in my hand [did not that hand tremble?] and fastened it around the body of Morgan, just above the hips, using all my skill to make it fast, so that it would hold. Then,

> in a whisper, I bade the unhappy man to stand up, and after a momentary hesitation he complied with my order. He stood close to the head of the boat, and there was just length enough of rope from his person to the weights to prevent any strain, while he was standing. I then requested one of my associates to assist me in lifting the weights from the bottom to the side of the boat, while the others steadied her from the stern. This was done, and, as Morgan was standing with his back toward me, I approached him, and gave him a strong push with both my hands, which were placed on the middle of his back. He fell forward, carrying the weights with him, and the waters closed over the mass. We remained quiet for two or three minutes, when my companions, without saying a word, resumed their places, and rowed the boat to the place from which they had taken it."[173]

Valance struggled for years with the voice of Morgan, who prior to being killed had begged not to be murdered. Valance said:

> "Go where I would, or do what I would, it was impossible for me to throw off the consciousness of crime. If the mark of Cain was not upon me, the curse of the first murderer was--the blood-stain was upon my hands and could not be washed out."[174]

The murder of Morgan is one of many documented examples that Freemasons follow through with oaths to murder in order to protect secrets. Catholic Church Cardinal Rodriguez published the stories of other Masonic assassinations in *The Mystery of Freemasonry Unveiled.*[175]

Morgan's murder became widely known. The murder led to a decline in U.S. Masonry and the creation of the Anti-Masonic party in 1828. The conviction of Freemasons involved in Morgan's murder resulted in an estimated 45,000 of the 50,000 Freemasons in America resigning as they realized they were in the service of organized evil.[176] The public opposition to Freemasonry helped many politicians who were opposed by Brotherhood affiliated secret societies win elections. One example is anti-Mason Millard

Fillmore who won the New York State Assembly election in 1828 and became the 13th President of the United States in 1850.[177]

Freemasons tried to confuse the public and counter the membership resignations through the publication of altered versions of Morgan's Exposé.[178] Attempts to bury the truth were met with the National Christian Association's placement of a large monument in honor of Morgan in New York's Batavia City Cemetery on September 13, 1882. The monument states that Captain William Morgan was killed because he revealed Masonic secrets.

The text on the monument reads:

> "Sacred to the memory of Wm. Morgan, a native of Virginia, a Capt. in the War of 1812, a respectable citizen of Batavia, and a martyr to the freedom of writing[,] printing[,] and speaking the truth. He was abducted from near this spot in the year 1826, by Freemasons and murdered for revealing the secrets of their order. The court records of Genesee County, and the files of the Batavia Advocate, kept in the Recorders office contain the history of the events that caused the erection of this monument."

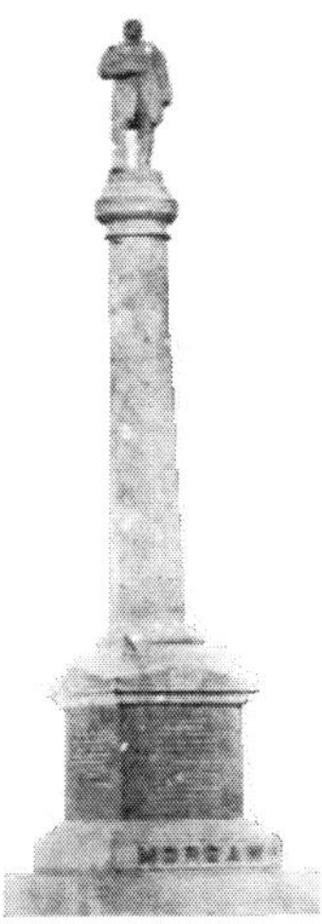

Monument for William Morgan.[179]

The monument in memory of Captain William Morgan is a reminder of the price courageous people have paid to provide first-hand testimony of how evil is organized in our world.

President of Ecuador Gabriel Garcia Moreno (December 24, 1821 - August 6, 1875) was also a victim of Masonic assassination. Cardinal Rodriguez wrote:[180]

> "Garcia Moreno himself wrote to Pius IX, bidding him farewell, aware that the American Lodges, incited by the Germans, were going to murder him. The man who had rid Ecuador of the evil of the Masons, was not afraid to stop the dagger which lurked treacherously for him in the shadows, nor even to know from where it was to strike his breast. The day before the crime they advised him that the crime was to be committed shortly, that he should take precautions, that he should surround himself with guards, and he replied, and who will rid me of the guards if they are those bought to strike me? When by writing or by words they advised him of new indications or signs that the decree of the lodges was to be fulfilled, that he should take precautions, he would answer: 'One only can I take, and I have taken it, that is to give myself up to God and to prepare myself to die in a Christian manner.'"[181]

In 1875 Garcia Moreno asked Pope Pius IX for his blessing and divine protection.[182] He wrote:

> "Today, when all the Masonic lodges, excited by those in Germany and Belgium, utter against me the vilest and most horrible of calumnies, and are moving heaven and earth to find means to assassinate me, I need more than ever the power of Divine protection, so as to live and die for the defense of our holy religion and of this dear Republic which God has called upon me to govern. What greater happiness can be awarded to me, most Holy Father, than to see myself detested and calumniated for the love of our Divine Redeemer? But what still greater happiness it would be if your benediction could obtain from the heaven the grace to

shed by blood for Him, who, being God, has deigned to shed every drop of his at the pillar and upon the Cross."[183]

Garcia Moreno was assassinated on August 6, 1875 while leaving the Cathedral of Quito.[184] The assassins used a messenger to summon Moreno from prayer in the Cathedral. Moreno was "wounded in the shoulder by a machete and riddled with bullets by the assassins from the Lodges."[185] An assassin yelled "Die, scourge of liberty," and Moreno replied, "God does not die!"[186]

Levels of Secrecy

Secret societies routinely have levels of secrecy. Members on the lower levels do not even know about the upper levels. Few Freemasons know the upper level, called Palladium, even exists.

Freemasons pay thousands of dollars and wait probationary periods of 15 years or more to learn the secrets of Freemasonry. Exposing the levels and religion of Freemasonry does not mean most Freemasons know about the one-world agenda. In fact most Freemasons, including 33rd degree Freemasons, do not know. The highest level secrets are reserved for the Palladium inner circle level. This means almost every Freemason, and probably every Freemason most people would likely meet in their lifetime, will learn Palladium-level secrets for the first time by reading this book.

The Thirty-third Degree Masonic symbols.[187]

There are over 100 degrees of Freemasonry, and members can generally disclose their degree title to the general public.[188] The degrees are not a progression of 100 levels, but choices a Mason can make along three main paths. One path is the American Rite or York Rite which has 13 degrees. A second path is the Scottish Rite which has 33 degrees. The third path is the Egyptian Rite which has 96 degrees. In addition to degrees are levels including the Mystic Shrine and Palladium. The Mystic Shrine level is available to any Master Mason; however, less than one Master Mason out of 100,000 is estimated to be selected for the Palladium-level.[189]

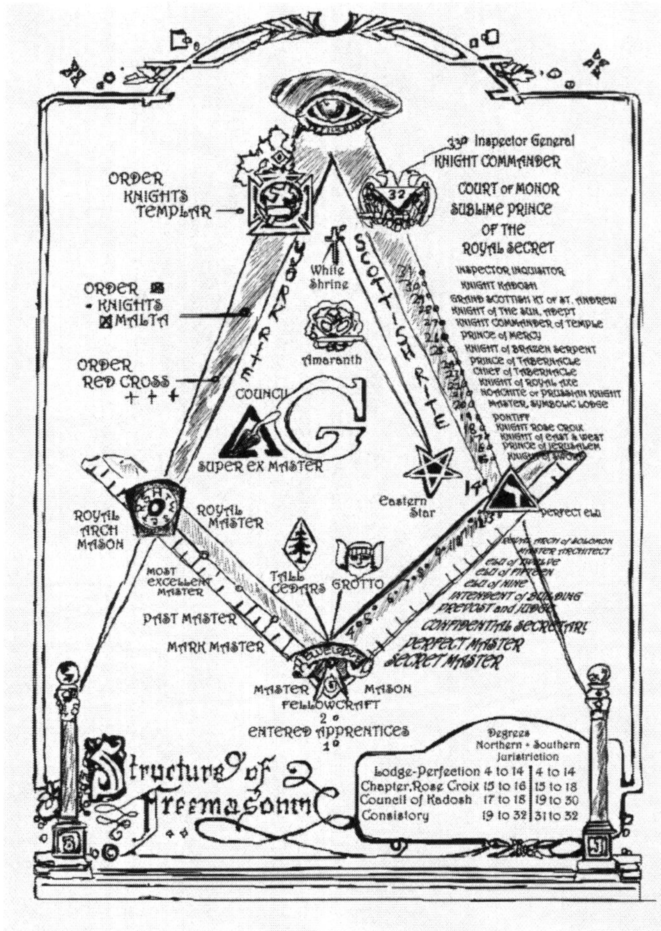

The structure of Freemasonry below the All-Seeing Eye.[190]

The drawing is the structure of Freemasonry below the All-Seeing Eye. The image shows Lucifer is the head of Freemasonry and the infrastructure of the secret society which conceals the religion of Freemasonry.[191] The Masonic square and compass are used to list the York Rite and Scottish Rite branches along with the levels in each branch. Regardless of the branch or path of Freemasonry, at each level the Mason learns he was previously misled. Only the few members who reach the Palladium level are entrusted with the full knowledge of the religion and its purpose. This means secrets are withheld even from 33rd degree members.

The Secret god of Freemasonry

The secret god of Freemasonry is Lucifer. In 1889 Albert Pike wrote to the 23 Supreme Councils of World Masonry, "The Masonic religion should be, by all of us initiates of the highest degrees, maintained in the purity of the Luciferian doctrine."[192] Elite Freemasons do not want their secret rituals explained or revealed. Even most Freemasons do not know Lucifer is the god of Freemasonry. Fortunately, this confusion evaporates rapidly when a person knows where to find the secrets of Freemasonry. When Freemasons do learn the truth, they frequently leave; this is a key reason membership is currently decreasing.[193]

Luciferians believe after attaining illumination or gnosis they rise above the human race.[194] Many Freemasons have confirmed they worship Lucifer to obtain illuminating knowledge. The secret that Lucifer is the god of Freemasonry is explained by Manly Hall in his book *The Lost Keys of Freemasonry.*[195] Hall wrote:

> "When the Mason learns that the key to the warrior on the block is the proper application of the dynamo of living power, he has learned the mystery of his Craft. The seething energies of Lucifer are in his hands and before he may step onward and upward, he must prove his ability to properly apply energy."[196]

The god of Freemasonry, Lucifer, is taught to be both female and male. Palladium-level Masons are told that Lucifer was the god of Atlantis and the god appearing as both Isis and Osiris in Egypt.[197] Isis is the female half and Osiris is the male half. Their child, Horus, is the third part of the Luciferian unholy trinity.

Jahbulon is Lucifer

Secret words used in Freemasonry often have their origin in the Bible.[198] In the Royal Arch degree shown in the following diagram, the secret word is not a Biblical name. The password is Jahbulon, a secret name for Lucifer. Jahbulon is an unholy trinity of names for the Masonic god. Freemason Albert Pike wrote that this name "has been for more than two thousand years an appellation of the Devil."[199] Mirroring the Hindu trinity of Brahma, Vishnu, and Shiva, Freemasonry teaches Jahbulon is creative, preservative, and annihilative.[200]

The following is a Holy Royal Arch Masonic altar-top and shows the Jahbulon letters which are scrambled before and after secret society meetings.[201]

Scrambled altar-top.[202]

Many Freemasons will never see the altar-top unscrambled. The unscrambled version is shown intentionally only to high-level Freemasons. If anyone not authorized views the unscrambled version, they are presented with a false translation. The unscrambled meaning of the symbol and letters, confirmed by former Freemasons and official documents, is shown in the next picture.

Unscrambled altar-top.[203]

According to the Freemasons, the circle in the above picture is an emblem of eternity and "a type of God" because it has no beginning or end. The circle is a reminder of the endless reward for Freemasons who advance the plan for a New World Order. The word on the circle in the above picture, Jehovah, is a name Freemasons use for I Am, that I Am, or the God of Abraham.[204]

In the triangle, the word Jahbulon is a name for the Masonic god. Freemasons believe Jehovah is divine but Jahbulon is also divine.[205] For Palladium-level Freemasonry the name Jahbulon, the enemy of Jehovah, is to be worshipped.

The Hebrew characters at the angles of the triangle in the picture are Aleph, Beth, and Lamed. In English, the corresponding letters are A, B, and L. Aleph and Beth combined, or AB, means Father.[206] The Beth, Aleph, and Lamed combined or BAL, means Lord.[207] The placement of the Hebrew characters on the triangle corners announces the inner and true god of Freemasonry is Jahbulon, which is synonymous with Lucifer.

The name Jahbulon is derived from four languages.[208] Jah is the Chaldee name of God and a Hebrew word signifying "I am and shall be."[209] The Syriac Bul or the Assyrian Baal means Lord or Powerful. On is an Egyptian word for Father of all.[210] Not surprisingly, the god of the Chaldee, Syriac, and Egyptian mystery religions was the enemy of the God of Abraham. While few people know about the Chaldee or Syriac religious beliefs, Moses and the exodus of the Jewish people from Egypt highlight that the senior god of the pharaohs was the enemy of the God of Abraham.

Freemasons still agree to be killed and kill fellow members if the name Jahbulon is correctly explained by their brother Masons. This is a key reason why a Freemason who does know this secret will lie when asked by an unauthorized person to explain Jahbulon.

Darkness Visible

Walton Hannah published the entire Masonic ritual of the three Craft degrees and of the Royal Arch in his *Darkness Visible* book.[211] Following this 1952 publication many Freemasons stepped forward to renounce their blood oaths and confirm the accuracy of the secrets published. At that time the worldwide Masonic membership was approximately 5.2 million men with 30.8% living in the United States.[212]

The publication of the Masonic secrets resulted in a massive disinformation campaign in an attempt to confuse the general public.[213] As a result, hundreds of publications falsely claim to expose the secrets of Freemasonry, but are actually written by Freemasons who seek to confuse and conceal secrets. In fact, a book about Freemasonry written after 1952 that does not mention *Darkness Visible* is an indicator the author may be serving a clandestine purpose.

Hanna's detailed explanation put the pieces of the puzzle together completely. The secrets he published made it clear that only people uninformed or comfortable with an anti-Christian religion could remain practicing the Craft. With the full rituals in plain view and validated by former Freemasons, elite Freemasons simply hope to never discuss *Darkness Visible.* Even one Freemason reading a single copy of *Darkness Visible,* or the book you are now reading, has the potential to hurt Masonic recruiting efforts.

Palladium

The official name of the elite level in Freemasonry is the New and Reformed Palladian Rite. Palladium is a continuation of the Knights Templar secret society.[214] It is this group of Freemasons who are most likely to interact directly with Brotherhood of Death "Wise Men." Wise Men are explained in Chapter 5.

The name Palladium is derived from the Latin "pala" or "phallus" and Hindu "pala" meaning male sex organ. In many secret societies, including Freemasonry, the phallus is a symbol of the generative force within man. The phallus symbol has been used to communicate ruling as a prince or king for thousands of years. Freemasons designed and built the Washington Monument phallus symbol. The Washington Monument is at the base of the Masonic triangle in the following picture. This triangle in the Washington, D.C. street design has its apex at the U.S. Capitol. Palladium-level members are entrusted with the full meaning of the Washington, D.C. city design which is explained in Chapter 9.

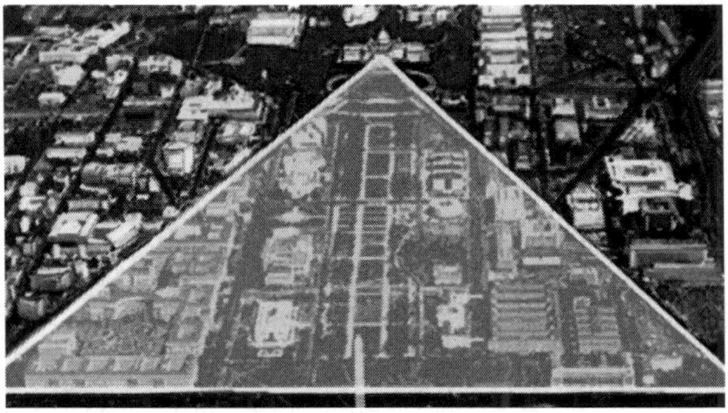

Hidden symbols are found throughout Washington, D.C. [215]

Charleston, South Carolina was selected as the birthplace for Palladism and is the Mother Supreme Council of all Masonic

Lodges of the World. Charleston was selected because it is geographically located near the 33rd parallel of latitude. This is important to Luciferians for several reasons, including that Ancient Babylon was geographically linked on the 33rd parallel.[216]

The Palladium secret society exists today and is a continuation of an ancient secret society, known as the Brotherhood of Death or the Brotherhood of the Snake. The three Freemasons working with Albert Pike (1809-1891) to run the Palladium order were Giuseppe Mazzini (1805-1872), Otto von Bismarck (1815-1898), and Henry Palmerston (1784-1865).[217] These four men united elite Freemasonry in the 19th century and laid the groundwork for much of the organized evil the world would experience, including the Civil War, World War I, and World War II. While each man was dead by the start of World War I, Pike taught that three world wars were needed to condition humanity to accept world government.[218] Appendix A explains Pike's plan for three world wars.

Pike's 1871 Letter to Mazzini

Multiple credible authors reported Albert Pike wrote a letter dated August 15, 1871 to Giuseppe Mazzini that described the Brotherhood of Death strategy.[219] Mazzini was a top Freemason and founded the Young Italy secret society. Young Italy became the Cosa Nostra, which is better known in the United States as the Mafia.[220] Since the late 19th century Freemasons have claimed that Pike's letter is a fabrication and the Palladium-level does not exist. The most obvious reason to deny the letter is to conceal that the Palladium-level exists and has planned a third world war.[221]

Former Freemasons have claimed that Pike's letter to Mazzini is authentic, and one credible example is Paul Joseph Copin (1851-1939) who used the pseudonym Copin-Albancelli.[222] He used a pseudonym because he violated his Masonic blood oath and knew Masons would attempt to murder him. Copin was a Rose-Croix Knighthood Freemason when he renounced his membership and revealed the secret society threat to Christianity.

Cardinal Rodriguez of Chile is another source that Pike's letter to Mazzini is authentic.[223] In Cardinal Rodriguez's 1925 book, *The Mystery of Freemasonry Unveiled*, he explained that the letter was kept at the British Museum Library.[224] Earlier sources that Pike's letter is authentic include the 1920 book titled *The Cause of the World Unrest*.[225]

An early claim that Pike's letter is authentic is in the 1895 book *Le Palladisme - Culte de Satan-Lucifer dans les Triangles maçonniques*.[226] The author, Domenico Margiotta, renounced Freemasonry after attaining the 33rd degree.[227] Cardinal Rodriguez concluded Margiotta was an insider although a carefully crafted 1897 hoax is cited by Freemasons as discrediting Margiotta.[228]

Albert Pike, author of the plan for three world wars.[229]

What is extremely noteworthy is the accuracy of what is claimed to be written in 1871 and was absolutely published by 1895. Cardinal Rodriguez died in 1958 and William Carr died in 1959. The accuracy of what these authors alone have explained about Pike's letter is mind-blowing. Starting with Cardinal Rodriguez, he reported Pike's 1871 letter explained a secret plan to create terrorism that would both destroy Christianity and deceive the world to accept world government.[230] Cardinal Rodriguez published the following text from Pike's 1871 letter.

> "We shall unleash the Nihilists and Atheists, and we shall provoke a formidable social cataclysm which in all its horror will show clearly to the nations the effect of absolute atheism, origin of savagery and of the most bloody turmoil. Then everywhere, the citizens, obliged to defend themselves against the world minority or revolutionaries, will exterminate those destroyers of civilization, and the multitude, disillusioned with Christianity, whose deistic spirits will be from that moment without compass (direction), anxious for an ideal, but without knowing where to render its adoration, will receive the TRUE LIGHT, through the universal manifestation of the pure doctrine of Lucifer, brought finally out in the public view, a manifestation which will result from the general reactionary movement which will follow the destruction of Christianity and Atheism, both conquered and exterminated at the same time."[231]

Carr reported that Pike wrote to Mazzini informing him he had received a vision that three world wars would be needed to help advance world government. In the 1954 book *Pawns in the Game*, William Carr wrote: "Between 1859, and 1871, he [Pike] worked out the details of a military blue-print, for three world wars, and three major revolutions which he considered would further the conspiracy to its final stage during the twentieth century."[232] Carr's explanation of each world war is provided in Appendix A. Carr's interpretation of Pike's plan is amazing.

Carr wrote in 1954:

> "World War Three is to be fomented by using the differences the agentur of the Illuminati stir up between Political Zionists and the leaders of the Moslem world. The war is to be directed in such a manner that Islam (the Arab World including Mohammedanism) and Political Zionism (including the State of Israel) will destroy themselves while at the same time the remaining nations, once more divided against each other on this issue, will be forced to fight themselves into a state of complete exhaustion physically, mentally, spiritually and economically. Can any unbiased and reasoning person

deny that the intrigue now going on in the Near, Middle, and Far East is designed to accomplish this devilish purpose?"[233]

What is now happening in the Near, Middle, and Far East may lead to World War III. As this book is published, some U.S. political leaders are calling for war with Iran, which could start World War III.

Freemasonry and Christianity

The Brotherhood of Death benefits greatly when people are deceived to believe Christianity officially approves of Freemasonry. The official public position of Freemasonry is that it is compatible with Christianity because the secret society is not a religion. This lie is told in order to protect Lucifer's identity. Freemason Sir John Cockburn, the Past Grand Deacon of England and Past Deputy Grand Master of Australia, explained that Freemasonry is a religion and claims to the contrary are "merely a war of words."[234]

Catholics and other Christians, even pastors, are sometimes Freemasons. For centuries, initiation for a Roman Catholic was an ipso facto excommunication, but increasingly we find Christian leaders are silent. The vast majority of these good people in Freemasonry are fooled by the lies and do not know the nature of the information withheld from them. A far smaller number of Freemasons are people who are committed Luciferians who infiltrate Christian organizations to help achieve the Brotherhood objective of destroying Christianity.

The following is an excerpt in which Sir John Cockburn elaborates on why Freemasonry is a religion, and simultaneously highlights how deceptive language can be when used to convince lower level members that the purpose of this hidden belief system is noble:

> "Perhaps the best way of arriving at a conclusion [on the question is Freemasonry a religion] would be first of all to enumerate the points which are common to most religions and then to enquire in what respect Masonry differs from them. Religion deals with the relationship between man and his Maker and instills a reverence for the Creator as the First Cause. Religions abound in observances of worship by prayer and praise. They inculcate rules of conduct by holding up a God or Hero as a pattern for imitation. All true religions denounce selfishness, extol mutual service and, if necessary, self-sacrifice. It would be difficult to say in which of these characteristics Freemasonry is lacking. Surely it abounds in all. Its ceremonies are elaborate and are unsurpassed for beauty and depth of meaning. They are interspersed with prayer and thanksgiving. In no religion is the reverential attitude of the Creature to the Creator [the Masonic god Lucifer] more clearly displayed."[235]

Freemasonry is a religion with altars, oaths, temples, priesthood, consecrations, anointings, creed, morality, and a god who is the enemy of God. Freemasonry is condemned by Christian faiths around the world. The leading opponent of Freemasonry for many centuries has been the Roman Catholic Church. The rumor that a Freemason can be a Roman Catholic in good standing is just that, a rumor. In 1983 the Congregation for the Doctrine of the Faith confirmed Catholics are prohibited from joining Masonic organizations.[236]

A comprehensive series of Roman Catholic condemnations of Freemasonry exist. The following is a list of the important and well-known condemnations:

1738 - Pope Clement XII issued *In Eminenti*

1751 - Pope Benedict XIV issued *Providas Romanorum*

1821 - Pope Pius VII issued *Ecclesiam a Jesu Christo*

1826 - Pope Leo XII issued *Quo Graviora*

1829 - Pope Pius VIII issued *Traditi Humilitati*

1832 - Pope Gregory XVI issued *Mirari Vos*

1846 - Pope Pius IX issued *Qui Pluribus*

1873 - Pope Pius IX issued *Etsi Multa*

1884 - Pope Leo XIII issued *Humanum Genus*

1917 - Pope Benedict XV issued the *Codex Iuris Canonici*

The leading opponent of Freemasonry for many centuries has been the Roman Catholic Church. Pope Clement XII described Freemasonry as "Satan's synagogue."[237] Pope Leo XIII also accurately identified Freemasonry's important role in the Brotherhood of Death, equating Freemasonry with the domain of Satan and warning the "partisans of evil" were united and seeking the destruction of Christianity.[238]

Pope Leo XIII[239]

"The Human Race, by the malice of the devil, it had departed from God, the Creator and Giver of heavenly gifts, divided itself into two different and opposing parties, one of which assiduously combats for truth and virtue, the other for those things which are opposed to virtue and truth. The one is the Kingdom of God on earth - that is the Church of Jesus Christ; those who desire to adhere to which from their soul and conducively to salvation must serve God and His only begotten Son with their whole mind and their whole will. The other is the kingdom of Satan, in whose dominion and power are all who have followed his sad example and that of our first parents."[240] Pope Leo XIII

Christians and non-Christians are encouraged to carefully read *Humanum Genus* which is the 1884 encyclical by Pope Leo XIII warning the world about Brotherhood of Death secret societies in the service of the kingdom of Satan.[241]

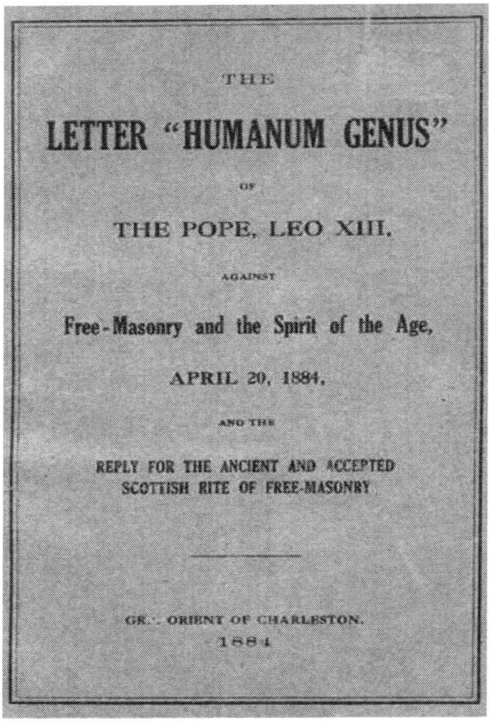
THE

LETTER "HUMANUM GENUS"

OF

THE POPE, LEO XIII,

AGAINST

Free-Masonry and the Spirit of the Age,

APRIL 20, 1884,

AND THE

REPLY FOR THE ANCIENT AND ACCEPTED SCOTTISH RITE OF FREE-MASONRY

GR∴ ORIENT OF CHARLESTON.

1884

The 1884 Masonic response by Albert Pike.[242]

The Humanum Genus encyclical is unique for two important reasons. The Masonic "Pope" for the kingdom of Satan, Albert Pike, delivered his response in October 1884 stating: "It was a declaration of war, arraying all faithful Catholics in the United States not only against their fellow-citizens, the Brethren of the Order of Freemasons, but against the principles that are the very life-blood of the government of the people of which they were supposed to be a part, and not the members of Italian Colonies, docile and obedient subjects of a foreign Potentate, and of the Cardinals, European and American, his Princes of the Church."[243]

The state of open war between Freemasonry and the Catholic Church is highly noteworthy as explained in the documentary *The Secret of Nagasaki* because 61 years later the center of Catholicism in Japan was destroyed by Freemasons using the atomic bomb.

Roman Catholic, Greek Orthodox, and many other Christian denominations condemn Freemasonry for teaching that multiple gods are equal, that killing people for disclosing secrets is appropriate, and for blasphemous religious rituals. The Palladium-level secrets, declaring Lucifer as god, present additional problems for anyone trying to claim Freemasonry is compatible with Christianity.

The Greek Orthodox Church is very clear that Freemasonry is a direct offspring of mystery religions spawned by the Brotherhood of the Snake. The Bishops of the Church of Greece concluded unanimously on October 12, 1933 that Freemasonry was ancient evil organized in modern times. An excerpt from the December 4, 1933 *Ekklesia* follows:

> "Thus, the incompatible contradiction between Christianity and Freemasonry is quite clear. It is natural that various Churches of other denominations have taken a stand against Freemasonry. Not only has the Western Church branded for its own reasons the Masonic movement by numerous Papal encyclicals, but Lutheran, Methodist, and Presbyterian communities have also declared it to be incompatible with Christianity. Much more has the Orthodox Catholic Church, maintaining in its integrity the treasure of Christian faith, proclaimed against it every time that the question of Freemasonry has been raised. Recently, the Interorthodox Commission which met on Mount Athos and in which the representatives of all the Autocephalous Orthodox Churches took part, has characterized Freemasonry as a 'false and anti-Christian system.'"[244]

The "anti-Christian system" condemnation by the Bishops of the Church of Greece is correct. Lutheran condemnation of

Freemasonry includes the Missouri Synod, which explained the god of Freemasonry is not the God and Father of our Lord.[245] The Lutheran denunciation stated that the Masonic path to salvation does not require faith in Jesus Christ.[246] Lutherans are to "admonish their pastors and congregations to testify against the sin of lodgery."[247]

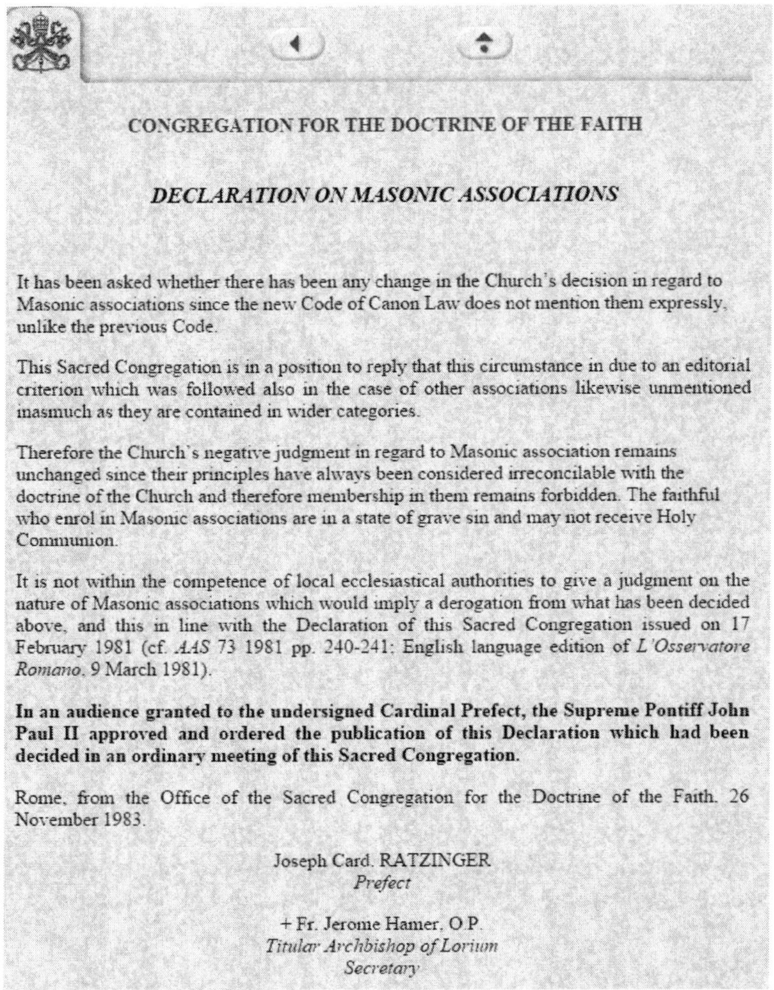

CONGREGATION FOR THE DOCTRINE OF THE FAITH

DECLARATION ON MASONIC ASSOCIATIONS

It has been asked whether there has been any change in the Church's decision in regard to Masonic associations since the new Code of Canon Law does not mention them expressly, unlike the previous Code.

This Sacred Congregation is in a position to reply that this circumstance in due to an editorial criterion which was followed also in the case of other associations likewise unmentioned inasmuch as they are contained in wider categories.

Therefore the Church's negative judgment in regard to Masonic association remains unchanged since their principles have always been considered irreconcilable with the doctrine of the Church and therefore membership in them remains forbidden. The faithful who enrol in Masonic associations are in a state of grave sin and may not receive Holy Communion.

It is not within the competence of local ecclesiastical authorities to give a judgment on the nature of Masonic associations which would imply a derogation from what has been decided above, and this in line with the Declaration of this Sacred Congregation issued on 17 February 1981 (cf. *AAS* 73 1981 pp. 240-241; English language edition of *L'Osservatore Romano*, 9 March 1981).

In an audience granted to the undersigned Cardinal Prefect, the Supreme Pontiff John Paul II approved and ordered the publication of this Declaration which had been decided in an ordinary meeting of this Sacred Congregation.

Rome, from the Office of the Sacred Congregation for the Doctrine of the Faith, 26 November 1983.

Joseph Card. RATZINGER
Prefect

+ Fr. Jerome Hamer, O.P.
Titular Archbishop of Lorium
Secretary

The 1983 Catholic Church declaration confirming a Catholic who is a Freemason is in a state of grave sin.[248]

The English Methodists have condemned Freemasonry. One example is the 1927 Bradford Conference, finding that Freemasonry "is wholly incompatible with the claims which have often been put forward by Freemasons.[249] Presbyterians' condemnations include those made by the Free Presbyterian Church of Scotland, the Reformed Presbyterian Church of Ireland, and the Orthodox Presbyterian Church of America. In Scotland, the "Original Secession" opposed Freemasonry as early as 1757.[250]

Padre Pio's Special Assignment

Saint Padre Pio was a Roman Catholic mystic in the Order of Friars Minor Capuchin.[251] He became famous for being able to often know what people thought and bearing the stigmata for most of his life.[252] Padre Pio received the bodily marks and bleeding of Jesus on September 20, 1918. The blood with the odour of sanctity flowed from these marks until 1968 when he died.[253]

Padre Pio met Fr. Luigi Villa in 1956 at San Giovanni Rotondo in southeastern Italy. In this initial meeting, Padre Pio informed Fr. Villa of his special mission to protect the Catholic Church from the Brotherhood of Death. Padre Pio said "you must dedicate your entire life to defend the Church of Christ from the work of Freemasonry, especially the ecclesiastical."[254] As part of this special assignment, Fr. Villa was officially tasked to identify all Freemasons in the Catholic Church leadership.[255]

In 1963 Fr. Villa met for a second time with Padre Pio. Padre Pio said: "Courage, courage, courage! for the Church is already invaded by Freemasonry. Freemasonry has already reached the Pope's slippers."[256] This statement from a recognized Saint is paradigm changing and explains why the Blessed Virgin wanted the full Fatima Secret disclosed in 1960. On June 21, 1963 Cardinal Montini became Pope Paul VI.[257] Padre Pio is saying Pope Paul VI was being influenced by Satan.

Fr. Villa's writings including his book, *Paul VI beatified?*, exposing Pope Paul VI as a Freemason are often cited as the reason Pope Paul VI was stopped from becoming a saint.[258]

Franciscan priest Charles Madden wrote in 1995 that Freemasonry is "mankind's hidden enemy," and the Catholic Church opposition in the 21st century has not changed.[259] He sums up Freemasonry as existing to establish a religion of blasphemy.[260]

Freemasonry is both a Luciferian religion and a parasite on the Christian religion. In Christianity, Jesus is the cornerstone of salvation. In Freemasonry, the Masonic savior Hiram is the cornerstone.[261] As highlighted by Walton Hannah, "No [Christian] Church that has seriously investigated the religious teachings and implications of Freemasonry has ever yet failed to condemn it."[262]

5

INTERLOCKING EVIL

"For more than a century ideological extremists at either end of the political spectrum have seized upon well-publicized incidents such as my encounter with Castro to attack the Rockefeller family for the inordinate influence they claim we wield over American political and economic institutions. Some even believe we are part of a secret cabal working against the best interests of the United States, characterizing my family and me as 'internationalists' and of conspiring with others around the world to build a more integrated global political and economic structure–one world, if you will. If that's the charge, I stand guilty, and I am proud of it."[263]

David Rockefeller

David Rockefeller is one of the most visible leaders of the Brotherhood of Death.[264] In the quote above he admits to participating in "a secret cabal working against the best interests of the United States."

Rockefeller's 2002 admission of participating in a secret cabal shines light on the Brotherhood as a cartel of interlocking evil. He is a leader in at least three of the five top Brotherhood of Death front organizations that are corrupting the United States government. The largest organization, Freemasonry, is explained in the prior chapter. The organizations David Rockefeller helps lead are the Council on Foreign Relations, the Bilderberg Group, and the Trilateral Commission which are explained in this chapter. Yale's Skull and Bones Society is the fifth key Brotherhood front influencing the U.S. government, and is also explained in this chapter.

David Rockefeller is not the only Brotherhood of Death insider who revealed all or part of the one-world agenda in a published book.[265] Other notable insider authors include: Albert Pike in *Morals and Dogma* (1872), Cecil Rhodes in *Confessions of Faith* (1877), Madame Blavatsky in *The Secret Doctrine* (1888), Edward Mandell House in *Colonel House's Diary* (1919) and his lightly veiled fiction *Philip Dru Administrator: A Story of Tomorrow 1920-1935* (1912), Frederick Howe in *The Confessions of a Reformer* (1925), Manly P. Hall in *Lectures on Ancient Philosophy* (1929), H. G. Wells in *The New World Order* (1940), Carroll Quigley in *Tragedy and Hope* (1966), and Walter Isaacson & Evan Thomas in *The Wise Men* (1986).[266]

Quigley Confirmation

Carroll Quigley, a professor at Harvard, Princeton, and Georgetown documented the existence of the Brotherhood in *Tragedy and Hope.*[267] His book was suppressed after the first 1966 printing but reprinted in 1974. Quigley's book title communicates his perspective that it is a tragedy rule by the elite cartel had not yet arrived and his hope that it would one day arrive. Quigley concluded an educated elite would govern better than ordinary people. What he failed to realize is the danger of absolute power, the kind of power sought by the Brotherhood, threatens humanity. History teaches us that absolute power in the hands of humans corrupts absolutely.[268]

Quigley wrote, "I know of the operations of this network because I have studied it for twenty years and was permitted for two years, in the early 1960's, to examine its papers and secret records."[269] He also wrote: "It is not easy to write the history of a secret group of this kind, but...it should be done, for this group is, as I shall show, one of the most important historical facts of the twentieth century."[270]

Quigley is famous for his significant influence on New World Order insider Bill Clinton. In a 1991 presidential campaign speech, Clinton referred to Quigley as an important influence in his life.[271] Clinton also mentioned Quigley at other times, including his 1992 acceptance speech at the Democratic National Convention.[272]

Interlocked Across Economic Systems

Exactly how Brotherhood of Death affiliated secret societies interlock across vastly different economic systems, including capitalism and communism, is often not clearly understood. Leaders of interlocking economic systems are depicted in the following picture from the Potsdam conference.

Churchill, Truman and Stalin at the Potsdam Conference.[273]

British Prime Minister Winston Churchill, U.S. President Harry S. Truman, and Soviet Leader Josef Stalin were Brotherhood of Death members.[274]

Brotherhood of Death member,[275] bank robber, creator of Birobidzhan[276] and the Order of Sword-Bearers,[277] Iosif Vissarionovich Dzhugashvili is better known as Joseph Stalin.

The Tsar's Secret Police arrested Stalin for his secret society activities.[278] Stalin is shown in the following mug shot.[279]

Police photograph of Joseph Stalin.[280]

Stalin used many different names to conceal his secret society service including: Bars, Besoshvili, David, Gayoz Nizheradze, Ogoness Vartanovich Totomyants, and Zakhar Gregoryan Melikyants.[281]

Stalin had a blood loyalty oath to the Brotherhood of Death which superseded his loyalty to the Soviet Union.[282] After Stalin's death, Soviet leaders concluded it was impossible to fully suppress the evil that he inflicted on the world.[283] The term as "de-Stalinization" means suppression of Stalin's agenda to create a society in the service of Satan and political reforms to change policies that he established.

The Cold War successfully distracted many people from seeing how evil is organized. Properly identifying the role of Brotherhood of Death agents is necessary to understanding World War I, World War II and the Cold War.[284] The fact that major wars are routinely led by members of Brotherhood of Death affiliated secret societies can be eye-opening.

U.S. Presidents and Brotherhood of Death Fronts

The following list shows recent U.S. presidents and their participation in one or more of the six Brotherhood of Death secret society fronts explained in this book (i.e., Freemasonry, Skull and Bones, the Council on Foreign Relations, Bohemian Grove, the Bilderberg Group, and the Trilateral Commission).

Name and years as president	Secret Society
Herbert Hoover (1929-1933)	CFR, Bohemian Grove
Franklin D. Roosevelt (1933-1945)	Freemasonry
Harry S. Truman (1945-1953)	Freemasonry
Dwight D. Eisenhower (1953-1961)	CFR, Bohemian Grove
John F. Kennedy (1961-1963)	CFR
Lyndon B. Johnson (1963-1969)	Freemasonry
Richard Nixon (1969-1974)	CFR, Bohemian Grove
Gerald Ford (1974-1977)	Freemasonry, CFR, Bilderberg, Bohemian Grove
Jimmy Carter (1977-1981)	CFR, Trilateral
Ronald Reagan (1981-1989)	Honorary Scottish Rite Mason, Trilateral, Bohemian Grove
George H. W. Bush (1989-1993)	Skull and Bones, CFR, Trilateral, Bohemian Grove
William J. Clinton (1993-2001)	CFR, Bilderberg, Trilateral
George W. Bush (2001-2009)	Skull and Bones
Barack Obama (2009-present)	CFR, Bilderberg

Skull and Bones

The Order of Skull and Bones is one of the older secret societies in the United States. Skull and Bones is located at Yale University in New Haven, Connecticut. Founded in 1832, the once male only society now includes both men and women. It is also known as The Brotherhood of Death because members perform occult rituals, including the blood oath to protect secrets. The

Russell Trust Association owns its properties and oversees student activities.

Many members of Skull and Bones have worked for the Central Intelligence Agency (CIA). Former presidents George H. W. Bush and George W. Bush are Skull and Bones alumni. Other prominent "Bonesmen" are former President and Supreme Court Justice William Howard Taft, former Supreme Court Justice Potter Stewart, former Secretary of War Henry Stimson, and former Secretary of Defense Robert A. Lovett. The CIA's James Jesus Angleton was one of the most important Skull and Bones insiders serving the Brotherhood of Death. His leadership in covering up the John F. Kennedy assassination is explained in *Vigilant Christian IV: 9/11 - The Secret War.*

Council on Foreign Relations

The Council on Foreign Relations (CFR) is the most visible Brotherhood of Death front in United States politics.[285] David Rockefeller became a CFR director in 1949. Dr. Carroll Quigley explained its inception, development, and current dominance in all U.S. branches of government.[286] He explained the CFR is a "front group" for a small but powerful group seeking to establish world government. Presidents who have been members of the CFR include Herbert Hoover, Dwight D. Eisenhower, John F. Kennedy, Richard M. Nixon, Gerald R. Ford, James E. Carter, George H. W. Bush, and William J. Clinton.[287]

Council on Foreign Relations members in top positions.[288]

Presidents	**Vice Presidents**	**CIA Directors**
Herbert Hoover	Richard M. Nixon	Walter Bedell Smith
Dwight D. Eisenhower	Hubert Humphrey	Allen W. Dulles
John F. Kennedy	Gerald R. Ford	John A. McCone
Richard M. Nixon	Nelson A. Rockefeller	Richard M. Helms
Gerald R. Ford	Walter Mondale	James R. Schlesinger
James E. Carter	George H. W. Bush	William E. Colby

George H. W. Bush
William J. Clinton

Richard B. Cheney
Joseph Biden

George H. W. Bush
Stansfield Turner
William J. Casey
William H. Webster
Robert M. Gates
R. James Woolsey
John M. Deutch
George J. Tenet
Michael V. Hayden
Michael J. Morell[289]
David H. Petraeus[290]

Secretaries of War/Defense

Henry L. Stimson
Robert P. Patterson
James V. Forrestal
Robert A. Lovett
Neil H. McElroy
Thomas S. Gates, Jr.
Robert S. McNamara
Melvin R. Laird
Elliot L. Richardson
James R. Schlesinger
Donald H. Rumsfeld
Harold Bown
Caspar W. Weinberger
Frank C. Carlucci
Richard B. Cheney
Leslie Aspin
William J. Perry
William S. Cohen
Donald Rumsfeld[291]
Robert M. Gates
Chuck Hagel

Secretaries of the Treasury

Andrew W. Mellon
Ogden L. Mills
William H. Woodin
Henry Morgenthau, Jr.
Robert B. Anderson
C. Douglas Dillon
Henry H. Fowler
David M. Kennedy
George P. Shultz
William E. Simon
W. Michael Blumenthal
G. William Miller
Donald T. Regan
Nicholas F. Brady
Lloyd Bentsen
Robert Rubin
Lawrence H. Summers
Henry M. Paulson, Jr.
Timothy Geithner
Neal S. Wolin[292]
Jacob "Jack" Lew

Secretaries of State

Henry L. Stimson
Edward Stettinius, Jr.
Dean G. Acheson
John Foster Dulles
Christian A. Herter
David Dean Rusk
William P. Rogers
Henry A. Kissinger
Cyrus R. Vance
Edmund S. Muskie
Alexander M. Haig, Jr.
George P. Shultz
Lawrence Eagleburger
Warren Christopher
Madeleine K. Albright
Colin L. Powell
Condoleezza Rice
Hillary Clinton

Many of the CFR members are "five year only members" and are not cognizant of the organization's history or hidden agenda. The individuals with "lifetime membership" are aware of the one world government objective. Similar to Freemasonry and all other

Brotherhood of Death fronts, the elite lifetime CFR members need the larger number of CFR members to serve as credible dupes. Appendix D in *Vigilant Christian I: The New World Order* provides additional information on the CFR.

Bohemian Grove

This Brotherhood of Death has a woodland hideaway in northern, California. This private facility is where multiple secret societies meet and work together.[293] Each July key Brotherhood of Death agents meet in Monte Rio, California to participate in a religious ceremony called "The Cremation of Care."[294] The occult ritual occurs at the 2,700-acre Bohemian Grove facility in front of a 40-foot Owl Shrine.

The Bohemian Club owl shrine.[295]

Many participants or guests serve as dupes and do not realize the ceremonies are derived from an ancient Babylonian religious ritual. Membership levels help conceal the meaning of the Cremation of Care ceremony and insiders can earn "Old Guard" status after 40 years of membership.[296]

Brotherhood of Death members value the owl as clever, a silent hunter in darkness, and often hidden in plain sight [297]

Weaving Spiders sign at the Bohemian Grove.[298]

The Bohemian Grove has been the epicenter for many Brotherhood of Death meetings to plot and execute their various plans for world domination. One example is the first atomic bomb meeting that took place in September 1942 at the Bohemian Grove.[299]

Bilderberg Group

The Bilderberg Group exists to help achieve a world government. The Bilderberg Group is named after the hotel in Holland where a highly secret meeting of Brotherhood of Death leaders took place in May 1954.[300] For decades the existence of the group was denied and, despite exposure, people expressing concerns were labeled by the mainstream media as conspiracy nuts. The Bilderberg Group's exposure continued, which prompted changes. No longer is the existence of this secret organization denied. The Bilderberg Group even launched a website with some meeting and participation information. A partial listing of people who have attended one or more Bilderberg conferences is in *Vigilant Christian I: The New World Order*, and demonstrates the powerful reach of the Brotherhood.[301]

Trilateral Commission

The Trilateral Commission (TC) was established in 1973 by David Rockefeller as a Brotherhood of Death front to create a federation among Asia, America, and Europe.[302] The TC is focused on creating a new economic world order by transforming nations to technocratic economies. A technocracy is a system where an elite control resources. The TC technocrats are architecting a new energy-based economic system to replace the current price-based system.

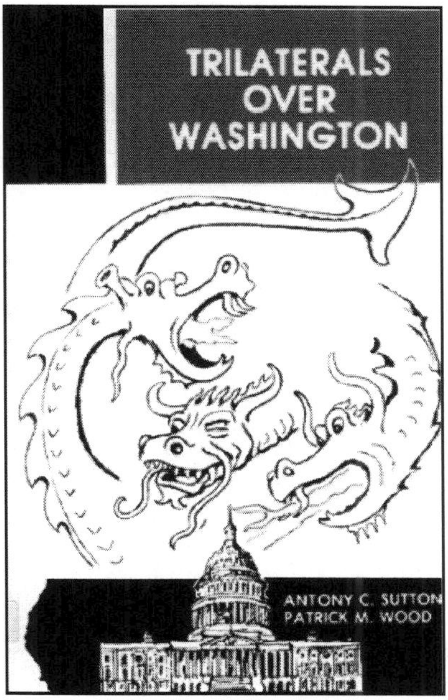

Wood and Sutton explained the dark purpose of the Trilateral Commission and dangers of technocracy.[303]

Senator Barry M. Goldwater wrote in his memoirs that the CFR and TC are international cabals working to replace the U.S. government with a one world government. He wrote: "The CFR is the American branch of a society which originated in England. Internationalist in viewpoint, the CFR believes national boundaries should be obliterated and one world rule established."[304] Goldwater explained the TC was doing the same thing as the CFR but with a Pacific Asian focus. He wrote that the Trilateral Commission views populations "as nothing more than producing and consuming units" in the pursuit of one world government.[305]

The 1871 Brotherhood of Death plan for world government called for three world wars and the establishment of ten economic zones. The ten zones or regions were published in the Brotherhood's Club of Rome report, "Regionalized and Adaptive Model of the Global World System."[306]

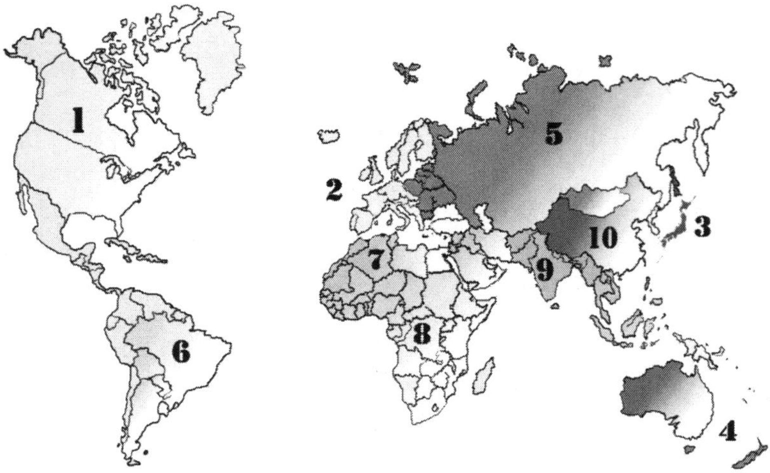

The one-world government ten economic zones.[307]

Legend

1. United States, Canada and Mexico
2. The European Union
3. Japan
4. South Africa, Australia, and New Zealand
5. Eastern Europe, Pakistan, Afghanistan, Russia and the former countries of the Soviet Union
6. Central America, South America, Cuba and Caribbean Islands
7. The Middle East and North Africa
8. The rest of Africa except South Africa
9. South and Southeast Asia, including India
10. China (Mongolia is included with China)

The Trilateral Commission is charged with helping create six of the ten Brotherhood of Death regions. The Trilateral Commission Pacific Asian Group includes region 1 (United States, Canada, and Mexico), region 2 (the European Union), region 3 (Japan), region 4 (Australia, and New Zealand), region 9 (South and Southeast Asia including India), and region 10 China (including Mongolia). The Trilateral Commission has a similar purpose and operating methods as the Council on Foreign Relations with a key difference being that the CFR is only focused on regions 1 and 2.[308]

Freemasonry, Skull and Bones, the Council on Foreign Relations, the Bilderberg Group, and the Trilateral Commission are the tip of the iceberg. Other front organizations exist to diversify organized evil. When an insider in one secret society blows the whistle, that organization can be written off—although often these organizations go into hibernation and sometimes just change their name or reappear when the public attention has faded.

The number of organizations secretly used to advance the interests of the Brotherhood of Death exceeds several thousand. Organizations range from private mercenary companies such as the former Blackwater (renamed to Xe Services in 2009 and renamed to Academi in 2011) to occult publishing corporations such as the former Lucifer Publishing Company (now called the Lucis Trust).

Wise Men

The interlocking Brotherhood of Death strategy includes a layer of agents below the very top group, known as "Wise Men." Wise Men are often the offspring of top Brotherhood of Death agents. They serve as the hidden hand to interact with leaders in governments and Brotherhood of Death front organizations.

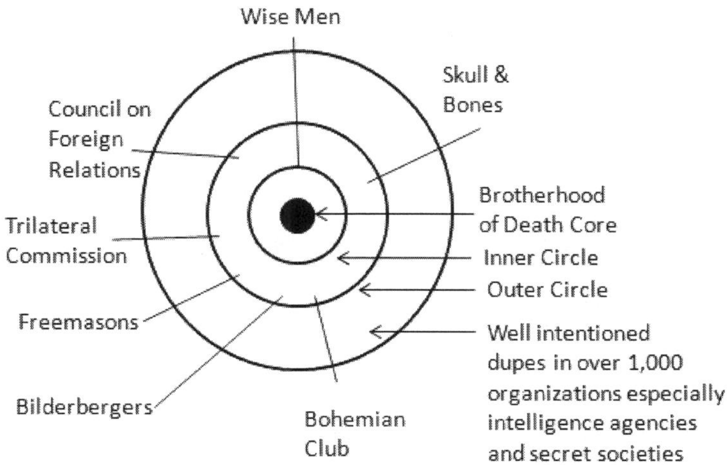

Wise Men are near the center and are extremely powerful.[309]

The top group, known as High Council members or Olympians, interact directly with the Wise Men to help conceal their control of secret societies. As noted in the beginning of this chapter, David Rockefeller is the most visible 21st century "Wise Man" and has acknowledged "conspiring with others around the world" to achieve world government.[310]

In the 19th century, August Belmont was a Wise Man who helped the Brotherhood of Death seize control of the U.S. monetary system.[311] In the 20th century, Edward Mandell House performed a key Wise Man role.[312] He was followed by Henry Stimson and Bernard Baruch.

Books have been written about the Wise Men, usually by authors in the service of the Brotherhood of Death. In the book *The Wise Men*, Henry Stimson is described as a savior and the "consummate American statesman and Wall Street lawyer."[313] In another Wise Men book, *Henry L. Stimson: The First Wise Man*, he is presented as the Wise Man who is responsible for the atomic bomb program.[314]

How the Wise Men interact with U.S presidents reveals much about how the Brotherhood of Death wields power. Finding the role of Wise Men is finding the Brotherhood of Death red thread running throughout history. Without understanding that Wise Men serve the Brotherhood of Death, not the governments they public affiliate with, historical events are often difficult to accurately decipher.

Two brief examples are highlighted. The first involves Harry S. Truman. In March 1941, Senator Truman led a United States Congressional investigative body called the Senate Special Committee to Investigate the National Defense Program.[315] Better known as the Truman Committee, the investigative body served to conceal, not reveal, war profiteering.

Interactions between Henry Stimson and lower level Brotherhood of Death member Harry Truman highlight who was the superior and who was the subordinate. In 1943 when Truman inquired about massive amounts of war spending, Stimson replied he would not tell him and it was "part of a very important secret development."[316] Truman was told "that he would have to trust me implicitly."[317] Truman replied "I herewith see the situation, Mr. Secretary, and you won't have to say another word to me. Whenever you say that to me, that's all I want to hear."[318] Another example is Stimson's conclusion that Truman "was a nuisance" and "a pretty untrustworthy man."[319]

In April 1945, Stimson decided to tell President Truman that within four months the United States would "have completed the most terrible weapon ever known in human history, one bomb of which could destroy a whole city."[320] Stimson did not tell Truman of his decision to take Kyoto off the target list and put Nagasaki on the list.[321] Stimson told General Groves, "This is one time I'm going to be the final deciding authority. Nobody's going to tell me what to do on this. On this matter I am the kingpin."[322]

Bernard Baruch, as is often the case with Wise Men, was the son of a top Brotherhood of Death agent.[323] Wise Men have access to information that enable them to become extremely wealthy. In Baruch's *My Own Story* memoir he explains his "first big deal" which greatly increased his wealth.[324] He wrote:

> "As our special roared past sleeping towns and hamlets it seemed to me that I was repeating on a smaller scale the financial feat which legend ascribed to Nathan Rothschild at the Battle of Waterloo.
>
> In honoring Wellington's drafts when the English government was unable to do so, Rothschild had staked his fortune on the overthrow of Napoleon. Wellington's campaign in Belgium started badly, which depressed English securities. Rothschild, who had crossed the Channel to get first news of events, is said to have been on the field of Waterloo when the tide of battle

turned against Napoleon. By getting word of this to London a few hours in advance of the official couriers he enabled the Rothschilds to make large purchases before shares rebounded.

As our train sped through the dark, it seemed that history was repeating itself. Thinking of how American arms had been victorious on land and sea from Cuba to the Philippines, halfway around the world, I felt the surge of empire welling within me. No thought entered my head of the problems and responsibilities that an "American Empire" might bring in years to come."

Baruch explains in his memoirs that advance information enabled him to make a killing by placing orders for American stocks on the London Exchange before the New York exchange opened.[325] He wrote: "The next morning when the Exchange in New York opened, stocks advanced all along the line. Our London purchases showed good profits immediately."[326]

Among Baruch's early Brotherhood of Death assignments was influencing the U.S to fight in World War I. His Brotherhood of Death service included leading the War Industries Board in 1918.[327] In 1919, he was one of the Wise Men at Versailles attending the Paris Peace conference.[328] Authors Isaacson and Thomas observed the Wise Men twentieth-century incarnation "began with the group of internationalists who acted as an informal brain trust for Woodrow Wilson at Versailles and returned home to found the Council on Foreign Relations."[329]

Winston Churchill, Bernard Baruch and Dwight Eisenhower.[330]

Soon after World War I the Brotherhood of Death began working to start a second world war. In control of these men was Baruch. Baruch was responsible for helping many people reach top military and civilian positions.[331] President Dwight D. Eisenhower said: "Twenty-five years ago as a young and unknown Major, I took the wisest step in my life - I consulted Mr. Baruch."[332]

President Dwight D. Eisenhower in 1967.[333]

Eisenhower was Baruch's man for many years, ranging from the rank of major, to World War II Supreme Commander, to President from 1953 to 1961. To further appreciate Eisenhower's "Twenty-five years ago..." statement a brief explanation of the Bonus Army is provided. The term "Bonus Army" is derived from a demand by World War I veterans for a bonus which led to the creation of the American Legion in 1919. The political movement partially succeeded in 1924 when the U.S. government approved the World War Adjusted Compensation Act. A bonus of $1.25 for overseas service and $1.00 for each day served in the United States was authorized to be made in 1945.

In the spring and summer of 1932 the Great Depression intensified prompting approximately 43,000 soldiers to occupy Washington, D.C. President Herbert Hoover ordered the Army to remove the veterans who had proclaimed themselves the Bonus Expeditionary Force. A Brotherhood of Death officer, General Douglas MacArthur, commanded the mission. Major Dwight D. Eisenhower, MacArthur's Washington police liaison, orchestrated bayonet and tear gas attacks on veterans and their families. When the veterans' families retreated across the Anacostia River, Hoover ordered MacArthur to stop. MacArthur and Eisenhower, loyal to Bernard Baruch, continued the attack. Over one hundred people were seriously injured and two children died. The violence was covered up by a report, written by Eisenhower, endorsing MacArthur's use of force.

Baruch never ran or held a public office but nonetheless was more powerful than the various presidents he interacted with throughout his life.[334] A. K. Chesterton wrote: "Now Americans believe, and they are not alone in their belief, that the most powerful man in the United States is the President. Bernard Baruch, giving evidence before a Congressional Committee, disposed of that polite fiction. In answer to a question he affirmed that during the war he, Baruch, had been the most powerful man in America."[335] A key point Chesterton makes is Baruch was the most powerful person in the United States during World War I and his power, albeit unofficial, only expanded during and after World War II.

The hidden hand of how U.S. presidents are selected is less hidden when the role of Wise Men is understood. For example, the great-grandfather of former U.S. President George W. Bush and grandfather of former U.S. President George H. W. Bush was Samuel Prescott Bush.[336] Samuel Prescott Bush worked for Bernard Baruch. Bush and Baruch had created a sea of blood long before thousands of woman and children died from the atomic bombs dropped on Japan.[337]

A second example of Wise Men Baruch and Stimson working with a lower level Brotherhood of Death agent is Harry Hopkins.[338] Hopkins served the Wise Men by arranging for the Soviet government to receive Top Secret code breaking information and the materials needed to build an atomic bomb.[339] As background, after World War II ended, the Brotherhood of Death needed to have another credible enemy for people to focus on, so the Wise Men went to work to create a Cold War. Bernard Baruch is the person who literally created the term "Cold War."[340] Hopkins is the person who Major George Jordan revealed was responsible for sending the nation's most sensitive atomic bomb information to Stalin.[341] The fact that two Freemason presidents, FDR and Truman, gave Freemason Joseph Stalin communications and atomic bomb secrets is illogical without understanding the role and purpose of the Wise Men.

Reece Committee Confirmation

You may wonder if the existence of a powerful elite advancing one-world government was ever uncovered by Congress. The answer is yes, and the 1954 Reece Committee is a prime example. Norman Dodd was the chief investigator for U.S. Congressman B. Carroll Reece's Special Committee on Tax Exempt Foundations. He testified that the Reece Committee concluded that the Rockefeller Foundation partnered with the Carnegie Endowment for International Peace to rewrite history for a powerful banking elite seeking to control the education of American students and to achieve one-world government.[342]

In a 1977 interview Dodd said:

> "They decided that the success of this program lay in an alteration in the manner in which American history was to be presented. They then approached four of the then most-prominent historians -- such as Mary and Charles Beard -- with the suggestion that they alter the manner in which they were accustomed to presenting the subject. They [were] turned down flat, so ... they decided they [had] to build a coterie of historians of their own selection."[343]

In 1982, G. Edward Griffin interviewed Norman Dodd. In this interview Dodd explained how America's major non-profit foundations have a hidden agenda to create a one-world government.[344] According to Dodd, in the archives of the Carnegie Endowment for International Peace was the following statement of purpose:

> "The only way to maintain control of the population was to obtain control of education in the U.S. They [the Brotherhood of Death leadership] realized this was a prodigious task so they approached the Rockefeller Foundation with the suggestion that they go in tandem and that portion of education which could be considered as domestically oriented be taken over by the Rockefeller Foundation and that portion which was oriented to International matters be taken over by the Carnegie Endowment."[345]

The Reece Committee also found that the American Historical Association (AHA) was controlled by a secretive elite. This meant that even if concrete evidence of the Brotherhood of Death shadow government were presented to the American people, agents of the elite in education would brainwash people to the point that they would dismiss this information as a "conspiracy theory."[346]

The AHA's disclosure about its history and influence provides the specifics on how an elite group seized control of the history taught in schools. The following AHA excerpt summarizes how the Brotherhood obtained control: [347]

> "The teaching of history has been an AHA concern since its inception. At the K-12 level, the AHA took a leadership role in the National Education Association's Committee of Ten (1893), which established the importance of history in the emerging secondary school curriculum. The Association followed this with further suggestions for revision and improvement from the Committee of Seven (1899), the Committee of the Social Studies (1916), the AHA Commission (1929-34), and the establishment in 1969 of AHA's History Education Project, funded by the Office of Education."

The Reece Committee also revealed a relationship between the Guggenheim Foundation and the AHA. The Guggenheim Foundation, founded in 1937, had a direct role in selecting "a coterie of twenty historians" for AHA leadership positions.[348] The historians were approached early in their academic careers and offered comfortable and prestigious futures as long as they redefined history to serve the interests of their sponsors.

In addition to what the Reece Committee discovered in 1976, the U.S. Senate Church Committee revealed that the Central Intelligence Agency was used to routinely publish books suppressing the truth.[349] CIA agents who are journalists, think tank staff, and broadcasters present incomplete information to the public in the false belief that they are serving U.S. interests. In 1976, the Church Committee confirmed over a thousand books have been sponsored by the CIA to redefine history.[350]

6

BROTHERHOOD RELIGION

"The Masonic religion should be, by all of us initiates of the highest degrees, maintained in the purity of the Luciferian doctrine."[351] Albert Pike

The religion of the New World Order needs to be explained because a belief of becoming a god guides their actions. The Brotherhood of Death religion has different names, but whether it is called Freemasonry, Luciferianism, or something else, a common unifying thread is the belief that possessing secret knowledge is the way to transform people into gods.

The All-Seeing Eye capstone is added to this picture of the Brotherhood of Death temple in Washington, D.C.[352]

The religion, as illustrated by Freemasonry, is directly related to the Egyptian mysteries as evidenced by shared secret hand grips, signs, symbols, postures, and apron that harken back to ancient Egypt.[353] The apron is presented during the first initiation and the pictures of Harry Truman and George Washington in Chapter 4 show both men wearing the apron.[354]

The Brotherhood of Death religion predates ancient Egypt by thousands of years, originating with the Brotherhood of the Snake claimed to predate ancient Babylon. In this belief system, members are initiated and pledge their soul to Lucifer, or Satan, or another god of deception. The concept of "selling your soul to the Devil" is often dismissed as a myth, but it is a very real part of the Brotherhood belief system.

Satanism vs. Luciferianism

Although Satanists and Luciferians ultimately end up in the same place, they have notable differences. Satanists believe they are evil and worship Satan, while Luciferians believe they are good and worship Lucifer. Luciferians believe they worship a good god and Satanists believe they worship an evil god. Luciferians believe that Satan does not exist, while Satanists believe that Lucifer does not exist because Lucifer became Satan. Luciferians believe that good and evil acts should be balanced while Satanists reject this notion. Satanists correctly view Lucifer as one of Satan's deceptions to drag more souls to hell. The differentiation seems minor at first pass, but understanding the difference is necessary to understanding how a person who would never join a Satanist group can be tricked into participating in Luciferian secret societies.

Luciferians and Satanists both believe they are worshipping a god that wants them to acquire power and wealth. Both religions teach that their god blesses the rich and the end justifies the means. For Luciferians wealth and power on earth are paramount, and only fools believe the materially poor are blessed. Jesus taught the poor are blessed. Unlike Luciferianism, a greed-justifying belief system, wealth and power are not to be life goals.[355]

Many people are surprised to learn that Satanism is officially sanctioned by the U.S. military. The Church of Satan and Temple of Set belief systems are in the *U.S. Army's Handbook for Chaplains* and are religious options available to soldiers. In 1997, the Pentagon approved witchcraft occult rituals at Fort Hood. The U.S. government approval of the Fort Hood Open Circle was the first official Wiccan authorization, although clandestine occult worship at military bases such as Fort Hood existed long before the official recognition.[356] Wicca is a modern pagan religion that routinely involves witchcraft. Wiccans, Satanists, Luciferians, and other occult followers are often attracted to the military because it legalizes their desire to serve their god with human sacrifice.

Satanists in the U.S. Army generally keep a low profile but Michael Aquino is an exception. This retired Lieutenant Colonel in Military Intelligence was a very public Satanist and a founder of the Temple of Set.[357] He was extremely proud of a black magic ceremony he led at Wewelsburg Castle in Germany. The Luciferian and ultimately Satanic rituals performed at Wewelsburg Castle are explained in detail in *Vigilant Christian III: The Occult Religion of the 9/11 Attackers*.

The Brotherhood of Death needs to maintain a positive military public image in order to use the U.S. and foreign military forces.[358] Nonetheless, headlines in the United States and other countries, including, "Royal Navy to Allow Devil Worship," are changing the notion that people in the military are killing for God.[359]

In the Book of Revelation Lucifer is described as a perfect angel who through his free will challenged God. The influence of Lucifer persuaded one-third of the angels to leave heaven and become demons.[360] Lucifer is described in the Bible as coming to earth like a lightning bolt.[361] The prophet Isaiah describes Lucifer's fall from heaven in order to forevermore become Satan, but Luciferians reject this account because they believe that Lucifer is the all-powerful grand architect of the universe.[362] Lucifer is the Latin word meaning light-bearer. Luciferians disguise their dubious efforts as those of people seeking light. 2 Corinthians 11:13-15 warns that Satan appears as an angel of light and his helpers deceive by appearing to be apostles of Christ.[363]

Illuminism and Gnosticism are in many respects just branches or subsets of Luciferianism, as both teach that people can become gods. Gnosticism is an integral part of Freemasonry.[364] Gnosticism dates from the first and second centuries A.D., although Luciferianism existed earlier. Gnosticism is the Greek word meaning knowledge. Gnosticism teaches that humans are divine souls trapped in a material world created by the demiurge which the Palladium-level Freemason describes as the Abrahamic God. Gnostic salvation is not from grace, faith, or good works but from attainment of gnosis. Freemasonry teaches the same lie that with gnosis a person can evolve into a god.

All secret societies promise access to secrets for the members who are worthy to receive them. The members of secret societies are gradually taught that Lucifer is the true path to enlightenment. The deception is sold through very real earthly rewards, including job opportunities and advancement. Members are motivated to become gods; once a god, they can make up their own rules, such as justifying great wealth disparity, slavery, and even murder.

In this worldview, non-illuminated individuals are called "uneducated" or "goyem" and are exploited without regard for suffering or needs.

Many Luciferians employ psychedelic drugs in order to experience moments of illumination. While Muslims, Jews, and Christians view drug use for spiritual illumination as harmful, Luciferians encourage it. The practice of using drugs to connect to demons or spirit powers is found throughout history. For ancient

Greeks, rituals at the Oracle in Delphi routinely involved the priestess practicing pharmakia. The word pharmaceutical is derived from Pharmakia. Today, the Brotherhood of Death is connected to the drug trade, both legal and illegal, in order to make profit and to destroy people spiritually.[365]

Why Operate Secretly

Sir John Cockburn was an elite Freemason with "about forty-seven years in the Craft," when he answered the question as to why they operate in secret.[366] He explained: "Allegory, moreover, has a further advantage in enabling great truths [Lucifer is worshipped as god] to be transmitted through indifferent or even hostile hands when the naked truth would be instantly suppressed."[367]

Many people find it impossible to comprehend that some of those in power are part of secret societies, even in the face of overwhelming evidence such as that presented in Chapter 4 of this book. Fortunately many people are courageous, smart, and willing to evaluate the evidence. People are waking up, and elite Brotherhood members fear that until Christianity is erased from human memory, their one-world government agenda will always be revealed and defeated.

Christians are regularly the leaders in exposing how evil is organized, as demonstrated by multiple authors of the Bible starting around the 12th century B.C. In the last few centuries, many Christians have written books exposing secret societies and the New World Order agenda, including:

- John Robinson with *Proofs of a Conspiracy* (1798)
- Walton Hannah with *Darkness Visible* (1952)
- William Guy Carr, R.D., *Satan, Prince of This World* (Palmdale, CA: Omni Publications, 1979).
- William T. Still with *New World Order: The Ancient Plan of Secret Societies* (1980)
- David Rivera with *Final Warning* (1984)

- John Daniel with *Scarlet and the Beast* (3 Volumes, 1995)
- Bro. Charles Madden, O.F.M. Conv., *Freemasonry: Mankind's Hidden Enemy* (1995)
- G. Edward Griffin with *The Creature from Jekyll Island* (1998)
- Milan Martin with *Lucifer's Children* (2002).

All-Seeing Eye

The All-Seeing Eye symbol is the key symbol to identify the presence of the Brotherhood of Death. The All-Seeing Eye symbol signals that illuminated superiors or "Olympians" rule the world. For elite Brotherhood members, the Eye is a symbol of their god and evolution of man into a superman. The evolution of a person to a super-person is central to many mystery religions and secret societies. This oldest lie, described in Genesis 3:5 as "ye shall be as gods," is very seductive as it seeks to trap people with their desire for knowledge and eternal life.[368]

The All-Seeing Eye, commonly known as the "evil eye," appears on the Great Seal of the United States, the one dollar bill, buildings, and numerous other objects. It is also known as the Eye of Shiva, Eye of Horus, Eye of Freemasonry, Eye of Apollo, Eye of Lucifer, and the misleading Eye of Providence.[369]

In Freemasonry the Eye of Horus symbolizes an alternative to Christ named Hiram.[370] Freemasons teach that Hiram is the builder and light for the world. For Freemasons, their false savior Hiram came into the world in order to proclaim that godhood is attainable through secret knowledge. But as Christians know, it is Jesus who is the true light of the world to save humanity.

In ancient Chaldea and ancient Egypt the symbol of a single eye represented the god of the dead, god of human sacrifice, protector of mysteries, and ruler of the underworld. Countless additional names throughout history are associated with a Shiva-like god of the dead. Shiva or Siva is the Indian equivalent to the

Egyptian Osiris and Masonic Lucifer. Additional Shiva-like names include Amaru, Apollo, Anubis, Baal, Bacchus, Destiny, Dionysius, Isis, Jove, Jupiter, Kukulkan, Molach, Osiris, Pan, Phoebus, Quetzalcoatl, Solar, Satan, Saturn, and Sirius.[371] Whether it is Apollo, Phoebus, or some other Shiva-like name, when used by Brotherhood of Death front organizations, these names refer to their All-Seeing Eye god.

People are often deluded about the meaning of the All-Seeing Eye and do not understand the underlying evil it represents. For instance, how many Americans really recognize the meaning of the Eye on the U.S. dollar bill?[372]

The All-Seeing Eye is pervasive and additionally symbolizes that the Brotherhood of Death is in control. For example, the 2012 London Olympics Opening and Closing Ceremonies were framed with pyramids and centered on an eye with a cauldron as the pupil of the eye.[373] Other notable examples of the All-Seeing Eye in modern society include: the Prayer Room of the United States Capitol, the United Nations Meditation Room, the New York City Temple of Understanding, the Israel Supreme Court, and the Jonyas sculpture in Kennebunk, Maine. The Israeli Supreme Court is explained in the next section, while the Jonyas sculpture is described in *Vigilant Christian III: The Occult Religion of the 9/11 Attackers*.

Missing Capstone

When the All-Seeing Eye is separated from a pyramid or other structure, as it is on the U.S. dollar bill, it communicates that a one-world government is a work in progress. In ancient Egypt, the All-Seeing Eye was a hieroglyph of a human left eye. This is one reason why the Brotherhood of Death used Freemasons to place a left eye on the United States Great Seal and on the one dollar bill.

The All-Seeing Eye on the U.S. dollar bill.[374]

The most famous example of a pyramid missing a capstone is Egypt's Great Pyramid of Giza.[375] Diodorus Siculus was a 1st century B.C. Greek historian and author of *Bibliotheca Historica.* He traveled to Egypt during 60-57 B.C. and observed that the Great Pyramid apex was missing. He noted that the casing stones of highly polished white limestone were in pristine condition. His first-hand account supports the belief that a permanent capstone was never installed; if a capstone had been installed and then dismantled, the casing stones would likely have been damaged. However, there is evidence that a temporary and portable capstone was placed on the pyramid for special religious ceremonies. This is supported by the discovery of limestone blocks by Dr. Zahi Hawass the former Egyptian Minister of State for Antiquities.[376] He concluded that a capstone was used for the first Great Pyramid completion ceremony.

> "My interpretation is that, when the Ancient Egyptians finished building the pyramid, the king and government officials cased a capstone with gold and placed it [for the period of the completion ceremony only] on top of the pyramid. This symbolized completion of the pyramid, and everyone in Upper and Lower Egypt danced and sang because the national project of constructing the pyramid was successfully finished."[377]

The Great Pyramid was the tallest structure made by humans for over 3,800 years. In a very real way, the Great Pyramid replaced Nimrod's Tower of Babel. The Great Pyramid is the oldest of the Seven Wonders of the Ancient World, and the Brotherhood is waiting to complete the capstone. *Vigilant Christian III: The Occult Religion of the 9/11 Attackers* explains the Brotherhood religion dictates that the capstone cannot be permanently placed until a world government is established.

The following is the Egyptian hieroglyph for Sirius. Sirius is also known as the "Dog Star" because of its prominence in the Canis Major or Greater Dog constellation.

> This hieroglyph helps explain the meaning of the missing capstone for both ancient Egyptians and many Brotherhood of Death affiliated secret societies.[378]

The Egyptian hieroglyph for Sirius is a central message of the Washington, D.C. street layout. Osiris (often depicted as a red right-angled triangle) and Isis (the womb-like dome) create a star which mystery religions call Horus, Hiram, and the Antichrist.[379] The symbols depict the Washington Monument (Osiris) and the womb-like dome of the Capitol (Isis) connecting to produce Horus. Chapter 9 explains how the symbols unite in the Washington, D.C street design.

Freemasons use this same Egyptian symbolism and alternative Egyptian trinity symbolism to explain the Masonic trinity, which is the true meaning of the Masonic square and compass.[380] Osiris is the compass, Isis is the square and the letter "G" produced from this combination of male and female energy is Horus. The combination of the three components is a symbol for Lucifer, the Blazing Star of Freemasonry. Freemasons are deceived by their leaders with partial truths and lies that explain that the G stands for Geometry, the Great Architect of the Universe, gnosis or knowledge, the generative principle, or even the God of Christianity; but the accurate explanation is a symbol for Jahbulon or Lucifer.

Luciferian Calendar

Freemason teacher Sir John Cockburn explained that "the commencement of the historical age" began when the stars were aligned in a particular way.

> "It apparently took place when the Sun, then beginning to be the object of worship, entered the zodiacal sign of Taurus, at the Vernal Equinox about 4,000 years B.C. Since that time the position of the Sun at Easter has been the dominating factor in symbolism. Starting from the Bull of Assyria and Egypt, the object of adoration became successively the Ram and the Fishes, as, in the Precession of the Equinoxes, the Sun retrograded through the Signs of Taurus, Aries, and Pisces, whence it has recently emerged into Aquarius."[381]

Freemasonry and other Brotherhood of Death secret societies worshipping Lucifer have a distinct Anno Lucis (A.L.) or "Year of the Light" calendar vs. Anno Domini (A.D.) meaning "in the year of the Lord." As with every secret in Freemasonry, a false interpretation is crafted to conceal the Luciferian interpretation. To further deceive the public, Freemasons will sometimes show dates in both A.D. and A.L.[382] In addition, the Luciferian A.L. is sometimes concealed by building the letter L into the letter A.

Freemasons count years based on the date they believe Freemasonry started, which was the date Lucifer was cast out of heaven and arrived on earth.[383] They believe Lucifer is on earth in a spirit form. Generally, the way to convert the Christian calendar to A.L. is to add 4,000 years to a B.C. or A.D. date. The time difference between these dates is actually 4,004 years; however, lower level Freemason documents round that to 4,000 years.[384] For example, the year 1000 B.C. becomes 3000 A.L. and 2013 A.D. becomes 6013 A.L.[385]

The following is an official Masonic document for an American Indian Chief who was initiated into Freemasonry in a London ceremony in 1776 A.D. (5776 A.L.).

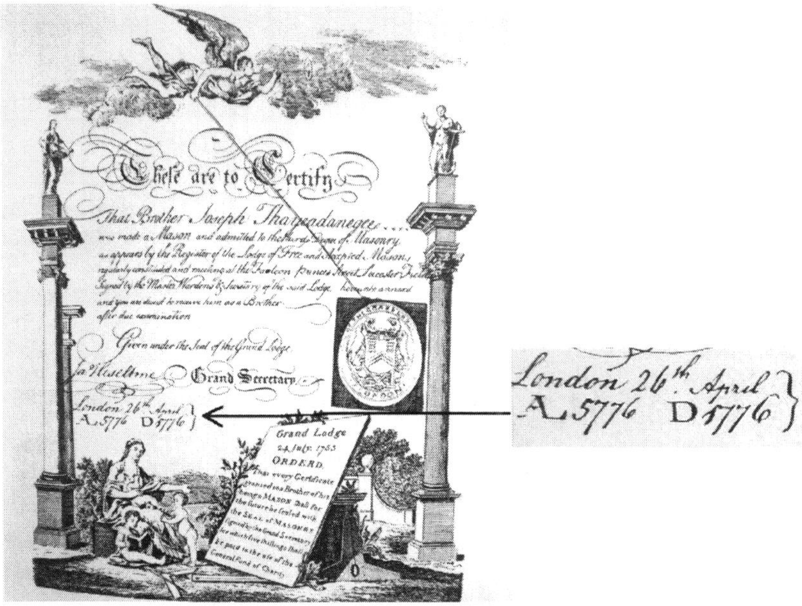

Joseph Brant was initiated as a Freemason in the U.S. in 1755 and issued the certificate from the Grand Lodge of England on April 26, 1776.[386]

The initiation of Chief Joseph Brant is well-known by many Masons because of his actions at the battle of The Cedars which saved the life of a brother Freemason. Brant received his Masonic apron directly from King George III.[387] The story of American Indians and their initiation into Freemasonry is fascinating. For more information read William Denslow's book *Transactions of the Missouri Lodge of Research, Freemasonry and the American*

Indian. [388] Today, Masons are taught the story of Indian Chief Brant as a reminder that the secret hand signals are important.[389]

Freemasonry teaches that the first "Holy Lodge" was opened Anno Lucis 2515. This is the date the secret society claims is two years after Moses led the exodus of the Israelites from Egyptian bondage. The second Lodge is called the "Sacred Lodge" and was opened in Anno Lucis 2992. This is the Lodge Freemasons claim King Solomon, Hiram Abiff, and Hiram the King of Tyre presided over. The third Lodge is called the "Grand Lodge" or "Royal Lodge." This Lodge was opened in Anno Lucis 3469 shortly after the return of the Israeli people from captivity in Babylon.

Secret Societies and Amaruca

The United States is the promised land to more than the restless refuse of the teeming shores; America is the promised land as well to the devotees of Lucifer. Palladium Masons learn that even before the United States of America was created, Brotherhood of Death affiliated secret societies forming in the United States began initiating Native Americans into Freemasonry.

According to Freemason Manly P. Hall, America is the New Atlantis deemed essential to establishing a New World Order.[390] This piece of the puzzle fits with Masonic claims that America has a secret destiny or purpose.[391] Freemasons teach that their Luciferian human sacrifice religion was practiced in America before the arrival of Christopher Columbus. Manly Hall writes: "In the Jungles of Yucatan, Guatemala, and Honduras are the ruined cities of a lost civilization on the North American continent a thousand years before the voyage of Columbus."[392]

When Columbus discovered what we now call America, he called his discovery Hispaniola. A name most likely chosen in honor of his royal Spanish sponsors, Ferdinand II and Queen Isabella.[393] Freemasons teach Columbus was really a Greek prince named Nikoloas Ypsilantis who selected a false Italian identity to hide his secret society service.[394] Supporting evidence for this claim includes that Columbus's ships sailed with the Knights Templar secret society red cross.

The story of the naming of America that is often taught in schools ignores the secret society involvement of Columbus. Children learn that America was named when an Italian mapmaker, Amerigo Vespucci, labeled the new land "America" after himself.[395] American students are deceived because map making and publishing companies of that time were often tightly controlled by secret societies, just as they are today. The far more likely version of history is that the Brotherhood chose Amerigo Vespucci as map maker in order justify its selection of the name America.

The name "Amaru" is another name for Quetzalcoatl, the ancient serpent-like god in the Aztec and Peruvian cultures.[396] Manly Hall taught that the serpent is often a symbol of Lucifer.[397] The serpent deity required human sacrifice. The land of Amaru in Peru was called Amaruca.[398] William T. Still observed it is not an "exaggeration to extrapolate from this that America may well mean "Land of Lucifer."[399]

In 2012, Amaru's fabled birthplace, known as the City of White, La Ciudad Blanca, was reportedly discovered deep in the rainforest of Honduras' Mosquitia region.[400] From a Christian perspective, if the La Ciudad Blanca claim were true, this could be the place Lucifer was initially cast from heaven to earth.

I realize many people will still find it difficult to believe that a cartel of people who maintain that the end justify the means, a key tenet of Luciferianism, seek to rule our world. The truth is sometimes hard to believe because people are taught a version of history in schools that is the careful fabrication of elitists aiming to establish a world government. To help make the hard to believe easier to believe, Chapter 9 of this book provides concrete evidence that Washington, D.C. was designed by Freemasons to be the "City of Lucifer."

7

NEW WORLD ORDER PLAN

"That the fundamental difference in the principles embodied in the historic creeds of Christendom and those of our modern secret orders has not been clearly thought out is indicated by the fact that many pledge themselves to both."[401] Theodore Graebner

The New World Order or Brotherhood of Death agenda, the "Secret Plan," is hidden in a flood of false information. The Brotherhood inner circle plan can be explained in a single sentence: Abolish representative government, abolish private property, abolish food independence, abolish the family, and abolish God. The plan is nothing new and is ultimately the plan designed by Satan to deceive and drag souls to hell.

In order to cloak its plan, Brotherhood agents create a problem, create a reaction, and condition people to accept the Brotherhood's solution to the problem. An example of this in action is the orchestrated 9/11 terrorism by the Brotherhood of Death. After 9/11, the public reaction was to fight people who were falsely believed to be responsible for the terrorism. The outcome people have become conditioned to accept includes forfeiting civil rights, collateral damage, murdering innocent people, torture, and assassinations.

The Brotherhood of Death agenda can be summarized with five points.

1. End national sovereignty with a world government.

2. Control the issuance of money and thereby control everything money is needed to buy.

3. Abolish family life, end the institution of marriage, and eliminate the primary influence of parents in raising their children.

4. Win souls in order to acquire the energy they believe is needed to enable the Antichrist to defeat Christ in the final battle.[402]

5. Abolish religion, or more accurately end Abrahamic religions and convert humanity to a Luciferian religion also known as Illuminism.

21st Century Pharaohs

The pharaohs of Egypt believed that regardless of how a pharaoh acquired wealth and power, a pharaoh could take it to the next life. Hence a dead pharaoh was placed in a pyramid with gold and other valuable possessions. The pharaohs believed they were the god of the whole world. The God of Abraham was the pharaoh's enemy because the pharaoh claimed to be god. Today, many of the same ancient Egyptian occult beliefs are held by the New World Order.

Researcher Fritz Springmeier invested years of his life to uncover the top 13 Brotherhood of Death families and their surnames.[403] Thirteen top Brotherhood family surnames include; Astor, Bundy, Collins, Dupont, Freeman, Kennedy, Li, Onassis, Reynolds, Rockefeller, Rothschild, Russell, and Van Duyn; in addition, other surnames also do appear.[404] While the Brotherhood elite are united against God, insiders compete with each other.

John Coleman, a former British intelligence officer, has also published top Brotherhood of Death family surnames as well as a subordinate group known as the Committee of 300.[405] Additional Brotherhood family surnames revealed by former insiders include: Baring, Erlanger, Fould, Lazard, Mallet, Mirabaud, Morgan, Schroder, Selingman, Speyers, and Warburg.[406]

Leaders of the elite 13 families are known as "Kings" or internally as "Olympians." In Greek mythology, twelve Olympians are the principal deities.[407] Some of the elite 13 families have claimed to be descendants of Nimrod who in the Bible was the great-grandson of Noah. Nimrod led a rebellion against God.[408] He sought to establish a "world order" in opposition to God, which continues to be the goal of the Brotherhood today.

Authenticated bloodlines are required for the top positions; however, specific family surnames are not required due to the fact that surname changes over the years are a part of a vast array of techniques the families have employed to deceive. The Brotherhood of Death also conceals lineages by altering public records such as birth certificates.[409] The key point is the surnames of Brotherhood members can change as well as assignments within the cartel.

The 13 heads of families, along with the lower level of 300 powerful individuals, direct over a thousand secret societies and corporations designed to advance the Brotherhood agenda.[410] Former insiders report the top 13 leaders are assisted by a 70 person "court" known as a Satanic Sandedrin, which has the power to order the death of opponents. Fritz Springmeier reported that a cartel computer called "the Beast" is located in Brussels and can also order an assassination.[411] Springmeier's book *Bloodlines of the Illuminati* describes the upper levels of the Brotherhood cartel as comparable to a 13 person Executive Branch, 300 member Congress, and 70 member Judiciary.[412]

The inner circle of the Brotherhood of Death is in the service of evil to the extent that the differences between Luciferianism and Satanism mean little. While the very top of front organizations (e.g., Freemasonry, Skull and Bones, etc.) are Luciferian, researchers including Fritz Springmeier are correct to conclude the very top of the Brotherhood is Satanic. Springmeier discovered the inner circle, known as the Olympians, participates in Satanic rituals, including a Feast of the Beast which is held every 28 years.[413] During this ritual, Satan is called upon to help shuffle the top 13 leaders and everything below.[414]

Jewish Persecution

Even though Christianity has been the target of infiltration by the Brotherhood of Death for over two millennia, Judaism was infiltrated by Satan's forces long before the establishment of the Christian religion. Today, Jews who uphold God's Ten Commandments are persecuted by the Brotherhood.[415] This chapter will help people understand why Zionists were used in the 9/11 ritual.

Sir John Cockburn was an elite Freemason with "about forty-seven years in the Craft," when he explained the connection of Judaism and the Brotherhood front of Masonry.[416]

"Masonry derives much of its ceremonial from the Collegia of Rome and their prototype the Eranoi of Greece. In these societies the patter for imitation was the Sun God under the name of Dionysus, Hercules, or Bacchus, whose death and resurrection formed the main theme. In Masonry their place has been taken by Hiram, whose name is derived from a word signifying light [Lucifer]. In addition to the adoption of Hiram as the type of the Sun there are other traces of Jewish influence in the Craft. Perhaps the reason for this may lie in the fact that when the Bacchanalia were suppressed in Rome, Caesar permitted the Jews, 'and these only,' to continue their rites."[417]

Part of Satan's plan to undermine God includes transforming Judaism into the Brotherhood of Death religion. The corruption of Judaism began thousands of years ago when those who serve Satan infiltrated the Sanhedrin, which was then the Jewish high court. These infiltrators were key actors in the condemnation of Jesus. The Sanhedrin was destroyed when the temple of Jerusalem was destroyed in 70 AD.[418] Throughout history the original tribes of Israel have had subversives in the service of evil rise up among them in attempts to undermine God's spiritual message.

Zionism to Destroy Judaism

Satan wants people to persecute Jews who worship the God of Abraham, and that is why the Brotherhood inner circle routinely uses supporters with false Jewish identities to conduct atrocities.

The secret war against not only Jews but all the Abrahamic religions is being conducted by members of Brotherhood-affiliated societies that encourage the public to support Zionism. The Zionist political movement exists to drive a dagger into the heart of Judaism.

Zionism is an ideology that justifies violating the Ten Commandments and should not be confused with Judaism, which values the Ten Commandments.[419] The Ten Commandments forbid coveting anything that belongs to your neighbor, taking a neighbor's property, and killing people in order to take their property.

This is why the Ten Commandments, cherished by Jews, Christians, and Muslims, are of little value to top Zionists. Many secular Zionists see the Ten Commandments as ten suggestions to be thrown to the wind. Killing Palestinians and taking their homes is a central component of the Brotherhood strategy to divide the Abrahamic faiths. Nothing Jesus ever said justifies stealing the homes of Palestinians, intentionally making them suffer with economic sanctions, or killing them in order to expand the Jewish homeland.

There exists a deep moral and political divide today among the Jewish people. What follows is an explanation of how that divide came to be and its underlying cause.

The Brotherhood needs Zionism to foster anti-Semitism.[420] Author and one-time Israeli citizen Jack Bernstein observed that Sephardic Jews and followers of Judaism are being persecuted by an elite group of atheist Ashkenazi Zionist Jews who are in firm control of Israel. Bernstein, an Ashkenazi Jew, explains:

> "There are two distinct groups of Jews in the world, and they come from different areas of the world. The Sephardic Jews are from the Middle East and North Africa, and the Ashkenazi Jews are from Eastern Europe."[421]

Bernstein explains that the Khazars, a semi-nomadic people, were forced to go west and settled in Eastern Europe and Russia. The Khazars, a coalition of Turkic or Hunnic-Bulgar clans with knowledge of King Solomon and the Babylonian Talmud, began in the fourth century AD.[422] *The Encyclopedia Judaica* (1978) confirms the progeny of the Edomite became part of the Khazar kingdom between the seventh and ninth centuries.[423] In 730 to 737 AD Caliph Marwan II fought to conquer Khazaria and forced Khazars to convert to Islam.[424] During the eighth to ninth centuries the Khazars officially converted to Judaism. The conversion occurred in stages and a formal conversion decree was issued during the reign of King Bulan.[425] The kingdom was officially

Jewish from two to four hundred years.[426] This Jewish Khazar kingdom was defeated in 1016 AD by a joint Byzantine-Russian force.[427]

Khazar "six-pointed star" relics have been found in Sarkel and Khazarian grave fields in Upper Saltov.[428]

The Khazar Empire was vast, reaching modern day Georgia to Kazan in Russia, Kiev in the Ukraine, Yalta in Crimea and Mosul in Iraq.[429] The empire was ruled from Itil on the Caspian Sea.[430] A Khazar Indo-Turk mystery religion continued to be practiced by Khazar's elite even after King Bulan decreed the Judaic religion was the official religion. The sacred language of the Khazar elite was Hebrew.[431]

Judaism as practiced by Khazars was very different from Judaism as practiced by Sephardic Jews. Khazar-Judaism was rooted in Babylonian shamanism and occult Karaite rituals.[432] Khazar-Judaism is a continuation of the mystery of iniquity or Brotherhood of Death religion.

Here is an example of a Khazar-Judaism ritual: A Khazar king was empowered by putting a silk cord around his neck, bringing him to the point of suffocation. A religious official would ask the soon-to-be king how many years he wished to reign. The reply was binding, and should a king live beyond his answer, he was put to death. Another example, the Judaic-Karaism chief occult symbol is the flag of Israel today. The flag of the Khazar's chief magician and sorcerer, David el Roi, became the Star of David.[433] Contrary to popular belief, the Star of David or Shield of David hexagram was not used as the symbol of Judaism before the Khazars.[434]

Jewish scholar Abraham Harkavy wrote in 1867 that the first Jews to arrive in southern Russia came from "the Greek cities on the shores of the Black Sea and from Asia, via the mountains of the Caucasus."[435] Norman Golb and Omeljan Pritsak provided additional evidence in their 1982 book *Khazarian Hebrew Documents of the Tenth Century*.[436] Historian Peter Golden contributed to historical evidence with his 1970 doctoral dissertation and 1980 book *Khazar Studies: An Historico-Philological Inquiry into the Origins of the Khazars*.[437]

The Thirteenth Tribe

The book of Genesis explains God changed Jacob's name to Israel and his twelve sons became the twelve tribes of Israel. Eleven of the sons of Jacob or Israel and the two sons of Joseph, Ephraim and Manasseh, became tribes of Israel. The Book of Revelation counts the tribe of Joseph as one, and therefore describes twelve tribes.[438] The Thirteenth Tribe, as labeled in this section, is not a tribe originating with a son of Jacob. The term is used here to discuss a separate bloodline originating from Nimrod. Regardless of the bloodline issue, all humans are created in the image of God, so concluding a person is not as holy or sacred in the eyes of God because he is not a descendant of Jacob is wrong.

Arthur Koestler explained the false tribe of Israel in his book *The Thirteenth Tribe*. Author Shlomo Sand confirmed Koestler's book was kept out of Israel because the publisher felt the Israeli people were not ready to handle the truth.[439] The truth Koestler dared share is that the large majority of Jews in the world are "of Eastern European - and thus perhaps mainly of Khazar - origin...genetically they are more closely related to the Hun, Uigur and Magyar tribes than to the seed of Abraham, Isaac and Jacob."[440] He concludes: "The story of the Khazar Empire, as it slowly emerges from the past, begins to look like the most cruel hoax which history has ever perpetrated."[441]

Tel Aviv University Professor of Mediaeval Jewish History, A. N. Poliak, confirmed what other historians have disclosed. In his 1944 book *Khazaria*, he wrote: "The descendants of this [Khazar] settlement -- those who stayed where they were, those who emigrated to the United States and to other countries, and those who went to Israel -- constitute now the large majority of world Jewry."[442]

The historical record that the Khazars decided to convert to Judaism as a strategy to avoid fighting with nearby Christians and Muslims is often unknown due to aggressive efforts by Zionists to suppress this information. Jewish historian Shlomo Sand explained in *The Invention of the Jewish People* that from 1951 to the present not a single historical work about the Khazars has been published in Hebrew.[443] He wrote: "The Israeli academic world has been mute on this topic, and no significant research has taken place. Slowly and consistently, any mention of the Khazars in the public arena in Israel came to be tagged as eccentric, freakish and even menacing."[444]

Sand wrote: "Israel's high priest of memory in the 1950s did not hesitate to describe Khazaria as the "diaspora mother" of the Eastern European Jewry."[445] Sand further explained: "There was anxiety about the legitimacy of the Zionist project, should it become widely known that the settling Jewish masses were not the direct descendants of the "Children of Israel" -- such delegitimization might lead to a broad challenge against the State of Israel's right to exist."[446] An excerpt from Jack Bernstein follows.

> "The Ashkenazi Jews, who now comprise 90 percent of the Jews in the world, had a rather strange beginning. According to historians, many of them Jewish, the Ashkenazi Jews came into existence about 1200 years ago. It happened this way: At the eastern edge of Europe, there lived a tribe of people

> known as the Khazars. About the year 740 AD, the Khazar king and his court decided to adopt a religion for their people. So, representatives of the three major religions, Christianity, Islam, and Judaism, were invited to present their religious doctrines. The Khazars chose Judaism, but not for religious reasons. If the Khazars had chosen Islam, they would have angered the strong Christian world. If they had chosen Christianity, they would have angered the strong Islamic world. So, they played it safe - they chose Judaism. It wasn't for religious reasons the Khazars chose Judaism; it was for political reasons."[447]

The explanation of Khazar-Judaism provides insights on the secret war the Brotherhood is waging against the Jews. Brotherhood agents that often appear to be religious Jews are using Sephardic Judaism as a front. Khazar-Judaism places a supreme value on the Babylonian Talmud. This information also helps explain the many conflicting messages between the Torah and Babylonian Talmud.

Upholding Ten Commandments

One way to determine if a person is knowingly or unknowingly serving the Brotherhood is their position on honoring the Ten Commandments. The Ten Commandments should not be twisted so that killing enemies is desirable, which is what is advocated in the November 2009 publication of *Torat Hamelech* by rabbis Yitzhak Shapira and Yosef Elitzur.[448] The book promotes killing gentiles using Jewish law as the justification. Rabbis Dov Lior and Yacob Yousef endorsed the book, which even includes the King's Torah justification for killing non-Jews who are not involved in violence. They even justify the murder of babies if it is believed they will grow up to pose a threat. By Lior's and Yousef's standard, anyone who writes anything that puts Israel in a bad light, even if true, is a valid assassination target.[449] This standard is used to help justify Israeli sponsored assassinations and terrorism. Opposing the truth is the opposite of the Ten Commandments, as well as everything God represents.

Jack Bernstein was correct to conclude the Brotherhood Zionist front is the enemy of Jews like himself. He wrote, "The ultimate goal of the Zionists is one-world government under the control of the Zionists and Zionist-oriented Jewish International Bankers."[450] To understand Bernstein, it is critical not to confuse "Zionist" with "the Jewish people." Bernstein is saying the Brotherhood top leadership includes people with Jewish names who are using the camouflage of a Jewish identity in their secret war against Jews, Muslims, and Christians.

The Brotherhood's Communist Creation

In 1917 the Blessed Virgin accurately predicted "Russia will spread its errors." The errors of Russia or Communism are the errors of the Brotherhood of Death. This fact is clear when people learn the Bolshevik Revolution in Russia was not a movement of downtrodden masses demanding freedom.

The 1917 Bolshevik Revolution was planned, staffed and funded by the Brotherhood of Death.

Tsar Nicholas II, the last Emperor of Russia, abdicated power on March 15, 1917.[451]

To pressure Nicholas II to resign, Brotherhood of Death secret societies implemented food shortages, transportation breakdowns and riots in Petrograd. President Woodrow Wilson served the Brotherhood of Death and promptly complied when he was instructed to send the U.S. military to Russia. Nicholas II was betrayed on multiple fronts as part of the Brotherhood's plan to topple his regime.

Murmansk was founded in 1915 as a supply port in World War I for the British, French, and American expeditionary forces in 1918.[452]

American troops were primarily deployed in Archangel (Arkangelsk), Murmansk, and Vladivostok. At the time many people were unable to explain why troops from the 339th Infantry, 310th Engineers, 337th Field Hospital, and 337th Ambulance Company were deployed to Russia. This U.S. forces in the direct service of the Brotherhood of Death became known as "The Polar Bear Expedition."

U.S. soldiers arriving in Vladivostok, Russia.[453]

When Nicholas II abdicated, Prince Lvov established an interim democratic government which was followed by the Kerensky regime. The Kerensky regime was replaced during the Bolshevik revolution with Communist rule under Lenin, Trotsky and Stalin. Lenin had previously attempted to overthrow Nicholas II in 1905. In 1917 the Brotherhood was supporting Lenin in Switzerland and helped him to return to Russia on a "sealed train" with $5 to $6 million in gold.[454] Prior to returning to Russia, Trotsky was a reporter for a Brotherhood newspaper in New York City. On March 27, 1917, Trotsky traveled on the S.S. Christiania with 275 revolutionaries and was arrested at the port of call in Halifax, Nova Scotia. President Woodrow Wilson's advisor, Colonel Edward Mandell House, arranged for the Canadian government to release Trotsky.[455]

Authors Gary Allen and Larry Abraham observed: "Although it was not their main purpose, by nationalization of Russia the [Brotherhood] Insiders bought themselves an enormous piece of real estate, complete with mineral rights, for somewhere between $30 and $40 million. Lord Alfred Milner, wealthy front man for the Rothschilds, served as paymaster for the international bankers in Petrograd during the Bolshevik Revolution. Milner later headed The Round Table secret society which was dedicated to establishing a world government whereby a clique of super-rich financiers would control the world under the guise of Socialism. The American subsidiary of this conspiracy is called the Council on Foreign Relations and was started by, and is still controlled by [Brotherhood of Death] Leftist international bankers."[456]

W. Cleon Skousen wrote in his book, *The Naked Capitalist* "the secret society became the main support for the Communists."[457] Skousen reported "members of the dynastic banking families had been financing the Russian-oriented revolutionists for many years. Trotsky, in his biography, refers to some of these loans from British financiers going back as far as 1907. By 1917 the major subsidies for the revolution were being arranged by Sir George Buchanan and Lord Alfred Milner (of the Brotherhood's Morgan-Rothschild-Rhodes confederacy)."[458]

According to his grandson John, his grandfather Jacob Schiff helped financed the Communist Revolution in Russia to the tune of $20 million.[459] Jacob Schiff was a leader in the Brotherhood of Death.[460] This is why Lenin's government immediately went to war against Christianity.[461] Understanding that the Brotherhood of Death created Communism is fundamental to understanding the Fatima Communism warning.

This information was confirmed by the White Russian General, Arsene de Goulevitch.[462] He wrote: "The important part played by the wealthy American banker, Jacob Schiff, in the events in Russia, though as yet only partially revealed, is no longer a secret... From the day that he was placed at the head of Kuhn, Loeb & Co., one of the influential American banking houses, Schiff's behavior was that of an avowed enemy of Russia... It is worth noting that in his "Diary of an Author," Dostoievsky foresaw the creation of a similar [Brotherhood of Death] syndicate... Mr. Bakhmetiev, the late Russian Imperial Ambassador to the United States, tells us that the Bolsheviks, after victory, transferred 600 million roubles [rubles] in gold between the years 1918 and 1922 to Kuhn, Loeb & Co."[463]

Communism and the Fatima Truth

Understanding the satanic nature of Communism, using the smokescreen of Judaism, is very important to understanding what the Blessed Virgin is telling us. That is one reason earlier in this chapter it was explained that Zionism was created to destroy Judaism. This information also helps people explain why much of the great evil in the world, with the September 11, 2001 attacks in New York City as a prime example, come from people who were born in Russia, but are now living or buried in Israel.

People providing education about the Brotherhood of Death or the Fatima solution are sometimes surprised when they are attacked as an anti-Semite. The false attacks are for the same reason that people speaking against Communism in the 20th century were accused of being anti-Semites. If a speaker or organization is a direct threat to the plans for a New World Order, a Brotherhood of Death attack is launched.

The Brotherhood document, the *Permanent Instruction of the Alta Vendita*, had its authenticity guaranteed by Pope Pius IX.[464] The document explains how to attack enemies. "If he is already a declared enemy, an Albani, a Pallotta, . . . envelop him in all the snares you can lay under his feet; create for him one of those reputations which will frighten little children and old women; . . . paint him cruel and sanguinary; recount regarding him some trait of cruelty which can easily be engraved in the minds of people."[465]

The *Permanent Instruction of the Alta Vendita* also explains a plan to infiltrate and corrupt the Catholic Church in the 20th century. At the core of the plan is control high levels in the Catholic Church so that corruption can spread and ultimately explode. At the same time the lower levels would be attacked. The Liberal ideas would be broadly disseminated to deceive new priests to reject the foundations of the faith while thinking they were making improvements. Catholic historian Rev. E. Cahill, S.J., acknowledged the seriousness of the Alta Vendita plan observing that this group was "commonly supposed to have been at the time the governing centre of European Freemasonry."[466]

The most common character assassination attack involves using a mutual friend who is Jewish. A Brotherhood agent will casually mention to the Jewish friend to spread the word that a person is anti-Semitic. The friend might be told about web sites that were created with false information to make the allegation appear accurate. Often without a word said to the person attacked, friends become former friends.

If a person is deemed a credible threat, then a Brotherhood "civil liberties" front organization leads the character assassination attack.[467] If the speaker of truth is a serious threat, the Mossad may be used to eliminate the individual.

One example of a Brotherhood front organization falsely attacking people is the Southern Law Poverty Center or SLPC. The SLPC is secretly at war with Christ and His people. Using the smokescreen of fighting extremism and hate, the SLPC works to character assassinate people speaking the truth. Christians who are not anti-Semites are listed by the SLPC next to people who are anti-Semites. This technique is unethical, but when you remember the Fatima solution will defeat the kingdom of Satan, you should expect the Brotherhood of Death to use every dirty trick possible.

Baptist preacher Colonel Gordon "Jack" Mohr was surprised when he was attacked for being an anti-Semite.[468] He said in 1996: "Whenever I spoke on Communism the media immediately labeled me as anti-Semitic. I never mentioned Jews, I never mentioned Judaism, I never mentioned Zionism but they called me anti-Semitic."[469] Colonel Mohr said that within a few years of being labeled anti-Semitic, "every single Baptist pastor in the state of Missouri would no longer talk to me."[470] Colonel Mohr statement is on YouTube and worth making the effort to watch as he explains how he discovered Communism was created by the Brotherhood of Death using primarily Ashkenazi Jews.[471]

At Fatima in 1917 the Blessed Virgin specifically warned that evil from Russia would spread to other nations. A careful examination of great evil in the 20th and 21st century confirms this prophecy. *Vigilant Christian IV* exposes the September 11, 2001 terrorism as one example. The shocking truth is Muslims were not responsible and most of the destruction was executed by the Mossad. As foretold by Our Lady, key terrorist leaders were born in Russia. Isser Harel, the Director of the Mossad from 1952 to 1963, was born in Vitebsk, Russia and is an example.[472] He was working as early as 1979 on the September 11, 2001 false-flag operation.[473]

The book, *Vigilant Christian II: Preventing an American Hiroshima* provides many other examples of false-flag operations. The key point to remember is the Fatima solution ends the kingdom of Satan. Anyone who stands up for the Fatima truth will be persecuted on earth and should remember heavenly rewards are eternal.

The Report from Iron Mountain

In 1963 the Brotherhood formed a 15-member special study group in order to write *The Report from Iron Mountain*.[474] This report was leaked, and became a *New York Times* best seller. In this report, wars were described as necessary for the elite to maintain power. In the absence of war, *The Report from Iron Mountain* recommended the public be distracted with terrorism, increasingly violent sports, a global climate change threat, and an alien threat.[475]

On November 20, 1967 the *U.S. News and World Report* published an article claiming *The Report from Iron Mountain* was confirmed as a secret document by an unnamed government official.[476] The official was quoted as saying that upon learning the report was leaked to the public, President Lyndon B. Johnson "hit the roof" and ordered it to be suppressed for all time. Not surprisingly, *The Report from Iron Mountain* has been attacked as false. Evidence that the report is genuine came on November 26, 1967 in *The Washington Post,* where Harvard professor John Kenneth Galbraith wrote that he had first-hand knowledge of the report's authenticity and that he was "part of the conspiracy."[477] Galbraith confirmed the authenticity on three separate occasions and with at least one tape-recorded confirmation.[478] Hubris and support for the report's conclusion may be the reason for Galbraith's confirmation.

There is evidence supporting that Brotherhood of Death members Leonard Lewin, Dean Rusk, and William F. Buckley, Jr. were among the 15 authors. Buckley stated to *The New York Times* that he helped write it.[479] Galbraith was asked to keep the project secret but broke this agreement when in 1967 he wrote:

> "As I would put my personal repute behind the authenticity of this document, so would I testify to the validity of its conclusions. My reservation relates only to the wisdom of releasing it to an obviously unconditioned public."[480]

Be Vigilant

The Report from Iron Mountain does provide an accurate summary of how many people were distracted in the 20th century and are now being distracted in the 21st century. We must be vigilant and not consent to the Satan's mystery of iniquity.

A summary of future events is explained in 2 Thessalonians.

> "And we beseech you, brethren, by the coming of our Lord Jesus Christ, and of our gathering together unto him: That you be not easily moved from your sense, nor be terrified, neither by spirit, nor by word, nor by epistle, as sent from us, as if the day of the Lord were at hand. Let no man deceive you by any means, for unless there come a revolt first, and the man of sin be revealed, the son of perdition, Who opposeth, and is lifted up above all that is called God, or that is worshipped, so that he sitteth in the

temple of God, shewing himself as if he were God. Remember you not, that when I was yet with you, I told you these things? And now you know what withholdeth, that he may be revealed in his time. For the mystery of iniquity already worketh; only that he who now holdeth, do hold, until he be taken out of the way. And then that wicked one shall be revealed whom the Lord Jesus shall kill with the spirit of his mouth; and shall destroy with the brightness of his coming, him, Whose coming is according to the working of Satan, in all power, and signs, and lying wonders, And in all seduction of iniquity to them that perish; because they receive not the love of the truth, that they might be saved. Therefore God shall send them the operation of error, to believe lying: That all may be judged who have not believed the truth, but have consented to iniquity."[481]

8

CONCRETE EVIDENCE

"Maintain humanity under 500,000,000 in perpetual balance with nature." New World Order

Before advancing with the next two chapters I want to pause and make a personal appeal. What you are about to enter upon is sort of like a basement discovered in a house you've long lived in but never knew existed. This dark cellar, full of nooks and crannies obscured by purposely laid cobwebs, is enough to strain the patience of anyone. So I ask that you summon the reserves of your utmost patience as you proceed through the dark recesses. Pleasure reading is dear to us all, but there is a time for all things. Now the time has come to unearth a very uncomfortable truth. "And you shall know the truth, and the truth shall make you free."[482]

Nor should the truth be a source of lament. Just because misguided occultists have been successful in developing occult symbols does not mean they have won. The blasphemous symbols can be removed or changed. In Germany, the Nazis used many occult symbols, and people once thought the Nazi symbols would be impossible to eliminate. Transforming Washington, D.C. and other cities from honoring Lucifer or Satan to honoring God is not only possible, it is essential for the survival of the United States.

Legislative Evidence

Because the Brotherhood of Death is generally unknown, the United States has changed for the worse at a very fast pace since September 11, 2001. Legislative evidence includes the Patriot Act, Military Commissions Act, Department of Homeland Security, a series of Executive Orders, and the National Defense Authorization Act. The draconian National Defense Authorization Act was signed into law on December 31, 2011 by President Barack Obama. With people celebrating the New Year and distracted, Obama terminated key provisions in the 1791 Bill of Rights prompting almost no public outcry.

The National Defense Authorization Act sweeps away the First Amendment. Free speech can now be interpreted as propaganda helping terrorists.[483] The National Defense Authorization Act eliminated both the Fifth Amendment of due process and the Sixth Amendment guaranteeing a speedy trial by a jury of peers. The Seventh Amendment, a civil trial, is also eliminated.[484] On a related note, the Fourth Amendment, protection from unreasonable search and seizure, was previously eliminated by the Patriot Act.

The legislative changes have redefined what it means to be an American. Americans can now be searched without a warrant, held without evidence, imprisoned indefinitely, denied access to a lawyer, deprived of a trial, tortured, and assassinated.

Legislative evidence since September 11, 2001 highlights that there is a very real battle for the United States. One group, the vast majority of the people, want the Constitution safeguarded, and children to have the same opportunities and ideally greater opportunities than their parents. The agents of the Brotherhood want to eliminate Constitutional protections and widen the gap between rich and poor.

Financial Evidence

Following the money exposes the Brotherhood of Death in a way that is tangible. Many Americans do not know Brotherhood of Death financial influence was proven to exist by Congress during the Money Trust Investigation of 1912 or that the Federal Reserve

System is privately owned.[485] The industries under the control of the Brotherhood of Death elite, then and now, include: financial, manufacturing, mining, telecommunications, transportation, and war production.

Monetary System Ownership

An early version of the Federal Reserve Act of 1913, called the Aldrich Bill, was opposed by Congress.[486] People increasingly became educated about the "Money Trust" and in 1912, Congress commissioned an investigation.[487] A special subcommittee was convened by the Chairman of the House Banking and Currency Committee, Arsene P. Pujo. The hearings were conducted between May 16, 1912 and February 26, 1913.

The Money Trust investigation showed a small group of men served as fronts for international banking families. The Money Trust bag men identified by Congress in 1913 include George F. Baker, J. P. Morgan, Frank E. Peabody, William Rockefeller, Jacob H. Schiff, James Stillman, Benjamin Strong, Jr., Felix M. Warburg, and Paul Warburg. A century later, the descendants of these men are some of the most powerful people influencing the U.S. government today.

Federal Reserve System

After Congress proved a shadow government existed, the Brotherhood of Death took steps to make the Money Trust problem go away. The solution was to begin to use organization names that were not mentioned in the Congressional records and obtain Congressional approval for the cartel.[488] The Money Trust, renamed the Federal Reserve System, was unwittingly legalized by a majority of Congress with passage of the Federal Reserve Act of 1913.[489] The sad reality is the name change and public deception campaign worked.

The Federal Reserve in Washington, D.C.[490]

The name "Federal Reserve System" was selected to appear government owned, but is not federal, does not have reserves, and is 100% privately owned. Federal Reserve System stock cannot be publicly traded, and the precise ownership details are concealed from the American people. Bank owners include: JPMorgan Chase, Citigroup, Bank of America/Merrill Lynch, Wells Fargo, Morgan Stanley, Goldman Sachs, Bank of NY Mellon, and State Street.

The Federal Reserve was created for the benefit of the Brotherhood of Death leading families. Dynastic banking families include: Abell, Astor, Bundy, Collins, Dupont, Freeman, Goldsmid, Kennedy, Krupp, Kuhn-Loeb, Li, Mocatta, Morgan, Onassis, Reynolds, Rockefeller, Rothschild, Russell, Van Duyn, Montagu, Pixley, Warburg, and Wilkins. By owning large percentages of U.S. banks that own Federal Reserve shares, the leading families own the Federal Reserve. The "pinnacle" Federal Reserve owner and global monetary system leader is the Rothschild family.

The term New World Order was increasingly used after the Federal Reserve System was established. One example of the New

World Order name being used was on November 27, 1915 when Nicholas Murray Butler said to the Union League of Philadelphia:

> "The old world order changed when this war-storm broke. The old international order passed away as suddenly, as unexpectedly, and as completely as if it had been wiped out by a gigantic flood, by a great tempest, or by a volcanic eruption. The old world order died with the setting of that day's sun and a new world order is being born while I speak, with birth pangs so terrible that it seems almost incredible that life could come out of such fearful suffering and such overwhelming sorrow."

Representative Charles August Lindbergh observed: "When the President signs this act [the Federal Reserve Act of 1913], the invisible government by the money power – proven to exist by the Monetary Trust Investigation – will be legalized. The new law will create inflation whenever the trusts want inflation. From now on, depressions will be scientifically created."[491]

Jekyll Island Meeting

To understand how the Money Trust cartel was deceptively reborn as the Federal Reserve System, the secret 1910 Jekyll Island meeting is explained.[492] In the late 19th century, Americans increasingly learned an elite cartel, called the Money Trust, was responsible for great suffering. In 1910, seven men representing the Money Trust agreed to meet because members of Congress were increasingly demanding action be taken against the Money Trust. The seven men that met represented dynastic banking families that controlled a large portion of the world's wealth.[493] The seven men were Nelson Aldrich, Abraham Piatt Andrew, Frank Vanderlip, Henry Davison, Charles Norton, Benjamin Strong Jr. , and Paul Warburg. The objective of the meeting was to seize even greater control of the U.S. monetary system with the guise of a government agency.

People who spoke out against the Jekyll Island conspiracy to seize control of the U.S. monetary system were ridiculed as paranoid.[494] Even today this sometimes happen. Nonetheless, the Jekyll Island meeting and its creation of the Federal Reserve System are confirmed.

The benefits of the Federal Reserve System for the descendants of the Money Trust, now in control of the Federal Reserve, are obvious. For example, JPMorgan Chase & Co. (JPMC) is the combination of J. P. Morgan and Rockefeller banks which served as fronts for the Rothschild family. JPMorgan Chase is the largest U.S. bank, with assets over $2 trillion and operations in more than 60 countries.[495] Fortunately money is auditable, and this forces the head of the Federal Reserve to be secretive.

<u>Debt Enslavement</u>

Governments acquire debt by spending money which is accelerated by the purchase of weapons. The Brotherhood of Death leading families own influencing interests in weapons manufacturers. Weapon sales accelerate if a government is faced with a perceived or real threat.

Freedom from mandated debt is possible as proven by Iceland in 2010. Iceland's success story is explained in *Vigilant Christian V: Perfect Money Planning*. When you realize the Great Depression was designed, triggered, and maintained by the Brotherhood of Death cartel Federal Reserve owners, you can better appreciate their need to keep their wealth concealed.[496] The same is true for the 2008 financial crisis that the Brotherhood set in motion. The passage of the *Consolidated Appropriations Act of 2000*, by design, led to the 2008 crisis which in many ways is equivalent to the 1920's naked option trading.[497]

Money Issuance

The founding fathers of the United States understood the importance of who had control of the issuance of money. When money is issued by privately owned banks, over time many homeowners become homeless. This is why Congress specified in Article 1 Section 8 of the U.S. Constitution that private banks could not issue currency.[498] However, today the Brotherhood of Death issues money via the 100% privately owned Federal Reserve System.

The kingdom of Satan's efforts to control money issuance started long before the Federal Reserve Act of 1913. The privately-owned First Bank of the United States was chartered by Congress in 1791 with a 20-year expiration date. The First Bank of the United States did not control issuing money. The Second Bank of the United States was also chartered by Congress in 1816 with a 20-year expiration date. The Second Bank of the United States was also not allowed to control issuing money.

Physical Evidence

Buildings and monuments are mediums for the Brotherhood of Death to perpetuate, communicate, and in their belief system generate occult power. In the words of Freemason Manly Hall, "Architecture remained a chosen instrument for the perpetuation of the Grand Design — the building of the perfect world."[499] For the Brotherhood, architecture is sacred. This is why the Brotherhood is aggressively building edifices around the world to honor their god.

In the United States, concrete or physical Brotherhood of Death evidence is visible at every Masonic Lodge, which means in most major cities. Ten of the more obvious examples present and past are:

- New York - World Trade Center Buildings

- New York - United Nations
- Colorado - Denver Airport
- Texas - San Jacinto Monument
- Virginia - Jamestown Colony 1607 Design
- Virginia - Washington Masonic Monument
- Washington, D.C. - Pierre L'Enfant's 1794 City Design
- Washington, D.C. - U.S. Capitol Building
- Washington, D.C. - Washington Monument
- Georgia - Georgia Guidestones

Books in the Vigilant Christian series explain why each of the above are examples of Brotherhood influence. In this chapter, the Georgia Guidestones example is explained.

Georgia Guidestones

The Georgia Guidestones are the Antichrist's ten commandments and a smaller version, also engraved on stone tablets, is to placed in a counterfeit Ark of the Covenant. The commandments communicate the misguided New World Order agenda for a post-Apocalypse world. The Georgia Guidestones are engraved on a stone as part of a large Brotherhood of Death monument in Elbert County, Georgia.[500] Additional occult objects are waiting for a time when the public is conditioned to accept them. For this reason the monument is unfinished and is planned to have an outer ring of "moon stones."[501]

> The Elberton, Georgia Masonic Lodge plays a key role in the management of the Georgia Guidestones.[502]

On March 22, 1980, there were two Georgia Guidestones unveiling ceremonies. The first was to help conceal the dark purpose of the monument from the public. The second unveiling ceremony dedicated the stones to the god of the New World Order. High priestess Jodi Minogue, using the name Lady Galadriel. drew a circle around the guidestones.[503] Working with her husband, John Minogue, pentagrams were drawn on the stones using sandalwood oil.[504] Witches and Satanists continue to acknowledge the occult purpose of the Georgia Guidestones for multiple reasons. One key reason is the monument "X" shape is an occult symbol for Osiris or Lucifer. The "X" shape is further explained in the next chapter.

The Georgia Guidestones are in close proximity to what the Cherokee Indians called "Ah-Yeh-Li A Lo-Hee," which means the center of the world.[505] The stones are oriented with each line of the axis in relation to the moon's annual rotation around the Earth. The capstone or top stone has a hole that employs the noon sunlight in order to identify the day of the year. Another hole, in the center support, is designed to locate the North Star.[506] A third hole, known as the "mail slot," is positioned for sunlight to pass through on an equinox or solstice.[507]

Sunlight passing through the third Georgia Guidestone hole.[508]

Six astrologically aligned "X" pattern granite stones evoke a Stonehenge-like familiarity. Ten "guides" or commandments are etched in the granite and are written in eight different languages.[509] The man who engraved the messages on the stones, Charlie Clamp, reported hearing "strange music and disjointed voices" as he carved.[510] The four outer faces of the capstone communicate "Let these be guidestones to an Age of Reason" in Babylonian cuneiform, Egyptian hieroglyphics, Sanskrit, and Classical Greek. The quote at the beginning of this chapter, "Maintain humanity under 500,000,000 in perpetual balance with nature," is the first commandment. If adhered to, this commandment would mean the extermination of at least 6.5 billion people.

This is one of the most bizarre and occult monuments in the United States because it calls for the elimination of billions of people. The abomination to humanity, increasingly known as the Ten Commandments of the Antichrist or Dajjal, communicates horrific messages.[511] The Georgia Guidestones validate prophecies in holy books that the Antichrist will seek to resemble Christ but with an opposing message.

The "mystery" of the stones was intended to provide Freemasons and other Brotherhood of Death creators plausible maneuvering room to both avoid answering questions and deceive people. To illustrate this point, the "master builder" of the project, Joe H. Fendley, is portrayed as someone who just "happened" to get involved. The following is from his company's 1981 *The Georgia Guidestones* book:

> "What started out as a usual Friday afternoon mid-summer has ended in the production erection of one of the world's most unusual monuments produced under the most unusual conditions.
>
> "Joe Fendley, president of Elbert Granite Finishing Company, Inc. in Elberton, Georgia, was spending Friday afternoon in June 1979 as he spends most Friday afternoons ... studying his weekly reports and generally closing up shop for a weekend ... and then it all started.
>
> "A neatly dressed man walked into Fendley's Tate Street office and said he wanted to buy a monument. Since everyone else in the office was busy, Fendley decided to talk to the stranger himself and explained that his company does not sell directly to the public, but only on a wholesale basis.
>
> "Not to be discouraged, the middle-aged man, who identified himself only as Mr. Robert C. Christian, said he wanted to know the cost of building a monument to the conservation of mankind and began telling Fendley what type of monument he wanted. With this he outlined the size in metric measurements."

The story that was put out for public consumption was that the mysterious Mr. Christian represented a secret group that had been working on the monument design for more than 20 years. The deceptive story continued with Fendley introducing Mr. Christian to banker Wyatt C. Martin, who promised to keep the project source anonymous and take the true identity of Mr. Christian to the grave.[512] The third party involved in the transaction, Wayne Mullinex, provided the land for the monument.

The key facts presented in this book, omitted from the official story and *The Georgia Guidestones* book, dispel the secrecy as well as the nonsense that the messages are to help humanity. The mysterious story becomes less mysterious when you realize Fendley, the self-acknowledged builder of the stones, was a 32 degree Freemason.[513] Fendley, Martin, and Mullinex were supporting the Elberton Philomathea Masonic Lodge #25.[514] Martin stated after meeting R. C. Christian that he dismissed the meeting as a hoax organized by brother Freemason Joe Fendley.[515]

Martin said R. C. Christian told him "If you were to tell who put the money up for this, it wouldn't be a mystery any more, and no one would come and read it."[516] This is an accurate statement because when light is shined on the secrets of the Brotherhood of Death, people see evil is organized and must be defeated. As Woodrow Wilson observed, "Everybody knows that corruption thrives in secret places, and avoids public places, and we believe it is a fair presumption that secrecy means impropriety."[517]

The eugenic messages on the polished granite prompt thoughts of Hitler and Nazi Germany (e.g., "maintain humanity under 500,000,000" and portraying people as "a cancer on the earth"). Could the Brotherhood seriously seek to eliminate billions of people? Unfortunately the answer is yes, and in 2000, Aaron Russo reported that Nick Rockefeller specifically informed him of a plan to decrease the global population.[518] Russo knew he had risked his life by disclosing what he had learned from Rockefeller. In 2001 Russo was diagnosed with bladder cancer, and he died on August 24, 2007.

The Georgia Guidestones are designed to appear wise, but each message has a dark hidden meaning.[519]

The Bible explains counterfeit commandments are an abomination.[520] Each Georgia Guidestone commandment is explained in *The Georgia Guidestones*.[521] The Georgia Guidestones are written with a primary audience that is not most people living today. The primary audience is the people who survive World War III. The Brotherhood of Death Ten Commandments are focused on killing the unfit, perpetual population reduction, maintaining totalitarian rule, eliminating opposing religions, and violating God given rights.

Satan often misleads with a single lie that is mixed with multiple truths. At first glance the Georgia Guidestones may appear to be multiple good commandments with only a single bad directive to kill most people. However, each of the Georgia Guidestones statements or commandments are evil when the primary audience and post-apocalyptic meaning of what is written is understood.

The Georgia Guidestones	Commandments Deciphered
1. Maintain humanity under 500,000,000 in perpetual balance with nature.	Exterminate most human life on the planet.[522]
2. Guide reproduction wisely - improving fitness and diversity.	Kill babies, the disabled, and people deemed mentally unfit - alter God's creation with genetic engineering.[523]
3. Unite humanity with a living new language.	A world government and religion with occult symbols as part of the living language.[524]
4. Rule passion - faith - tradition - and all things with tempered reason.	Judicial control of faith and religion teaching blessed are the powerful.[525]
5. Protect people and nations with fair laws and just courts.	Protect the elite and one world government regions with laws and courts approving torture and the death penalty.[526]
6. Let all nations rule internally resolving external disputes in a world court.	Nations are subordinate to a world court and government.[527]
7. Avoid petty laws and useless officials.	Void God's laws and eliminate officials seeking to safeguard people from tyrants.[528]
8. Balance personal rights with social duties.	Social duties, also camouflaged as Socialism, strips individual incentive and leads to enslavement.[529]
9. Prize truth - beauty - love - seeking harmony with the infinite.	Seek harmony with the god of the New World Order. Ignore God's laws and "do what you want" corrupting truth, beauty, and love.[530]
10. Be not a cancer on the earth – leave room for nature – leave room for nature.	People who worship the God of Abraham are a cancer on the earth. Leave room for nature is repeated because plants and other components of nature are valued more than most humans.[531]

Population reduction of billions of people requires a global Hiroshima. While a nuclear false-flag attack could be used in the United States, on the global scale the Brotherhood actually needs non-nuclear alternatives so that the planet is habitable for the elite and their servants.

This occult monument demonstrates that the goals of the Brotherhood are very serious.[532]

A global Hiroshima requires secrecy, control of central banks, control of the biggest media corporations, control of major drug corporations, control of the food supply, people to influence government laws, leadership infiltrations in the World Health Organization, and a means to manage people who communicate the truth. Unfortunately, much of everything needed is already waiting in the wings due in part to legislation passed after September 11, 2001.

9

A NEW ROME

"And they had a king over them, which is the angel of the bottomless pit, whose name in the Hebrew tongue is Abaddon, but in the Greek tongue hath his name Apollyon."
Revelation 9:11

I commence this chapter with a key. When the chapter is done the key should be firmly placed in lock position. Here is the key: This Palladium-level secret, that Washington D.C. is a welcome mat for the Apollyon or the Antichrist, is one reason why the Brotherhood of Death sometimes will commit murder to maintain secrecy.

Completed in 1884, the Washington Monument was at that time the tallest building in the world.[533]

Even before the birth of the United States, Brotherhood of Death affiliated secret societies were working to design a new Rome which we know today as Washington, D.C. David Ovason wrote, "I know of no other city in the world with such a multitude of public zodiacs displayed in so small a space."[534] Washington, D.C. is a spiritual center for the Brotherhood religion. The city plan continues to secretly evolve for a future time when the symbols, including the incomplete inverted pentagram to the north of the White House, will be completed.[535]

Chapter 4 of this book explained that earlier in 1884 a formal declaration of war was publically announced by the Pope for the Church of Christ and "Pope" for the kingdom of Satan. On December 6, 1884, the Brotherhood's symbolically communicated that Lucifer is greater than God by setting the Washington Monument capstone. Immediately prior to the Brotherhood's Washington D.C. 555 feet tall phallus monument, the tallest building in the world was the 515 feet tall Cologne Cathedral in Germany.[536] The Brotherhood of Death conceals the number 666 by using 555. This is because 555 feet equals 6660 inches and the zero in their belief system can be ignored. The Brotherhood's "Mark of the Beast" 666 as warned in the Bible is in this way both revealed and concealed.[537]

To keep the Washington Monument blessed only by the power of darkness, the blessed brick sent by Pope Pius IX in 1853 was stolen in 1854. The blessed marble from the ancient Temple of Concord in Rome was smashed into pieces and the fragments were thrown into the Potomic River.[538] This rejected stone was destroyed by a well organized mob because the Brotherhood did not want it to overrule a planned Masonic religious blessing when the obelisk was completed. To distance direct Masonic involvement, the Brotherhood's secret society ordered to execute this crime was the "Know-Nothing" Party. The name of this secret society is derived from instructions to members to only answer "I know nothing" when asked about the organization's activites.

To solidify the deception, during the construction of the Washington Monument propaganda misled Christians. Stones from states, cities, foreign countries, organizations and individuals resulted in 194 memorial stones.[539] Some of these stones have Bible phrases and messages leading Christians to believe the Washington Monument is a Christian structure. The capstone is a prime example with the "Laus Deo" inscription on east side of the cap. When translated from Latin the words mean "Praise be to God." People ignorant of the Brotherhood of Death religion fail to realize that the god being praised by the Masonic builders was and is not the God of Abraham.

One example of propaganda to suppress Christian dissent is prior to bringing the capstone to Washington, it was displayed at Tiffany's in New York City. To increase the public support for this abomination, people were given the opportunity to jump over "the top of the Washington Monument." The aluminum apex was at that time only 8.9 inches tall so jumping over it was very easy.

The capstone was placed on December 6, 1884.[540]

The message of the Blessed Virgin warns us of a time when earthquakes will turn abominations into shattered pieces of rock. The time is approaching when the Washington Monument will be destroyed just as the abominations were destroyed in Axum, Ethiopia.

Axum's 33 meter Great Stelae is broken into pieces.[541] Shown in the background are smaller obelisks being held up with wires.

Evidence that supports Washington, D.C. is a Brotherhood of Death Rome is hard to ignore. Rosicrucianism, also known as the Order of the Rose Cross, is a Brotherhood of Death secret society. The society was publicly founded by a 13th century philosopher named Christian Rosenkreuz. Brotherhood insiders teach that Rosenkreuz was selected to be a secret name to conceal the identity of Francis Bacon and it is Bacon who should be considered the founder of modern day Rosicrucianism.[542]

The Rosicrucian presence in the United States since the 17th century was part of a plan activated after Bacon's death.[543] Evidence supporting Bacon's plan for a new Rome is substantial. One of the first signs that Rosicrucians were actively working to create a new Rome appears in 1663. Francis Pope, the owner of the Washington D.C. hill now known as Capitol Hill, called this hill

Rome. Pope prophesized a capital more powerful than Rome would occupy the hill. In addition, the name Pope may be a pseudonym in honor of Francis Bacon, who was the first Rosicrucian "Pope" or leader.[544]

William Tindall wrote in 1914 about Francis Pope:

> "It is told of this dreamer, that he predicted a greater capital than Rome would occupy that hill and that later generations would command a great and flourishing country in the new world. He related that he had a dream or vision, in which he had seen a splendid parliament house on the hill, now known to us as Capitol Hill, which he purchased and called Rome, in prophetic honor of the great city to be.
>
> "His title to the land may be somewhat convincive of his prophecy, as it was deeded under the name 'Rome,' June 5, 1663."[545]

The title of the official manuscript reads:

> "Do hereby grant unto him the s[ai]d Francis Pope, a parcell of Land called Rome, lying on the East side of the Anacostine River Beginning at a marked Oak, standing by the River side, the bound Tree of Robert Troop, and running North up the River for breadth Two hundred perches to a bounded Oak standing at the mouth of a Bay or Inlett called Tiber."[546]

The language of the title indicates what is now Capitol Hill was acknowledged as Rome and the Potomac River as the Tiber River even before Francis Pope acquired the land. While the evidence that the true purpose of the nation's capital is to be a new Rome, there is much more to this real-world story.

In 1938, Rosicrucian H. Spencer Lewis confirmed the organization was implementing Bacon's plan in 1693.[547] Since Francis Bacon died in 1626, it is reasonable that Francis Pope was an early scout to find property for Bacon's secret society. Lewis noted a larger group arrived thirty years after Pope and acquired additional land. Lewis wrote:

> "Many newspaper articles and many historical pamphlets issued in Pennsylvania, and particularly in Philadelphia, in the last fifty years have made very definite and pleasant references to the work and success attained and achieved by the early Rosicrucians who left Europe in 1693 under a plan originally outlined by Sir Francis Bacon and came to America purposely and deliberately to introduce the first form of Rosicrucianism in America."[548]

In 1693, Johann Jacob Zimmerman, a Master of a Rosicrucian Lodge, attempted to carry the secret society torch from Hamburg, Germany to America.[549] He died in Rotterdam, Holland on the eve of his embarkation to the U.S.[550] Johannes Kelpius continued Zimmermann's work, and about 45 people set sail on February 7, 1694 from London to America on the *Sara Maria.*[551] Kelpius and Zimmermann's family arrived in Philadelphia on June 23, 1694 and traveled to Germantown on June 24, 1694.[552] With knowledge that Zimmermann was seeking to bring the Rosicrucian secret society torch from Hamburg to establish a new Rome, it is less surprising to learn that part of what is today Washington, D.C. was once named Hamburg.

The story of how part of this new Rome became Hamburg is complicated by two men named Funk. In 1754 Frederick Calvert granted part of what is today Washington, D.C. to a person who may have assumed the pseudonym of Funk.[553] The specific area granted was called Foggy Bottom. The Foggy Bottom grantee was presented as a Dutch gun maker named Henry Funk. Another man, Jacob Funk, is the person who is identified as naming the land Hamburg.[554] The selection of the name Hamburg by a purported Dutchman is unusual since it is the name of a German city.[555] A small group of people lived on the land, and it was also known as Funkstown before it became part of Washington, D.C.

The selection and management of the land that is now Washington, D.C. was dominated by Freemasons and other individuals with secret society affiliations. Pierre L'Enfant, Andrew Ellicott, Benjamin Bannaker, and Thomas Jefferson are examples of people not acknowledged by Freemasonry as members but with close relationships to Brotherhood of Death affiliated secret societies and involved in planning Washington, D.C.[556] Nonetheless, an individual's membership status means little as long as the design, building, or location is dedicated to the Brotherhood's god.

The Brotherhood appears to have anticipated that one day they would need to insulate Washington, D.C. from the American people. Historian William Tindall observed, "The capital of the United States is the only national capital the establishment of which was to a material degree due to or influenced by the purpose of the national authority to protect itself from its own citizens."[557]

Federal Government Relocates

Prior to moving to Washington, D.C., the federal government was located in New York City and had previously been located in Philadelphia. On July 16, 1790, Congress approved "An Act for establishing the temporary and permanent seat of the Government of the United States," which is also called the Residence Act of 1790. Named in honor of George Washington, Washington, D.C. was founded in 1791 as the nation's capital. The Residence Act gave Freemason George Washington the authority to select the exact location along the Potomac River for the capital and set the completion date to be no later than December 1800.

On January 22, 1791, George Washington appointed a three-member commission in order to implement the Residence Act; it consisted of Daniel Carroll, Thomas Johnson and David Stuart.[558] Andrew Ellicott was appointed as surveyor. Parcels from the farms of David Burns, Daniel Carroll, Samuel Davidson, and Notley Young became federal land.

Daniel Carroll's participation in the three-member commission is sometimes cited as evidence that there was no anti-Christian purpose in the establishment of Washington, D.C. because he was a Catholic. Daniel Carroll, the owner of the land that became Capitol Hill and commission member, was first and foremost a Freemason.[559] He may have attempted to conceal his Masonic membership because the Catholic Church strongly condemns Freemasonry, and during his lifetime would excommunicate people for participating in this anti-Christian religion.

Every step of the way, Freemasons and other Brotherhood of Death affiliated secret society members controlled the design of Washington, D.C. Pierre L'Enfant is acknowledged as the lead architect.[560]

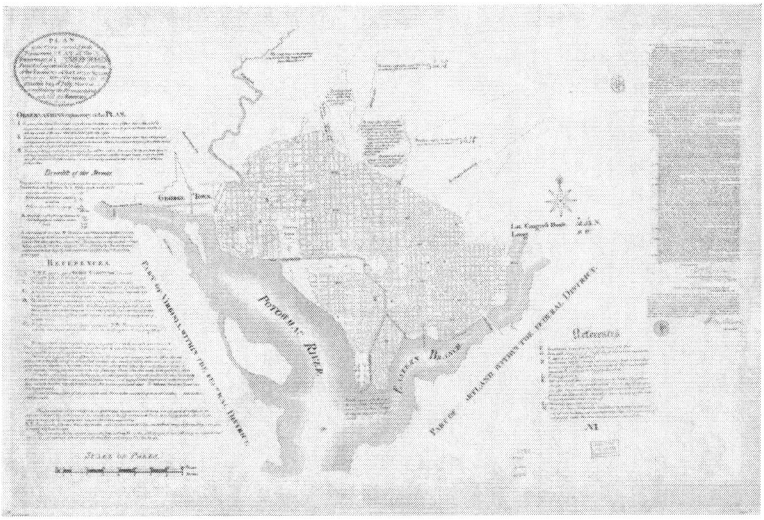

The earliest Washington, D.C. city plan in existence, "The L'Enfant Plan," is from 1791.[561]

At least 20 zodiacs were designed in the center of the city, along with over 1,000 Virgoan images.[562] Virgoan images are representations of the constellation Virgo, which contains the bright star Spica. Virgo is in the region of the celestial equator near

Leo and Libra. Examples of Virgoan images are explained in this chapter.

Washington, D.C., Layout

The Washington, D.C. street layout and architecture reveals one of the greatest Brotherhood of Death secrets. To help explain this "big secret" Brotherhood symbols are numbered and explained. The first three symbols are shown in L'Enfant's 1792 map. The three symbols are used by secret societies to represent Lucifer and can be easily found on modern Washington, D.C. maps.

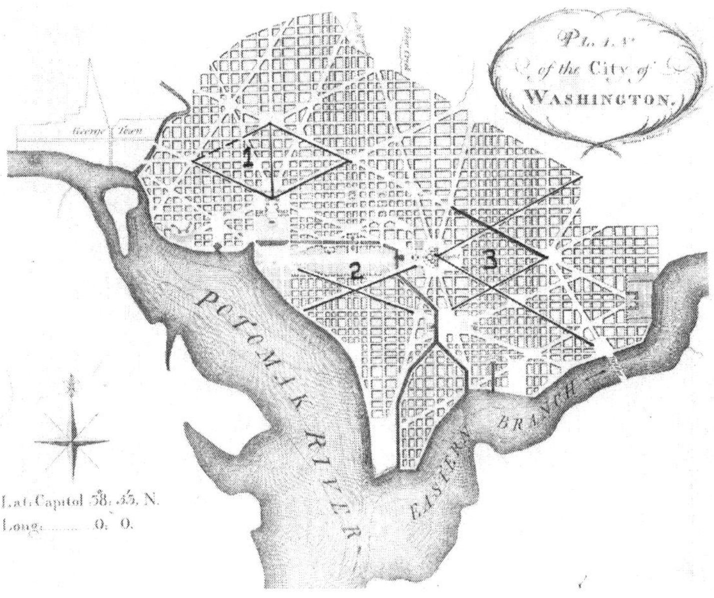

The L'Enfant's 1792 map with pyramid, X and Masonic symbol.[563]

The first highlighted symbol, #1 above, is a pyramid above the seat of power or White House. The placement of the White House, similar to an Egyptian pharaoh, is under a pyramid to optimize occult power. The number 2 is written on the city plan above an "X," which is a symbol for Osiris. Osiris, commonly signifying

Lucifer, is the "X" or "X factor" and unholy trinity. The number 3 on the city plan shows a Masonic square and compass, which are both commonly used by Freemasons.

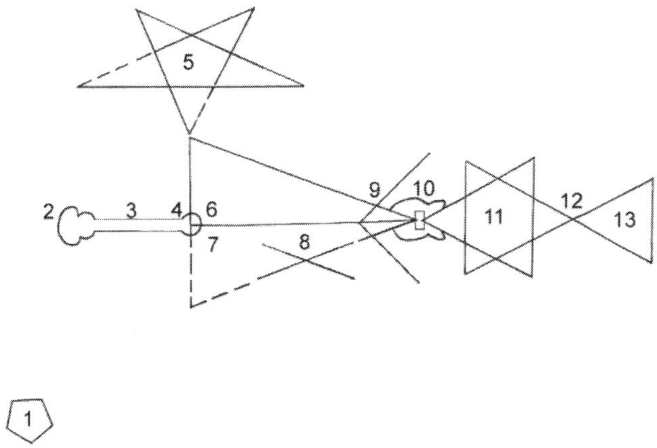

The image deciphers 13 Brotherhood of Death symbols near the U.S. Capitol.[564]

The nation's capital is situated where water forms a "Y." This is not shown above, but is easy to locate on a map by finding the Potomac River and locating the "Y" immediately below the center of Washington, D.C. The "Y" and symbols 1 to 13 on the tracing diagram are placed over a map of Washington, D.C. that is online at www.vigilantchristian.org/dcmap.html. The online map will help you see other occult symbols in Washington, D.C. The convergence of two rivers forming a "Y" is highly valued in the Brotherhood of Death religion as a location that can magnify spiritual power.

Number 1 shows the Pentagon, which is in the shape of the center of a pentagram. Numbers 2, 3, and 4, shown in the decipher diagram and in the below picture, are phallus symbols. The following is the Lincoln Memorial and Washington Monument.

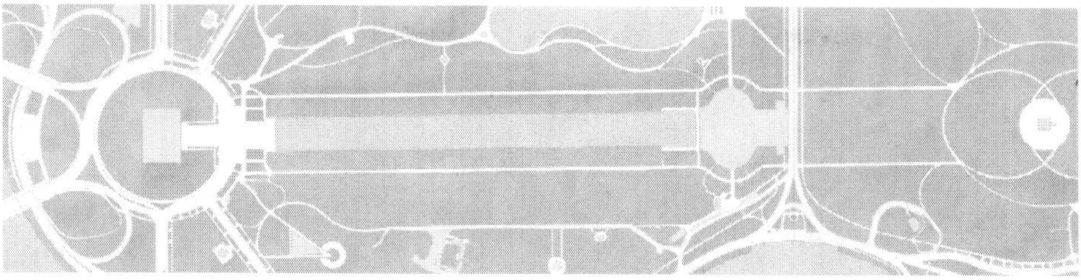

The phallus symbol combining decipher image numbers 2, 3, and 4 is traced below.[565]

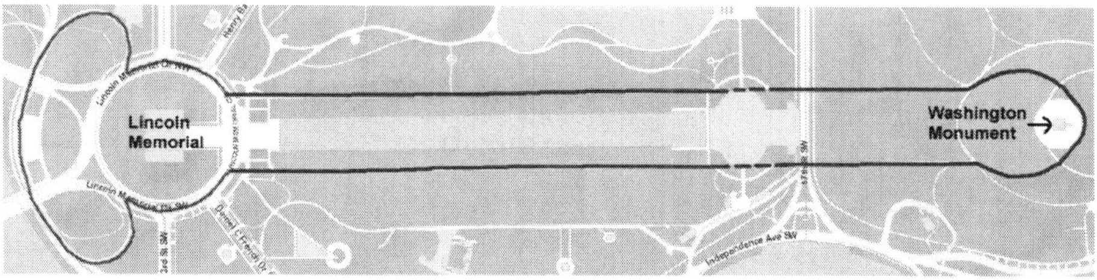

If you look carefully, you can see another "male energy" symbol.[566] The second symbol is visible by combining decipher image number 2 and number 3.[567]

Number 4 in the decipher image is the Washington Monument obelisk. The obelisk is an obvious phallus symbol. The cornerstone was laid on July 4, 1848 and dedicated with a Masonic occult ritual on February 21, 1885.

For all three phallus symbols, "male energy" is communicated, and when combined with "female energy" (the womb-like Semiramis or Isis symbol from combining numbers 6 and 7), the generative principal is represented. In history many names are used for the mythical male and female gods. Nimrod and Semiramis, Osiris and Isis, Bacchus and Venus, and Jupiter and Juno, Yin and Yang, are a few examples of male and female names. The male and female symbols are valued in the Brotherhood of Death religion because they believe occult symbols enhance a spiritual procreative force.

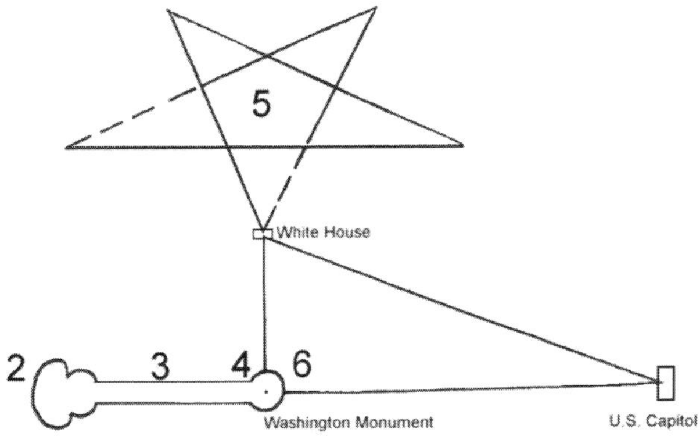

Number 5 in the decipher image shown below is an inverted pentagram with the tip formed at the White House.[568]

The inverted pentagram has many names associated with evil, including the Baphomet Star, Devil's Sign, Sirius Star, Satanic Pentagram, Witch's Foot, and Wizard's Star. Satanists believe that when the tip of the star is down or inverted, it is the symbol for Satan and can be used to conjure evil spirits. Witches teach that when the point is up, this pentagram can be used to conjure benevolent spirits. Christianity teaches that both black magic and white magic interfere with our relationship with God.

Manly Hall wrote, "In symbolism, an inverted figure always signifies a perverted power."[569] The pentagram is commonly found in the floor of Masonic lodges with the altar centered above it. Lower level Masons are told that the inverted pentagram represents the brightest star in the night sky, which is Sirius.

The inverted pentagram symbol is used by the female counterpart of Freemasonry, called the Order of the Eastern Star. This secret society publicly proclaims that the symbol is the Star of Bethlehem needed to locate the Savior. The star point that is down is explained as "indicating the light of the star is descending to Earth from Heaven."[570] The explanation beyond the public smokescreen is that the Masonic savior, who Freemasons openly call Hiram, is summoned from the spirit realm to earth.

The link between the pentagram symbolizing evil is confirmed by occultist Helen Petrovna Blavatsky.[571] For example, Blavatsky explained the link between Set and Satan. She wrote, "From Hermes, the god of Wisdom, called also Thoth, Tat, Adad, Seth, Set, and Satan, and in Greece as Kadmus. The kabalists identify him with Adam Kadmon, the first manifestation of the Divine Power, and with Enoch."[572]

Prior to Lucifer's fall from heaven, Freemasons teach that Lucifer's symbolic pentagram or star was pointed up. Manly Hall explained:

> "When used in black magic, the pentagram is called the 'sign of the cloven hoof,' or the footprint of the Devil. The star with two points upward is also called the 'Goat of Mendes,' because the inverted star is the same shape as a goat's head. When the upright star turns and the upper point falls to the bottom, it signifies the fall of the Morning Star [Lucifer being cast out of Heaven]."[573]

Freemasons teach that a five-pointed star signifies the interconnection of the four elements (Air, Fire, Water, and Earth) united by the fifth element called Aether or the Spirit.[574] A deceptive public Masonic explanation states that the five points on the star are the five points of Masonic fellowship.[575]

Number 6 in the decipher diagram is the Federal Triangle drawn by L'Enfant. The Federal Triangle is mirrored in the skies by the stars. Arcturus falls on the White House, Regulus falls on the Capitol, and Spica falls on the Washington Monument.[576] In 1999 David Ovason wrote a book explaining the significance of the Federal Triangle.[577] He observed:

> "To appreciate this stellar symbolism fully, we must look first of all at the nature of the triangle, set out in L'Enfant's plan

for Washington, D.C. Having done this, we must then relate it to a less obvious triangle, set in the stars around the constellation Virgo.

"L'Enfant set down his triangle on the Earth with great care. His Masonic Brothers who continued his work ensured that each of the three points of the figure was consecrated, and linked in a meaningful relationship with the stars. I will recapitulate:

- The White House cornerstone was laid at noon on October 13, 1796. The Moon and the Dragon's Head were in Virgo.
- The Capitol cornerstone was laid by George Washington on September 18, 1793. At that time, the Sun, Mercury and the Dragon's Head were in Virgo.
- The Washington Monument foundation stone was laid at noon on July 4, 1848. The Moon and the Dragon's Head were in Virgo.

"Besides the obvious connection with Virgo, the one thing which these foundation charts have in common is that they each have the Dragon's Head in that sign."[578]

Astronomy is important to most mystery religions, including Freemasonry. Freemason Robert Hewitt Brown revealed key secrets in his book *Stellar Theology and Masonic Astronomy*. While Christians conclude that predicting the future with astrology is misguided, Brotherhood of Death supporters value astrology in order to both predict and influence the future.

Freemasons teach that the triangle and the pyramid have been symbols of secret societies at least since Pythagoras.[579] The belief in pyramid power is why Egyptians placed a pharaoh's body in a pyramid. A pyramid is called a "sacred Delta." The picture in Chapter 4 of the Masonic altar depicts the name of Jahbulon, their god, in a triangle. Other Brotherhood of Death affiliated secret societies including the Rosicrucians and Illuminists mirror this use of the sacred Delta and pyramid.

Penned by THE ROSICRUCIAN
P. B. RANDOLPH, M. D.

BY REV. DR. R. SWINBURNE CLYMER
Director General Church of Illumination

Secret societies symbols are visible on Rosicrucian P. B. Randolph's seal on the left and Illuminist Dr. R. Swinburne Clymer's seal on the right.[580]

A further examination of the 13 symbols depicted previously shows that number 7 adds a mirror side to number 6, and if the north south line is moved east it becomes a triangle of equal lengths. When extended, as shown, the Washington Monument penetrates numbers 6 and 7. To fully appreciate this larger symbol, note number 9 symbolizes arms and number 10 is the symbol for a head. The significance of the arms and head will be explained shortly.

Number 8 is the "X" symbolizing Osiris, which was explained earlier in this chapter as a symbol for Lucifer.

Number 9 and 7 form a Masonic square and compass. There are multiple deceptive Masonic explanations for the square and compass. Albert Pike taught a partial truth of what the symbol means when he explained the compass was the male phallus and the square was the female vulva. He wrote, "And the hand on the male side holds a Compass, and that on the female side, a Square."[581] Pike continued to explain the Masonic symbols writing: "The Compass, therefore, is the Hermetic Symbol of the Creative Deity, and the Square of the productive Earth or Universe."[582] Freemasons view the square and compass symbol as a sex symbol as do Satanists, although Satanists generally associate the compass with female energy and the square with male energy.

The square and compass symbolize two parts of the unholy trinity of Freemasonry.[583] In the Egyptian version, the compass is Osiris and the square is Isis and they produce Horus. The combination of male and female energy to create Horus, or more commonly known as the "G" in the compass or Hiram in Freemasonry, is a Masonic secret. As noted in the quote at the beginning of this chapter, the entity created is Apollyon who is the Antichrist.

Number 10 in the decipher image is a head in the form of an owl, which represents Lucifer as being intelligent, a deadly hunter, and a stalker of prey in darkness. The owl is easier to see in the following map of the capitol, especially when the outline is traced.[584]

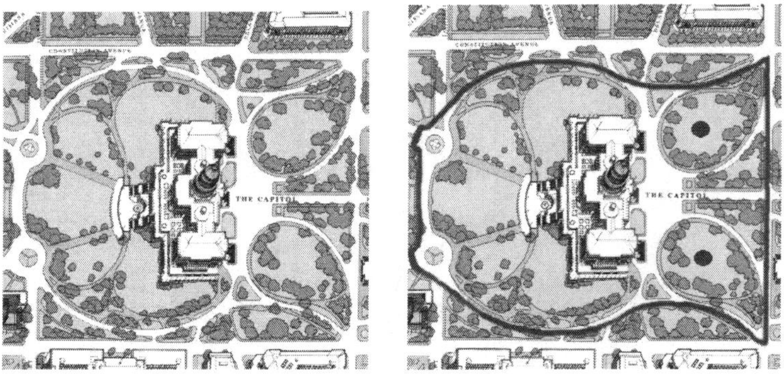

The owl, also called Athena's bird, is a key Brotherhood of Death Bohemian Grove symbol.[585]

The picture shows the owl on the front of a dollar bill.[586]

The owl grounds and U.S. Capitol building signify a spiritual center of the New Rome. On top of the Capitol dome is the Statue of Freedom atop a globe with "E Pluribus Unum" or "Out of Many, One." This statue is Columbia, a female allegorical god in the Brotherhood religion. The Columbia name of this goddess of democracy is why the nation's capital is in the District of Columbia.

Number 11 shows the hexagram, which is also called Crest of Solomon, Double Triangle, Hexalpha, Hexangular Seal of Solomon, Shield of David, Star of David, and the Talisman of Saturn. The hexagram, two triangles joined together, is a sexual union symbol, the combination of both male and female energy. A male energy example is the Egyptian god Osiris, and a female energy example is the Egyptian goddess Isis. This is also a mirror symbol with the message that the power below is equal to the power above. The mirror concept is why Washington, D.C. has reflection pools near key locations, including the Lincoln Memorial and Capitol. Lower level Masons are taught that the hexagram is the sign for the Great Architect, and Royal Arch Masons are taught that the symbol facilitates communication with a spirit realm.

Freemasons teach that the hexagram is similar to the interlaced Yin and Yang shapes.[587] The Masonic deception follows: "In one instance we have the interlaced triangles, one black, the other white; the white triangle [Lucifer] has its point up; the black triangle [God of Abraham and Lucifer's enemy] points down... The interlaced black and white triangles represent the forces of darkness and light, error and truth, ignorance and wisdom and good and evil; when properly placed they represent balance and harmony."[588]

The hexagram also symbolizes the number 666 because the inner hexagon and outer sides of each triangle has six sides. For witches, the hexagram is a fire and water symbol and is used to place a hex or curse on someone. [589] The Brotherhood of Death religion teaches the hexagram channels psychic energy to connect earth-plane consciousness with the spirit world. Brotherhood followers believe the hexagram must be present to summon a demon with a footprint similar to the symbol.[590]

Number 12 is the same square and compass explained as number 3 in the 1792 L'Enfant diagram. The square and compass extend from the Capitol or number 10 to number 13. The full symbol is not drawn in the decipher image to prevent confusion with number 11.

Number 13 in the decipher images is another pyramid. In the Brotherhood religion, the pyramid symbolizes the revival of sacred Egyptian knowledge and a bridge from the realm of flesh to the spirit realm.

Concrete Welcome Mat for Apollyon

In Chapter 4 it was noted that C. Fred Kleinknecht, the Sovereign Grand Commander of the Freemasonry Mother Council of the World, endorsed David Ovason's book and his notion regarding the origin of America's star.[591] What Kleinknecht and Ovason suggest, that the star symbol on the American flag is the Blazing Star or Lucifer's Star, is explained by Albert Pike in *Morals and Dogma*.[592]

> "...the BLAZING STAR of five points... Originally it represented SIRIUS, or the Dog-star, the forerunner of the inundation of the Nile;...the Blazing Star has been regarded as an emblem of Omniscience, or the All-Seeing Eye, which to the Egyptian initiates was the emblem of Osiris, the Creator."[593]

The Egyptian Osiris is the same god worshipped by Freemasons, although Albert Pike instructed that the name Lucifer be used only at the highest levels. The Blazing or Flaming Star is the Masonic Great Architect called Lucifer.

Ovason wrote about what is today Washington, D.C.:

> "Dominating this part of the skies would be the scorching dog star, Sirius, a brilliant white and yellow star. In 1800, this was the only star known to have been represented in the Egyptian hieroglyphics. Some modern scholars trace the name of the star in the hieroglyphic of a dog, evoking the god Anubis; however, the ancient Egyptians tended to call Sirius Spdt, and represented it with hieroglyphics that resembled an obelisk and a five-pointed star. The ancient Greeks, who took over so much of the Egyptian Wisdom, called Spdt by the name Sothis, yet it remained the dog star in their calendars, and it was used by both Greeks and Egyptians in the orientation of important temples. I pay attention to the five-pointed hieroglyphic here because, as we shall see, it seems to have been the source of the five-pointed star adopted for the American flag."[594]

Freemasons designed the Federal Triangle, number 6 in the decipher image, as a right triangle positioned to symbolize their alternative to Christ, called Horus in Egyptian mythology, Hiram by many Freemasons, and Apollyon at high levels in the Brotherhood religion. The basic logic is that the energy from Osiris and Isis create Horus. The logic of the energy has a mathematical formula of $a^2 + b^2 = c^2$ and is called the Pythagorean equation.[595]

Freemasons teach that the Babylonian mystery religion priests may have understood this formula before Pythagoras, who is acknowledged as a "highly advanced master in the knowledge of the secret schools of the Mysteries."[596] Pythagoras is claimed to have obtained much of his knowledge from Enoch.[597] The structure of Pythagoras' secret society, the Order of Pythagoras, mirrors Freemasonry with three degrees of membership (i.e., Novices, Nomothets, and Mathematicians).[598] Masonic authority Colin Dyer wrote that Pythagoras was a master of occult knowledge "of whose doctrine some small portion is enshrined for us in our Masonic system."[599]

The Federal Triangle is a secret symbol for the Masonic trinity and Antichrist. The symbol attempts to declare Washington, D.C. the "City of Lucifer." The Brotherhood of Death religion requires massive human sacrifices ordered from this location to create the spiritual energy to summon Apollyon, a human given spirit energy from the Masonic Lucifer's or Brotherhood's Satan. The following configuration of the symbols, in the religion of the Brotherhood, is to help usher in the rule of Apollyon.

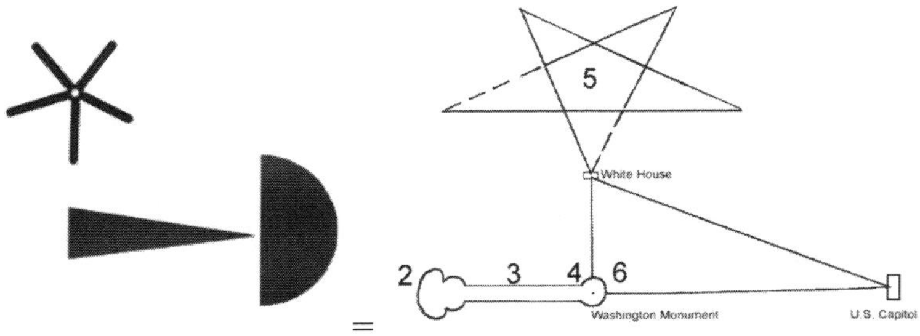

The Egyptian hieroglyphic for Sirius from Chapter 6 is modified slightly and oriented with the Washington, D.C. decipher image.[600]

The central message and secret of the Brotherhood, mirrored in the stars, is now in plain view.[601] Osiris (the right-angled triangle) and Isis (the womb-like half circle Benben) produce Horus.

The Washington D.C. decipher diagram shows Osiris is both the Washington Monument and larger phallic symbol starting with the Lincoln Memorial. Isis is the womb-like dome Capitol. The inverted pentagram, the third point of this right-angled triangle, is the White House. All three structures invoke dark energy into the mixture. Palladium-level Freemasons believe energy from Osiris is b^2 combined with energy from Isis to create c^2. The Pythagorean equation of $a^2 + b^2 = c^2$, with Palladium-level Freemasons believing c^2 is Apollyon (concealed as Horas and Hiram). From the Christian perspective, Apollyon is the Antichrist. The following image is the Brotherhood's unholy trinity and symbol for the Antichrist.

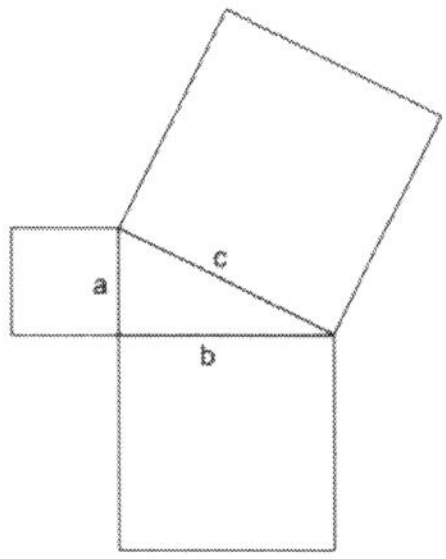

The big Masonic secret is that the nation's capital is a welcome mat for an unholy trinity and the Antichrist.

In the bizarre teachings of Freemasonry and the Brotherhood religion, the Washington Monument, the U.S. Capitol, and the White House direct energy that one day will give birth to the Antichrist.

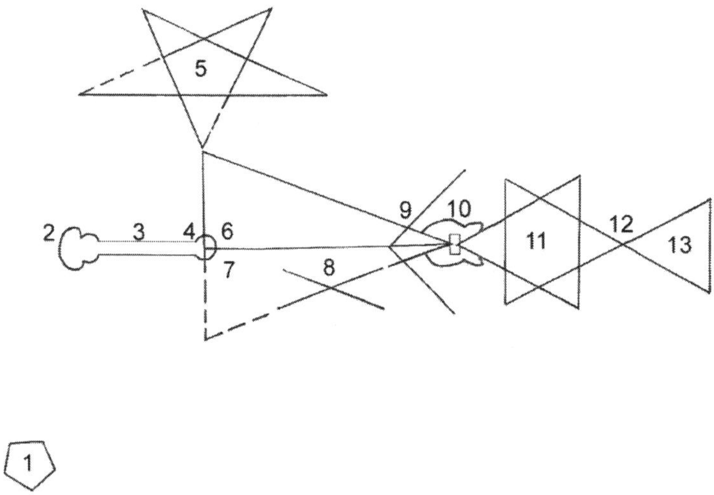

Other occult symbols serve to feed additional energy to summon the Brotherhood of Death Antichrist.[602]

Apollyon, is the missing capstone, and upon his arrival the Brotherhood seeks to complete symbols, including placing a permanent capstone on Giza's Great Pyramid.[603]

The fact that occultists have built symbols into Washington, D.C., does not mean the United States is doomed or Americans are evil. Christians have helped make the United States a great country and the land of opportunity for over two hundred years. All followers of the God of Abraham honor God by working to make their country better and loving people as Jesus loves us.

Occult names and symbols do need to change because people using them are sometimes unknowingly invoking occult powers. This is why for members of the Brotherhood the spelling of a name is less important than how the name is pronounced (e.g., Amaruca for America and Kukulkan for Ku Klux Klan). Eliminating the evil influence of secret societies in the U.S. government is achievable through prayer, education, and peaceful actions. When you share this book with others, you help to educate people and end or at least greatly reduce the influence of secret societies in government.

Believing the truth requires that you think critically and, when necessary, reject the mainstream programming of how the world works. Robert Kennedy was assassinated while campaigning to be president. Before his death he said:

> "It is from numberless diverse acts of courage and belief that human history is shaped. Each time a man stands up for an ideal, or acts to improve the lot of others, or strikes out against injustice, he sends forth a tiny ripple of hope, and crossing each other from a million different centers of energy and daring, those ripples build a current that can sweep down the mightiest of walls of oppression and resistance."[604]

I realize that most people will struggle with the information contained in this book. The Brotherhood of Death has followed its master plan so well that it makes the truth difficult to believe. I encourage you to conduct your own research. Following the millions of dollars spent by the Brotherhood on projects such as the Georgia Guidestones and occult symbols in Washington, D.C. does lead to answers.

10

OUR LADY'S VICTORY

"Blessed are the clean of heart: for they shall see God."
Jesus[605]

Saint Anthony of Padua is called the "hammer of the Heretics."[606] He provided easy-to-understand information that helped people go to heaven. This chapter is intended to be easy-to-understand and help you go to heaven.

Supernatural Solution - Fatima

In 1931, the future Pope Pius XII predicted: "I am worried by the Blessed Virgin's messages to Lucy of Fatima. This persistence of Mary about the dangers which menace the Church is a divine warning against the suicide of altering the Faith, in Her liturgy, Her theology and Her soul." Pope Benedict XVI declared in Bethlehem on May 13, 2009, "You promised the three children of Fatima that 'in the end, My Immaculate Heart will triumph.' May it be so!"

The 100th anniversary of this supernatural solution is October 13, 2017. Our Lady of Fatima has instructed people to pray the Rosary and ask God for help. When this happens, God will guide the Pope and Bishops to consecrate Russia to the Immaculate Heart of the Blessed Virgin. The result will be a miracle defeating the Brotherhood of Death.

Fatima and Daniel Prophecies

Christianity is unique for the accuracy of the prophecies specifically fulfilled and the prophecy that are yet to be fulfilled. The best example is Jesus predicted his suffering, death, and resurrection. All these events are fulfilled and Jesus said He would come again which has not yet been fulfilled.[607] The prophecies of Our Lady of Fatima and Daniel communicate that an evil person will seek to rule the world in the time before God's kingdom on earth is established. This person will appear when what Jesus and prophets in the Bible called the "abomination of desolation" is in the holy place.[608] In Matthew 24:15 Jesus said: "When therefore you shall see the abomination of desolation, which was spoken of by Daniel the prophet, standing in the holy place: he that readeth let him understand."

An abomination of desolation currently stands in the center courtyard of the Vatican Museum. This sculpture was specifically created for the Vatican in the 1960s. The Sphere abomination was prophesized at Fatima in 1917 and confirmed in Akita in 1973. The fact that all Pope's since it's installation have not removed speaks to the powerful influence of Satan and why people need to pray for the Pope.

The creator of the abomination of desolation sculpture, Arnaldo Pomodoro, has gone on to create a number of occult "Sphere within a Sphere" sculptures.[609] The explanation by the sculptor is very revealing. He explained that his sphere "is intended as a metaphor for the coming of a new millennium, a promise for the rebirth of a less troubled and destructive world."[610] In 1999, he confirmed what was suspected for decades. He said:

> "The sphere is a marvelous object, from the world of magic, wizards, whether it is of crystal or bronze, or full of water…It reflects everything around it, creating such contrasts that it sometimes is transformed, becoming invisible, leaving only its interior, tormented

and corroded, full of teeth, ...That's what drives me to make the spheres: breaking these perfect, magic forms in order reveal (find, discover) its internal ferment, mysterious and alive, monstrous and yet pure; so I create a discordant tension, a conflict, with the polished shine: a unity composed of incompleteness. In my sculpture, the shape of today's world contains within itself the form of the 'ideal city' as conceived by the artists of the Italian Renaissance. This, in turn, contains my hopes and dreams, and those of countless other citizens of the world."[611]

The blood shot All-Seeing Eye abomination of desolation is prominently on display in the center courtyard of the Vatican Museum.[612]

The monstrous Vatican's All-Seeing Eye, made from a wizard, or male witch, shows a new world emerging after tormenting and corroding Christianity. Pomodoro's Vatican Sphere within a Sphere communicates the mystery of iniquity, as explained in Catholic Cathecism 675, is being unveiled and third world war will tear the earth apart. Alternate versions of the Sphere within Sphere communicate various stages in the earth's healing process following World War III. The fact that this sculpture is at the

Vatican confirms Catholic priest Rev. Gabriele Amorth's statement that the reach of Satan is greater than people realize.[613]

Chapter 7 in *Vigilant Christian III: The Occult Religion of the 9/11 Attackers* provides additional information about Pomodoro's abominations located at the United Nations Headquarters in New York, in Washington, D.C., in Israel and other locations.

Luke 21: 17-22 explains that when Jerusalem is surrounded by armies the time of the abomination of desolation is near.[614] Mark 13:14-16 instructs people that when the abomination of desolation stands in the temple, people should know the great tribulation will immediately follow.[615]

When Jesus says the abomination of desolation is standing in the holy place, He is sharing with us that in the future the temple is rebuilt.[616] The abomination of desolation may not only be in the temple, but in the holy of holies, and placed on top of a counterfeit Ark of the Covenant. Chapter 2 explains the Brotherhood Ark was unveiled on September 9, 2001. Chapter 8 explains the Georgia Guidestones. The time is approaching when the stone tablets or commandments of the Antichrist will be placed in the counterfeit Ark of Hope.

Biblical scholars routinely conclude the location in Jerusalem where the abomination of desolation event occurs is either where the Dome of the Rock stands or very near this location. What is interesting to note is the Dome of the Rock is an abomination of desolation structure because it symbolizes rejecting Jesus as Lord and Savior.

The Dome of the Rock is on the site of the temple.[617]

For the followers of Jesus hearing him speak, the placement of a statue of Zeus by King Antiochus in the temple two centuries earlier was a clear example of what abomination of desolation meant.[618] Antiochus was a minor Antichrist that began his rule in 222 BC. Antiochus had the abominable idol of desolation placed on the altar of God.[619]

Antiochus III the Great coin.[620]

If not already happening in ways that we do not understand, when this temple referred to in the Bible is rebuilt, and subsequently an idol stands in this temple, the abomination of desolation is complete.

Furnishing for the temple are made and on display. For example, Exodus 25:31-39 explains the golden menorah was a solid one-piece of gold lampstand.[621] About 75 pounds of gold was used to make the temple lampstand.[622] Each branch of the lampstand held a cup in the shape of a flower that was soon to bloom. Candles were not used as light from the lampstand was fueled by oil.

This sign for this golden menorah in Jerusalem confirms parts of the temple are already rebuilt.[623]

The Fatima and Daniel prophecies have proven to be accurate and warn of a time when Satan would achieve a one-world government. Both the Fatima and Daniel prophecies communicate a final part that remains to be fulfilled. Daniel explained to King Nebuchadnezzar a future period of great trouble and a reborn Rome would be destroyed. Chapter 9 in this book explains Washington, D.C. was established by a secret society as a new Rome. All reborn Romes and their satellite occult branches, whether in the United States or in Italy, will be one day destroyed and followed by the everlasting kingdom of God.[624]

Many Catholics believe the last Pope will announce an extraordinary Jubilee before the return of Christ.[625] On a potentially related note, on March 13, 2015, Pope Francis announced an extraordinary Jubilee starting on December 8,

2015.[626] The perspective from Judaism is the Jubilee law no longer applies because the observance of this law ceased when the tribes were deported by Assyria in 722 BC.[627] The Catholic Church has continued the Jubilee law although *Vigilant Christian V: Perfect Money Planning* explains the Jubilee is no longer honored by the financial powers of our world.[628]

The idea that the Messiah will return during a year of Jubilee also comes from Rabbi Judah ben Samuel in AD 1217. According to the rabbi, there would be a certain number of Jubilees from ben Samuel's time to when the Messianic kingdom begins. Rabbi Judah ben Samuel predicted the year 2017. If he is correct or close by a few decades, the everlasting kingdom of God, preceded by a seven-year tribulation in which God's judgments are poured out on the earth, may happen in the lifetime of most people reading this book.

While the Bible warns to that But of that day or hour no man knoweth, neither the angels in heaven, nor the Son, but the Father (Mark 13:32). The return of the Lord and significance of a blood moon is explained in Joel 2:30–31 which says, "And I will shew wonders in heaven; and in earth, blood, and fire, and vapour of smoke. The sun shall be turned into darkness, and the moon into blood: before the great and dreadful day of the Lord doth come." In Revelation 6:12-14, John describes one of the seal judgments of the Tribulation: "And I saw, when he had opened the sixth seal, and behold there was a great earthquake, and the sun became black as sackcloth of hair: and the whole moon became as blood: And the stars from heaven fell upon the earth, as the fig tree casteth its green figs when it is shaken by a great wind: And the heaven departed as a book folded up: and every mountain, and the islands were moved out of their places."[629]

A tetrad of lunar eclipses—and the timing of those eclipses in the Jewish calendar—is fairly unusual, but not unprecedented. So the fact of the eclipses, while interesting, is no proof that Jesus will return by 2015. Furthermore, John's and Joel's descriptions of the signs of the Day of the Lord could refer to solar and lunar eclipses, but there are other possible explanations for those phenomena, such as changes in the atmosphere (mentioned in Revelation 6:12).

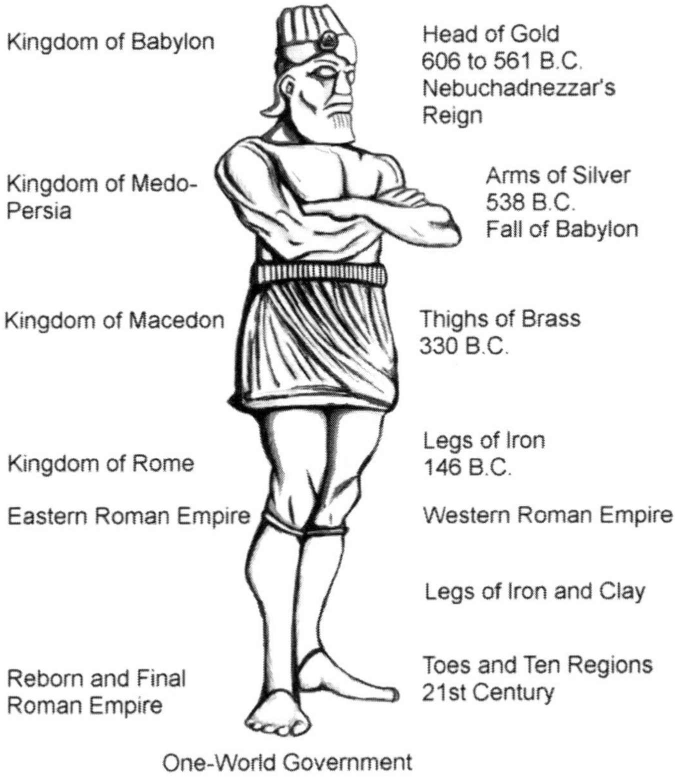

Babylon the Great empires in the prophecy of Daniel.[630]

Who is Deceived?

Satan has implemented a plan for a New World Order that is designed to fool almost every person on the planet. If we feel we are the rare exception and are not deceived, we may be wrong. A key principle to be on constant guard against Satan is never assume we cannot sin like those we are trying to correct. My advice is read this book from the perspective that you can learn from a person who knows that he makes mistakes.

I have taken great care to provide accurate information but do not claim to have all the answers. I feel called by God to share what I have learned to help people become Vigilant Christians. If a mistake in this book is discovered, please know I will provide a correction on the teachpeace.com website.[631] Anyone wishing an updated version of a book that I have written is encouraged to simply send the older book front cover page and $4.99 for shipping to the Teach Peace Foundation.[632]

An example is offered to consider that we may be doing something seriously wrong and not be aware of it. This "charging interest" example also shows how the truth is sometimes very inconvenient as it requires us to both change and work for justice.

Charging interest is explained as a serious sin in the Bible. Ezekiel 18:13 says the person who charges interest forfeits heaven and a righteous person helps others by making loans without charging interest.[633] The Law of Moses prohibited Israelites from charging interest. Jesus taught us to clarify, not revoke the Law of Moses.

People who claim that charging loan interest is problem-free are forgetting the guidance in Exodus, Leviticus, and Deuteronomy not to charge interest.[634] When money is needed for basic needs, the Old Testament and New Testament absolutely forbids charging interest. So how is it that Christians no longer consider the prohibitions against usury? Certainly it serves the princes of this world for people to conclude that charging interest is good.[635]

Charging interest on a loan is far below the Christian ideal of giving to the poor without seeking anything in return. Christians are called to free people burdened in debt with a debt-freeing Jubilee. Debt cancellation is the Biblical norm, which the princes of this world prefer to be forgotten. If we follow God's guidance in

Leviticus 25-26, the entire monetary system would be fundamentally changed resulting in a system freeing people enslaved in debt. The financial wisdom in the Bible, a Jubilee calling for this system to be reset every 50 years, reflects that even in the time of Moses people knew fractional banking and interest were direct threats to life, liberty, and the pursuit of happiness.

In the New Testament, Jesus builds upon the Law of Moses. Jesus also lifted the concept of a Jubilee to a far more significant meaning when he started his public ministry with text from Isaiah 61:1-2.[636] Jesus announces a Jubilee freeing people of all nations both spiritually and materially. The Lord's Prayer includes the material dimension of forgiving debts.[637] In Luke 16:9, the parable of the shrewd manager, we learn that we should use wealth to help people so that when it is gone we are welcomed in heaven.[638]

Jesus challenged the money-changers and Temple leaders with dangerous concepts including reminding people of the traditional teachings to periodically redistribute wealth via the Jubilee, forgive debts, and provide interest-free loans to the poor.[639] The financial system is aligned with the kingdom of Satan enabling the rich to become richer and the poor to become poorer via taxation and interest loans. How will God view violations of Ezekiel 18:13, the Law of Moses and the teaching of Jesus?

Perhaps you are aligned with God's monetary guidance. Satan has many other traps. Another example of a trap is deceiving people to believe Jesus was not serious when he said we should love our enemies.[640] As with the earlier financial deception example, billions of people are deceived and support militarism. Statements to "support our troops" are very popular. The truth is these statements often serve the agenda to establish the New World Order. On judgment day do you want to plead before God that you blindly supported Satan because you did not believe what Jesus said?

If you do not believe militarism is spiritually harmful or you have not been deceived by Satan, read *Vigilant Christian IV: 9/11 The Secret War*. Millions of people are following blind leaders regarding the September 11, 2001 terrorism and other lies that make militarism appear good. The Bible warns us that following blind leaders is eternally dangerous.[641]

Victory Soon?

When will the Brotherhood of Death be defeated? I do not know. Even when Jesus walked the earth He did not know.[642] While there are things we do not know, we do know that Jesus returns in a time of forgetfulness which means when He is not expected. We also know that no one on earth knows the day or hour because we are told in the Bible only "the Father alone" knows.[643]

We should be prepared for a supernatural event on October 13, 2017 to begin to usher in the 6th period of the Church. The reconstructed Third Secret in this book and the documentary *Akita and the Fatima Secret* makes a powerful case that we are living in extraordinary times and the period of peace in the Third Secret of Fatima is approaching.[644] With the information in this book, this film can help you understand why a shocking event in May 2014 prompted Pope Francis to declare the Year of Mercy.[645]

Knowledge of the seven Church periods is helpful. Luther's revolt began the fifth period of the Church in 1517.The year 2017 is 500 years later. The sixth period of the Christ's Church on earth is the Period of Peace explained in the Akita and the Fatima Secret documentary. The sixth period of the Church is advanced by a supernatural chastisement but formally initiated later by a Pope's consecration of Russia. The final period of the Church is the seventh period which is many years after the sixth period.

With knowledge of the Fatima and Akita miracles, we can begin to understand why Pope Francis is recommending people read *Lord of this World.*[646] We also gain insights on why he expects to soon die.[647] Chapter 9, *A New Rome*, also shines light on why he gave a historic speech in 2015 on Capitol Hill and why he believes World War III has begun.[648]

Satan wants people to think Fatima is no longer relevant. This is one reason leaks of the message often include some false information declaring the Fatima prophecies happened only in the 20th century. In addition, many good people made the mistake of predicting the event would happen within a range of years. This is understandable because the signs of our time do indicate that we are approaching what Christians ask for in the Our Father prayer.

Always Defeated

Physical and historical examples from around the world that the kingdom of Satan has always been defeated, however, are easy to identify.[649] One example is the European Parliament in Strasbourg, France.[650] The European Parliament building, an abomination completed in 1999, is a modern day Tower of Babel. The Tower of Babel is a relevant reminder that the Brotherhood is always defeated by God.

For the Brotherhood of Death, Rosslyn Chapel and the European Parliament were built to symbolizes their unfinished work. For Christians, all Brotherhood unfinished work and missing capstone symbols communicate the failure of the Brotherhood to achieve global domination.

Composite drawing of the Tower of Babel blended with the European Parliament.[651]

Drawing of an official European Union poster promoting the European Parliament.[652]

An aerial view of the building in the All-Seeing Eye European Parliament complex.[653]

Nimrod's Tower of Babel was stopped by God, and is a physical reminder that with God victory is not only possible, it is guaranteed. What is the hope for the United States and for the world? The answer is our Savior, Jesus Christ and the Christian Church. Depending on how the Christian Church (organized goodness) responds to the Brotherhood (organized evil), the United States will in the future be known as the land of the free or the land of the enslaved.

Understanding the Brotherhood can be initially depressing, but this is one step in the human grieving process that can be overcome. The five steps are shock/denial, bargaining, anger, depression, and acceptance.[654] With acceptance that the Brotherhood is real, great joy is possible because we can see solutions to defeat the Brotherhood. Furthermore, when you know that you are not part of the darkness but working to help others, you receive the joyful gift of knowing that you are serving God.

People often ask me how I can be so joyful even though I know Satan's Brotherhood is orchestrating death and suffering around the world. My answer is that Jesus died for us so that we sinners can triumph over evil. We are spiritually free beings who can have eternal living water by asking Jesus to be our Savior. When we accept Jesus into our lives, we are transformed, and nothing the Brotherhood can do can defeat God.

My knowledge of the Brotherhood of Death deepens my understanding and appreciation of the Bible. A deeper understanding of the Bible brings joy in a way that is difficult to describe. Instead of wondering why organized acts of evil are happening and having no answers, I often understand why, and as a result both see and value the solution. When you work for the truth, you are alive. Confusion leads to false solutions and depression. Truth brings clarity, joy, peace, and salvation.

Satan wants you to be paralyzed with fear. When you put your trust in God, you can overcome fear. God has no fear. The presence of God is the presence of pure love. We for whom the Bible is our guide are provided constant comfort and hope because evil was spiritually defeated by Jesus when He died for us.

Should we love people working for the Brotherhood? Jesus' answer is yes. For current and future generations we must never give up, especially as the Third Secret is fulfilled. Each and every person can defeat the Brotherhood of Death in their lifetime. What I mean is, if we try and fail to accomplish earthly objectives in our lifetime, this failure is only temporary, and the eternal rewards for trying are permanent.

With God, every day is a blessing, and a brighter future is possible. Daily acts of kindness, including towards people who we believe are our enemies, will help defeat the Brotherhood. Defeating evil is not only possible for each of us, it leads to an eternally rich life. As this book ends, 1 Corinthians 13: 1-13 is quoted.[655]

> "If I speak with the tongues of men, and of angels, and have not charity, I am become as sounding brass, or a tinkling cymbal. And if I should have prophecy and should know all mysteries, and all knowledge, and if I should have all faith, so that I could remove mountains, and have not charity, I am nothing. And if I should distribute all my goods to feed the poor, and if I should deliver my body to be burned, and have not charity, it profiteth me nothing. Charity is patient, is kind: charity envieth not, dealeth not perversely; is not puffed up; Is not ambitious, seeketh not her own, is not provoked to anger, thinketh no evil; Rejoiceth not in iniquity, but rejoiceth with the truth; Beareth all things, believeth all things, hopeth all things, endureth all things. Charity never falleth away: whether prophecies shall be made void, or tongues shall cease, or knowledge shall be destroyed. For we know in part, and we prophesy in part. But when that which is perfect is come, that which is in part shall be done away. When I was a child, I spoke as a child, I understood as a child, I thought as a child. But, when I became a man, I put away the things of a child. We see now through a glass in a dark manner; but then face to face. Now I know in part; but then I shall know even as I am known. And now there remain faith, hope, and charity, these three: but the greatest of these is charity."

Concluding Thoughts

The Fatima message is the answer to defeating the kingdom of Satan. The Fatima message explains why the Catholic Church before 1960 was absolutely viewed by the Brotherhood of Death as the true Church of Christ that led people to the narrow gate of salvation. As the Blessed Virgin foretold, there is now a war within the Catholic Church.[656] This is because the Catholic Church is still the greatest danger to the Brotherhood of Death.

The faithful are increasingly ignoring Our Lady and consenting to support the Brotherhood of Death. Important spiritual tools to help us go to heaven include saying the Rosary, confessing sins and the sacraments. We must be vigilant because each of us must battle against evil spirits.[657] The importance of Calvary cannot be forgotten and the reenactment of Calvary is necessary for our world to continue. With God all things are possible including supernatural solutions to defeat evil.

Accuracy Guarantee

To support my sincere belief that everything written in this book is true, I offer to publicly debate anyone. Should anyone ever find a mistake in this book, please send an email to contact@teachpeace.com. I will promptly publish the correction on the www.teachpeace.com/corrections.htm page. You are invited to join the Teach Peace Foundation in our mission to educate millions of people to defeat the Brotherhood of Death. Join us online at www.teachpeace.com.

Peace be with you.

APPENDIX A

THREE WORLD WARS

According to people who read the Fatima message. the Blessed Virgin warns a third world war will happen[658]. William Carr was a leader in exposing the New World Order. He wrote in 1954 "those who aspire to undisputed world domination will provoke the greatest social cataclysm the world has ever known."[659] Carr reported Albert Pike planned three world wars to help advance world government. Carr's explanation of the purpose of each world war is provided below.[660]

> "Pike's plan was as simple as it has proved effective. He required that Communism, Nazism, Political Zionism, and other International movements be organized and used to foment the three global wars and three major revolutions. The first world war was to be fought so as to enable the Illuminati to overthrow the powers of the Tzars in Russia and turn that country into the stronghold of Atheistic-Communism. The differences stirred up by agentur of the Illuminati between the British and German Empires were to be used to foment this war. After the war ended, Communism was to be built up and used to destroy other governments and weaken religions.
>
> "World War Two, was to be fomented by using the differences between Fascists and Political Zionists. This war was to be fought so that Nazism would be destroyed and the power of Political Zionism increased so that the sovereign state of Israel could be established in Palestine. During World War Two International

Communism was to be built up until it equaled in strength that of united Christendom.[661] At this point it was to be contained and kept in check until required for the final social cataclysm. Can any informed person deny Roosevelt and Churchill did not put this policy into effect?

"World War Three is to be fomented by using the differences the agentur of the Illuminati stir up between Political Zionists and the leaders of the Moslem world. The war is to be directed in such a manner that Islam (the Arab World including Mohammedanism) and Political Zionism (including the State of Israel) will destroy themselves while at the same time the remaining nations, once more divided against each other on this issue, will be forced to fight themselves into a state of complete exhaustion physically, mentally, spiritually and economically. Can any unbiased and reasoning person deny that the intrigue now going on in the Near, Middle, and Far East isn't designed to accomplish this devilish purpose?"[662]

APPENDIX B

BOOKS

The Teach Peace Foundation books are a light in the darkness, making the unseen shadow powers visible and providing readers with the information to see the truth.

A single book on the Brotherhood of Death offering concrete proof that this organized evil exists is sufficient for many people. Revealing multiple dimensions of the Brotherhood is helpful to better understand our world, safeguard our children, and deepen our faith in God.

The Vigilant Christian books are innovative in that it is essentially a tapestry of carefully explained events with each hair-raising assertion backed up with a thorough documentation of sources.

Understanding the Brotherhood of Death occult beliefs, control of monetary systems, and plans for a New World Order is essential to prevent a third world war. Understanding the Fatima solution is essential to defeating the kingdom of Satan. We invite you to not only read the books, but to join the nonviolent battle to defeat the Brotherhood of Death.

Book Title	**Purpose**
Defeating the Brotherhood of Death 	*Defeating the Brotherhood of Death* helps you better understand past, current and future world events. This book explains that the solution to defeat the Brotherhood of Death is within our reach. *Defeating the Brotherhood of Death* is recommended for a deeper understanding of the *Atomic Bomb Secrets* book and documentary.
Atomic Bomb Secrets 	The atomic bomb program was created and guided by a secret cartel that infiltrated the United States government. This startling fact is the first atomic bomb secret explained in this book. *Atomic Bomb Secrets* presents new evidence explaining why atomic bombs were used. This history-changing book is offered with the hope that revealing the truth will help prevent nuclear weapons from being used again.

Appendix B

<table>
<tr><th>Book Title</th><th>Purpose</th></tr>
<tr><td>

Vigilant Christian I
The New World Order

</td><td>

The New World Order explains the origin and development of the New World Order.

Concrete evidence is provided from authentic Brotherhood of Death source books and their lead spokespeople.

Book one explains how modern secret societies are a continuation of what is also known as the Egyptian mystery religion or mystery of iniquity.

</td></tr>
<tr><td>

Vigilant Christian II
Preventing an American Hiroshima

</td><td>

The agenda for a New World Order is advanced by planned chaos. From the chaos, fear is used to paralyze clear thinking and introduce incremental evil.

A top focus of the Brotherhood is weakening America by eliminating the protections in the Bill of Rights.

Preventing an American Hiroshima explains how global terrorism is orchestrated to help prevent an American Hiroshima.

</td></tr>
</table>

<table>
<tr><th>Book Title</th><th>Purpose</th></tr>
<tr><td>Vigilant Christian III
The Occult Religion of the 9/11 Attackers

</td><td>The religious motivations of the 9/11 attackers are difficult to believe.

The 9/11 terrorism was a Brotherhood of Death religious ritual to welcome demonic forces.

Analyzing the September 11, 2001 attacks from a spiritual perspective brings life to the warning by Jesus in Matthew 24:24 that if possible, even the elect are deceived.</td></tr>
<tr><td>Vigilant Christian IV
9/11 - The Secret War

</td><td>When people learn the truth that a secret Brotherhood of Death cartel is responsible for the 9/11 terrorism, clear thinking can return.

The smoking gun of 9/11 is Building 7. Building 7, also known as the Salomon Brothers Building, was the third World Trade Center building to collapse on 9/11.

This book accurately explains why 9/11 has helped the mass murderers responsible advance a New World Order.</td></tr>
</table>

Book Title	**Purpose**
Vigilant Christian V *Perfect Money Planning*  	*Perfect Money Planning* explains financial planning in the context of monetary systems controlled by an international banking elite. The advice offered will help you achieve financial stability and eternal treasure. Generous giving and socially responsible investing are key themes throughout the book. *Perfect Money Planning* will help you navigate how to use God's resources wisely as you provide for your family and future.

A discount is available at http://shop.teachpeace.com when ordering the book series at the same time.

APPENDIX C

CHURCH OF CHRIST

The Church Jesus established is an anchor to keep souls safe from Satan's stormy seas. This "how old is your church" information is modified from multiple sources and provided below.[663]

If you are a Lutheran, your denomination was founded by Martin Luther (November 10, 1483 - February 18, 1546). He was a German friar who was excommunicated by the Catholic Church in 1521.

If you belong to the Church of England, your denomination was founded by King Henry VIII (28 June 28, 1491 - January 28, 1547). He started this new religion in the year 1534 because the Pope would not grant him an annulment from his wife, Catherine of Aragon.

If you are an Eastern Orthodox, your church was created from the Catholic Church in 1054 when the Pope and an Eastern Patriarch excommunicated each other.

If you are an Anabaptist, your church started in Switzerland by Ulrich Zwingli in 1525.

If you call yourself a Mennonite, your movement was named after Menno Simons (1496 - January 31, 1561), a priest who left the Catholic Church to join the Anabaptists in 1536.

If you are a Presbyterian, your denomination was founded by John Knox (c. 1514 - November 24, 1572) in Scotland in the year 1560.

If you are a Congregationalist, your denomination was originated by Robert Browne (born c. 1550 - died October 1633) in Holland in 1582.

If you are a Baptist, you owe the tenets of your denomination to John Smyth (c. 1570 - c. August 28, 1612), who launched it in Amsterdam in 1605.

If you are of the Dutch Reformed church, you recognize Jonas Michaëlius (1577 - after 1638) as founder, because he originated your denomination in New York in 1628.

The Amish, started by Jacob Amman around 1693, are one of many different church bodies within the Mennonite community in the United States.

If you are a Methodist, your denomination was launched by John and Charles Wesley in England in 1744.

If you are in the Episcopal Church, your denomination was an offshoot of the Church of England. Founded by Samuel Seabury (November 30, 1729 - February 25, 1796), the Episcopal Church formally separated from the Church of England in 1789.

If you are LDS or "Mormon" (Church of Jesus Christ of Latter-day Saints), Joseph Smith Jr. (December 23, 1805 - June 27, 1844) started your religion in Palmyra, NY, in 1829.

If you are a Seventh Day Adventist, Ellen Gould White November 26, 1827 - July 16, 1915) inaugurated your group in the United States in 1863.

If you worship with the Salvation Army, your sect began with William Booth (April 10, 1829 – August 20, 1912) in London in 1865.

If you are a Christian Scientist, you look to 1879 as the year in which your religion was born and to Mary Baker Eddy (July 16, 1821 - December 3, 1910) as its founder.

If you are a Jehovah's Witness, your religion was invented by "Pastor" Charles Taze Russell (February 16, 1852 - October 31, 1916) in 1874.

If you are a worshipper at the Iglesia ni Cristo, Felix Manalo (May 10, 1886 - April 12, 1963) instituted your sect in the Philippines in 1914.

If you are a follower of the Church of Scientology, your group owes its origin to Lafayette Ronald Hubbard (March 13, 1911 - January 24, 1986) and was incorporated in 1953.

If you are a believer at the Vineyard Christian Fellowship, your denomination was started by Ken Guillickson (June 28, 1945 - present) in Santa Monica, California in 1974.

If you are a member of Calvary Chapel, Chuck Smith (June 25, 1927 - October 3, 2013) began your congregation in Costa Mesa, California in 1975.

If you are a traditional Roman Catholic, your Church was founded in the year 33 A.D. by Jesus Christ, the Son of God, true God and true man.

The Church of Christ builds on God's promise to Abraham circa 1711 BC. Jesus is the Messiah from the House of David and his Church will exist until the end of time. Matthew 16:18 – "And I say to thee: That thou art Peter; and upon this rock I will build my church, and the gates of hell shall not prevail against it."

APPENDIX D

APPARATIONS DIALOGUE

The following dialogue, modified for this book, is courtesy of *Fatima Network Essentials*.[664]

Spring 1916

In the spring of 1916, Lucy dos Santos and her cousins Francisco and Jacinta Marto, led their sheep to graze on a hill. Rain began to fall, so the children found a place on the hillside to serve as a shelter. Lucy was nine years old, Francisco was eight, and Jacinta was six.

As they were playing, a strong wind suddenly blew, shaking the trees, and the children saw a figure approaching above the olive trees. Lucy described the figure as having "the appearance of a young man of fourteen or fifteen, whiter than snow, which the sun rendered transparent as if it were of crystal, and of great beauty. "While coming closer to us, the Angel said: ‘Do not fear! I am the Angel of Peace. Pray with me.’ And kneeling on the earth, he bent his forehead to the ground. Prompted by a supernatural movement, we imitated him and repeated the words which we heard him pronounce: ‘My God, I believe in Thee, I adore Thee, I hope in Thee and I love Thee. I ask pardon for all those who do not believe in Thee, do not adore Thee, do not hope in Thee and do not love Thee.’

"Having repeated that prayer three times, he got up again and said to us: ‘Pray in this way. The Hearts of Jesus and Mary are attentive to the voice of your supplications.’ And he disappeared."

The Angel of Peace had come to speak to the children, to infuse them with this extraordinary grace through which they were penetrated with the Divine Presence, and to demonstrate to them the attitude, posture and fervor with which to pray to God. Interestingly, during the apparition Francisco could not hear the words of the Angel, and had to be told what 77was said afterward; this would be the case for all of the other apparitions as well.

Summer 1916

The second apparition of the Angel took place during the summer of 1916. While the children were playing around their favorite well, the Angel suddenly appeared. "What are you doing?" he asked. "Pray, pray a great deal! The Holy Hearts of Jesus and Mary have designs of mercy on you. Offer unceasingly prayers and sacrifice yourselves to the Most High."

Lucy asked the Angel how they were to make sacrifices. The Angel replied, "Make of everything you can a sacrifice and offer it to God as an act of reparation for the sins by which He is offended, and in supplication for the conversion of sinners. In this way, you will draw peace upon your country. I am its Guardian Angel, the Angel of Portugal. Above all, accept and bear with submission the sufferings which the Lord will send you."

The dominant theme in this second apparition of the Angel was the importance of making offerings to God through every possible action and sacrifice, even the smallest, and of making the offerings with special intentions, especially for the conversion of sinners.

Autumn 1916

In the autumn of the same year, the children took their sheep to the same place where the first apparition took place. There in the blessed place of the Cabeço, they were reciting the prayer the Angel had taught them when above them an unknown light appeared. Lucy relates, "We got up again to see what was happening, and we saw the Angel again, who had in his left hand a Chalice over which was suspended a Host, from which some drops of Blood fell into the Chalice."

Leaving the Chalice and the Host suspended in the air, he prostrated himself down to the earth near the children and repeated three times this prayer:

Most Holy Trinity, Father, Son, and Holy Ghost, I adore You profoundly, and I offer You the Most Precious Body, Blood, Soul and Divinity of Jesus Christ, present in the tabernacles of the world, in reparation for the outrages, sacrileges and indifferences by which He, Himself is offended. And I draw upon the infinite merits of the Most Sacred Heart of Jesus and of the Immaculate Heart of Mary, that You might convert poor sinners.

Then, getting up, the Angel took the Chalice and Host. He gave Lucy the Sacred Host on the tongue. Then while giving the Precious Blood from the Chalice to Francisco and Jacinta, he said:

"Eat and drink the Body and Blood of Jesus Christ, horribly outraged by ungrateful men. Make reparation for their crimes and console your God." Then, prostrating himself on the ground he repeated with the children three times the same prayer: Most Holy Trinity, etc., and disappeared.

This final apparition of the Angel was clearly the summit of the three, as the children were graced to see the Precious Blood of Our Lord fall from the Sacred Host into the Chalice, and then receive Holy Communion from the hands of the Angel.

The appearance of the Angel of Peace to three little Portuguese shepherds was a preparation for the signal grace that was about to be bestowed upon them: the appearance of the Queen of Heaven, the Blessed Virgin Mary.

May 13, 1917

By May of 1917 several months had passed since the final apparition of the Angel to the three children. They had continued their task of shepherding their flocks, and had resumed their former vivaciousness and playfulness. On the thirteenth of May, after Sunday morning Mass, they chose to lead their sheep to a property of Lucy’s parents called Cova da Iria. After eating their meal at noon and praying the Rosary, the children began to play. Suddenly they saw a kind of lightning, making them believe that a storm was approaching, and they began to descend the hill to make for home.

When about halfway down the slope there was another flash of light, and a Lady appeared above a holm-oak tree. Lucy says that the Lady was "all dressed in white, more brilliant than the sun, radiating a light clearer and more intense than a crystal glass filled with clear water pierced by the most burning rays of the sun." The children stopped and found themselves in the light that emanated from Her.

Lucy describes the apparition in this way: Then Our Lady said to us: 'Do not be afraid. I will do you no harm.' 'Where is Your Grace from?' I asked Her. 'I am of Heaven.' 'What does Your Grace want of me?' 'I have come to ask you to come here for six months in succession, on the 13th day, at this same hour. Later on, I will tell you who I am and what I want. Afterwards, I will return here yet a seventh time.' 'Shall I go to Heaven too?' 'Yes, you will.' 'And Jacinta?' 'Also.' 'And Francisco?' 'Also, but he will have to say many Rosaries.'

I remembered then to ask about two girls who had died recently. They were friends of mine and they used to come to my home to learn weaving with my eldest sister.

'Is Maria das Neves already in Heaven?' 'Yes, she is.' It seems to me that she was about sixteen years old. 'And Amelia?' 'She will be in Purgatory until the end of the world.' It seems to me that she must have been between eighteen and twenty years old. 'Are you willing to offer yourselves to God to bear all the sufferings He wants to send you, as an act of reparation for the sins by which He is offended, and for the conversion of sinners?' 'Yes, we are willing.' 'You are then going to have much to suffer, but the grace of God will be your comfort.'

It was in pronouncing those last words (the grace of God, etc.) that Our Lady opened Her hands for the first time, and communicated to us, as by a reflection which emanated from them, a light so intense that, penetrating our heart and even to the depths of our soul, it made us see ourselves in God, Who was this light, more clearly than we see ourselves in the best mirrors.

Then, moved by an interior impulse which was communicated to us, we fell on our knees and said repeatedly: 'O Most Holy Trinity, I adore Thee. My God, my God, I love Thee in the Most Holy Sacrament.'

The first moments passed, and Our Lady added: 'Recite the Rosary every day in order to obtain peace for the world and the end of the war.' 'Can You tell me whether the war will still last a long time, or if it will soon end?' 'I cannot tell you yet, as I have not yet told you what I want.'

Then She began to rise serenely, going up towards the east until She disappeared in the immensity of the sky.

During the apparitions, each child's part was distinct: Lucy was the only one who spoke to Our Lady; Jacinta saw and heard Her but did not speak; and Francisco saw Her but could not hear Her, and had to be told afterward what She said.

June 13, 1917

The children went to the Cova da Iria on June 13 as they had promised Our Lady, even though it meant missing all of the festivities for the Feast of St. Anthony, who was Patron Saint of their parish and of Portugal. When they arrived at the Cova that morning there were already several dozen people gathered there, mostly from the neighboring hamlets, where word of the apparition had spread.

By noon the number of spectators had risen to about fifty. The crowd had just finished praying the Rosary when Lucy cried out, "There is the lightning! ... Our Lady is arriving!" The crowd saw neither the lightning nor Our Lady, but one witness observed that "the branches of the tree gave way on all sides, as if the weight of Our Lady had really been supported on them." This observation demonstrates that Our Lady was in fact physically present, in Her glorified body, and that the children were not merely "seeing" a vision of questionable authenticity. Others present related that they had heard something like the sound of a very light voice, though they could not make out what was being said. Also observed was that the bright noontime sun had dimmed considerably.

Lucy gives an account of the second apparition of Our Lady in her Fourth Memoir: ... we saw Our Lady, on the holm-oak, just as in the month of May. 'What does Your Grace want of me?' I asked. 'I wish you to come here on the 13th of next month, to pray the Rosary every day, and to learn how to read. Later I will tell you what I want.' I asked for the cure of a sick person. 'If he is converted, he will be cured within the year.' 'I would like to ask You to take us to Heaven.'

'Yes, I will take Jacinta and Francisco soon, but you, Lucy, are to stay here some time longer. Jesus wishes to make use of you in order to make Me known and loved. He wishes to establish in the world devotion to My Immaculate Heart. To whoever embraces this devotion, I promise salvation; those souls will be cherished by God, as flowers placed by Me to adorn His throne.' 'Am I to stay here alone?' I asked painfully. 'No, My daughter. Are you suffering a great deal? Do not lose heart, I will never forsake you! My Immaculate Heart will be your refuge and the way that will lead you to God.'

It was at the moment when She pronounced those last words that She opened Her hands and communicated to us, for the second time, the reflection of that immense light. In it we saw ourselves as submerged in God. Jacinta and Francisco appeared to be in the part of that light which elevated itself to Heaven, and I in the part which spread itself on the earth.

In the palm of the right hand of Our Lady there was a Heart, surrounded by thorns which seemed to pierce it. We understood that it was the Immaculate Heart of Mary, outraged by the sins of humanity, which demanded reparation.

Then, as Our Lady left them, the crowd heard a sound like a firecracker in the distance. Lucy rose quickly and pointing, cried, "See, She is going, She is going!" The crowd did not see Her, but did note a small cloud that rose from above the tree and, moving toward the east, gradually disappeared. The holm-oak tree, on which Our Lady had stood, had its branches bent slightly toward the east.

Lucy wrote, "It seems to me that on that day, that reflection of light had as a principal goal to instill in us a knowledge and a special love towards the Immaculate Heart of Mary; in the same way as the other two times, it had that same goal, but with respect to God and to the mystery of the Most Holy Trinity. Since that day, we felt in our hearts a more ardent love for the Immaculate Heart of Mary."

July 13, 1917

The third apparition brought to the Cova da Iria a crowd of 5,000 people. Lucy led the Rosary and the crowd answered. At noon she rose and looked toward the east, crying, "Close the umbrellas! Close the umbrellas! (They used umbrellas to protect themselves from the intense noontime sun) ... Our Lady is arriving!"

The apparition then began in the usual way, with a flash of something like lightning and the appearance of Our Lady atop the holm-oak. Lucy relates the apparition in her memoirs: 'What does Your Grace want of me?' I asked. 'I want you to come here on the 13th of next month, to continue reciting the Rosary every day in honor of Our Lady of the Rosary, in order to obtain peace in the world and the end of the war, because only She can help you.'

'I should like to ask You to tell us who You are, and to work a miracle so that everyone will believe that Your Grace is appearing to us.' 'Continue to come here every month. In October, I will say who I am and what I want, and I will perform a miracle so that all might see and believe.'

Here I made some requests which I do not remember. What I do remember, is that Our Lady said it was necessary to say the Rosary in order to obtain these graces throughout the year. Our Lady continued: 'Sacrifice yourselves for sinners, and say often to Jesus, especially whenever you make a sacrifice: O Jesus, it is for love of Thee, for the conversion of sinners, and in reparation for the sins committed against the Immaculate Heart of Mary.'

As Our Lady spoke these last words, She opened Her hands once more, as She had done during the two previous months. The rays of light seemed to penetrate the earth, and we saw as it were a sea of fire. Plunged in this fire were demons and souls in human form, like transparent burning embers, all blackened or burnished bronze, floating about in the conflagration, now raised into the air by the flames that issued from within themselves together with great clouds of smoke, now falling back on every side like sparks in huge fires, without weight or equilibrium, amid shrieks and groans of pain and despair, which horrified us and made us tremble with fear. (It must have been this sight which caused me to cry out, as people say they heard me). The demons could be distinguished by their terrifying and repellent likeness to frightful and unknown animals, black and transparent like burning coals. That vision lasted only a moment, thanks to our good Mother of Heaven, Who, at the first apparition, had promised to bring us to Heaven. Without that, I think we would have died of terror and fear.

Terrified and as if to plead for succor, we looked up at Our Lady, who said to us, so kindly and so sadly: 'You have seen hell where the souls of poor sinners go. To save them, God wishes to establish in the world devotion to My Immaculate Heart. If what I say to you is done, many souls will be saved and there will be peace. The war is going to end; but if people do not cease offending God, a worse one will break out during the reign of Pius XI. When you see a night illumined by an unknown light, know that this is the great sign given you by God that He is about to punish the world for its crimes by means of war, famine, and persecutions of the Church and of the Holy Father.'

'To prevent this, I shall come to ask for the consecration of Russia to My Immaculate Heart, and the Communion of Reparation on the First Saturdays. If My requests are heeded, Russia will be converted and there will be peace; if not, she will spread her errors throughout the world, causing wars and persecutions of the Church. The good will be martyred, the Holy Father will have much to suffer, various nations will be annihilated. In the end, My Immaculate Heart will triumph. The Holy Father will consecrate Russia to Me, and she will be converted, and a period of peace will be granted to the world. In Portugal, the dogma of the Faith will always be preserved, etc. Do not tell this to anybody. Francisco, yes, you may tell him.'

'When you pray the Rosary, say after each mystery: O my Jesus, forgive us, save us from the fires of hell. Lead all souls to Heaven, especially those who are most in need.'

After this, there was a moment of silence, and then I asked, 'Is there anything more that You want of me?' 'No, I do not want anything more of you today.' Then, as before, Our Lady began to ascend towards the east, until She finally disappeared.

In the cycle of the apparitions, the apparition of July 13 is decidedly the most important. It was in this third apparition of Our Lady that the Secret was given to the seers. Also, the announcement of the October miracle was made for the first time, clearly indicating its date, time and place. Our Lady would reiterate the coming miracle in the August and September apparitions as well.

August 13 & 19, 1917

On August 13, between 10,000 and 20,000 people gathered at the Cova da Iria to await the arrival of Our Lady. The three little seers, however, were not present. The administrator of the district, Artur de Oliveira Santos, a prominent Freemason, had imprisoned the children on August 13, and for two days he used many means, including the threat of boiling them in oil, to pry from them either the Secret itself, or a confession that they were lying. Courageously the children refused to betray their confidence and remained steadfast under every tactic used. In fact, believing that they were soon to be killed, they were full of joy at the thought of soon being in Heaven. This willingness to suffer martyrdom is another proof of the truthfulness of the Message. Realizing that he was getting nowhere, after two days the administrator released the children.

While the seers were being held on August 13, Our Lady still came to the Cova da Iria and manifested Her presence to the large crowd. One faithful woman described the scene:

The clap of thunder was more or less similar to that of the preceding time. Some say that it came from the road, others from the holm-oak .... It seemed to me that it came from very far. Everyone kept quiet, frightened .... At the clap of thunder there followed lightning, and at once we began to notice a small cloud, very pretty, white in color, very light, which hovered some moments over the holm-oak, then rose towards the sky, and disappeared in the atmosphere.

While looking around us, we observed a strange thing, which we had already seen the previous time, and which we were going to see again in the future. The faces of the people had all the colors of the rainbow: pink, red, blue ... The trees did not appear to have branches and leaves but only flowers; everything seemed laden with flowers, and every leaf appeared to be a flower. The ground was covered with squares of different colors. Clothes were also of every color of the rainbow.

On the afternoon of August 19, Lucy and Francisco, accompanied by Francisco's older brother John, went to put their sheep to pasture. This is the account that Sister Lucy gave of what occurred:

I felt that something supernatural was approaching and enveloping us. Suspecting that Our Lady was going to appear to us, and feeling sorry that Jacinta would not be there to see Her, we asked her brother John to go and get her.

However John wished to stay and see Our Lady. Lucy, therefore, gave John one coin to fetch Jacinta, and promised him another when he brought her back. While he ran to get her, Lucy and Francisco saw the characteristic flash of light, and just as Jacinta arrived, Our Lady appeared above a holm-oak tree. Lucy's account continues: [Lucy asked:] 'What does Your Grace want from me?' 'I want you to continue going to the Cova da Iria on the 13th, that you continue praying the Rosary every day. On the last month, I will perform a miracle so that all may believe. If they had not taken you to the town, the miracle would have been greater. Saint Joseph will come with the Child Jesus, to give peace to the world. Our Lord will come to bless the people. Our Lady of the Rosary and Our Lady of Sorrows will come also.'

'What do You want them to do with the money the people leave at the Cova da Iria?' 'Have two litters made. You will carry one with Jacinta and two other girls dressed in white; the other one Francisco is to carry, with three boys, like him, dressed in white. It will be for the Feast of Our Lady of the Rosary. What is left over will help towards the construction of a chapel that is to be built.'

'I should like to ask You to cure some sick persons.' 'Yes, I will cure some of them during the year.' Then looking more sad, Our Lady said: 'Pray, pray very much, and make sacrifices for sinners, for many souls go to hell because they have no one to make sacrifices and pray for them.' As usual, Our Lady began to ascend towards the east.

After the apparition of August 19, the three children looked for ways to make more sacrifices to offer to Jesus, "for His love, for the conversion of sinners, and in reparation for the offenses against the Immaculate Heart of Mary."

Appendix D

September 13, 1917

On September 13 as many as thirty thousand people gathered at the Cova da Iria. While waiting for noon to arrive, Lucy led the Rosary for the crowd. At noon, a certain phenomenon announced the arrival of Our Lady to many in the crowd. As one witness relates,

The sky was blue, without any clouds. I also looked up, and began to scrutinize the immensity of the firmament, to see what other eyes, more fortunate than mine, had already contemplated. To my great astonishment, I then saw, clearly and distinctly, a luminous globe, traveling from the east to the west, and gliding slowly and majestically in space … Suddenly the globe, with its extraordinary light, disappeared from our eyes.

The light of the sun then dimmed, and the atmosphere became a yellow-gold color, like it had during the former apparitions. Some reported that they could see the stars, the sky had darkened to such an extent. Lucy then spoke to Our Lady, asking, "What does Your Grace want of me?"

'Continue to pray the Rosary in order to obtain the end of the war. In October, Our Lord will come as well as Our Lady of Sorrows and Our Lady of Mount Carmel, and Saint Joseph will appear with the Child Jesus in order to bless the world. God is satisfied with your sacrifices, but He does not want you to sleep with the rope. Wear it only during the day.'

'There is a little girl here who is a deaf-mute. Would not Your Grace wish to cure her?' Our Lady replied that a year from now, the girl would be better. 'I have many other requests, some for conversion, others for a cure.' 'I shall cure some, but others no, because Our Lord does not trust them.'

'The people would indeed like to have a chapel here.' 'With half of the money received so far, they should make litters and carry them on the Feast of Our Lady of the Rosary; the other half can be used to build the chapel.'

Lucy then offered Her two letters and a small flask of water with a fragrance, which had been given her by a man of the parish of Olival. In offering them to Our Lady, she said to Her: "They gave me that. Does Your Grace want it?" "That is not suitable for Heaven," Our Lady replied. "In October I will perform the miracle so that all may believe."

Our Lady then ascended toward the east and disappeared as usual. The crowd once again saw the luminous globe, which had accompanied Her upon Her arrival, rise up toward the east and disappear.

October 13, 1917

There were about 70,000 people present at the Cova da Iria for the October 13 apparition and Miracle of the Sun. Beginning the night before and persisting throughout the morning of the 13th, a cold rain fell on the crowd. The ground was muddy and the rain soaked everything. At the time when Our Lady was due to arrive, Lucy begged the people to close their umbrellas, which they did at once.

'What does Your Grace want of me?' [Lucy asked.] 'I want to tell you that a chapel is to be built here in My honor. I am the Lady of the Rosary. May you continue always to pray the Rosary every day. The war is going to end and the soldiers will soon return to their homes.' 'I had many things to ask You: to cure some sick people, to convert some sinners, etc.' 'Some yes, others no. They must amend their lives and ask pardon for their sins.'

Then taking on a more sorrowful air, Our Lady said: 'Do not offend the Lord Our God any more, for He is already too much offended!' 'You want nothing more from me?' [Lucy asked.] 'No, I want nothing more from you.' "Then I do not ask anything more of You either."

As Our Lady ascended into Heaven, Lucy shouted: "She is going! She is going! Look at the sun!"

The miracle announced by Our Lady then took place: the sky abruptly cleared and the sun "danced." The people were able to look at the bright sun directly, without it bothering their eyes at all. A physician, Dr. Almeida Garrett, testified: Suddenly I heard the uproar of thousands of voices, and I saw the whole multitude spread out in that vast space at my feet … turn their backs to that spot where, until then, all their expectations focused, and look at the sun on the other side … I turned around, too, toward the point commanding their gazes, and I could see the sun, like a very clear disc, with its sharp edge, which gleamed without hurting the sight … It could not be confused with the sun seen through a fog (there was no fog at that moment), for it was neither veiled, nor dim. At Fatima, it kept its light and heat, and stood out clearly in the sky, with a sharp edge, like a large gaming table. The most astonishing thing was to be able to stare at the solar disc for a long time, brilliant with light and heat, without hurting the eyes, or damaging the retina.

The testimony of Avelino de Almeida, editor-in-chief of O Seculo, Lisbon's anticlerical and Masonic daily newspaper, is similar: And then we witnessed a unique spectacle, an incredible spectacle, unbelievable if you did not witness it. From above the road … We see the immense crowd turn towards the sun, which appeared at its zenith, clear of the clouds. It looked like a plate of dull silver, and it was possible to stare at it without the least discomfort. It did not burn the eyes. It did not blind. One might say that an eclipse had occurred.

Others also testified:

"It shook and trembled; it seemed like a wheel of fire." (Maria da Capelinha)

"The sun took on all the colors of the rainbow. Everything assumed those same colors: our faces, our clothes, the earth itself." (Maria do Carmo)

The most terrifying aspect of the Miracle of the Sun then took place:

"We suddenly heard a clamor, like a cry of anguish of that entire crowd. The sun, in fact, keeping its rapid movement of rotation, seemed to free itself from the firmament and, blood-red, to plunge towards the earth, threatening to crush us with its fiery mass. Those were some terrifying seconds." (Dr. Almeida Garrett)

"The sun began to dance and, at a certain moment, it appeared to detach itself from the firmament and to rush forward on us, like a fire wheel." (Alfredo da Silva Santos)

"From those thousands of mouths I heard shouts of joy and love to the Most Holy Virgin. And then I believed. I had the certainty of not having been the victim of a suggestion. I had seen the sun as I would never see it again." (Mario Godinho, an engineer)

Yet another astonishing aspect of the Miracle was that all of the thousands of people, most of whom were soaked to the bone and dirty from the mud, suddenly found that their clothes were dry and clean.

"My suit dried in an instant." (John Carreira)

The academician Marques da Cruz testified: This enormous multitude was drenched, for it had rained unceasingly since dawn. But – though this may appear incredible – after the great miracle everyone felt comfortable, and found his garments quite dry, a subject of general wonder ... The truth of this fact has been guaranteed with the greatest sincerity by dozens and dozens of persons of absolute trustworthiness, whom I have known intimately from childhood, and who are still alive (1937), as well as by persons from various districts of the country who were present.

In one aspect, this is the most astonishing effect of the miracle and an indisputable proof of its authenticity: The amount of energy needed to accomplish this process of drying in a natural way and in such a short a time, would have incinerated everyone present at the Cova at that time. As this aspect of the miracle contradicts the laws of nature radically.

Finally, many miracles of conversion, the greatest miracle God can bestow, also occurred. Here are two examples:

The captain of the regiment of soldiers on the mountain that day – with orders to prevent the gathering of the crowd – was converted instantly. Apparently so were hundreds of other unbelievers, as their testimony will show.

"There was an unbeliever there who had spent the morning mocking the 'simpletons' who had gone off to Fatima just to see an ordinary girl. He now seemed paralyzed, his eyes fixed on the sun. He began to tremble from head to foot, and lifting up his arms, fell on his knees in the mud, crying out to God." (Fr. Lourenço)

A number of other cases of cures and conversions are documented in, among other places, the following books: Documentação Crítica de Fátima and Fatima from the Beginning.

The great Miracle of the Sun lasted for ten minutes. Many more accounts of the miracle have been taken and recorded from the masses of people present, which verify this incredible manifestation of the authenticity of the entire Fatima Message. (For more accounts, see Chapter 1 of *The Devil's Final Battle*.)

During the Miracle of the Sun, the three children were witnessing something else: the beautiful spectacle promised by Our Lady. Lucy writes: Our Lady having disappeared in the immensity of the firmament, we saw, beside the sun, Saint Joseph with the Child Jesus and Our Lady clothed in white with a blue mantle. Saint Joseph and the Child Jesus seemed to bless the world with gestures which they made with their hands in the form of a cross.

Soon after, that apparition having ceased, I saw Our Lord and Our Lady, Who gave me the impression of being Our Lady of Sorrows. Our Lord seemed to bless the world in the same manner as Saint Joseph. That apparition disappeared and it seemed to me that I saw Our Lady again, this time as Our Lady of Mount Carmel.

These three successive visions are connected to one of the dominant messages of Fatima: the Rosary. In each of Her six apparitions, Our Lady asked that the Rosary be prayed and here, in these visions granted to the three children, the mysteries of the Holy Rosary were represented. With the vision of the Holy Family we find the Joyful mysteries; the Sorrowful mysteries are represented by the vision of Our Lord and Our Lady of Sorrows; and the Glorious mysteries are represented in the vision of Our Lady of Mt. Carmel.

When the visions had disappeared and the sun was again normal, Lucy was placed on the shoulder of a man in the crowd and carried safely through the masses to the road. As she was moving past the people, she cried out to them, pleading one of the important themes in the Fatima Message: to convert, return to God and to flee sin. Her exact words were: "Do penance! Do penance! Our Lady wants you to do penance!" but Frère Michel states that in Portuguese this does not mean "performing mortifications." but rather "being converted, returning to God, fleeing sin." Through this plea Lucy was reiterating the sorrowful request Our Lady had made of humanity in Her final apparition: "Do not offend the Lord our God anymore, because He is already too much offended."

Thus the Miracle of the Sun, witnessed by 70,000 people, concluded the cycle of the apparitions at Fatima. Yet the Message of Fatima, with its great depth and scope, was to continue to be unfolded to the eldest of the three seers, Lucy. In the years to come Heaven's Messenger would be visited and, as promised by Our Lady in the July 13 apparition, would be instructed to reveal Heaven's plan for peace for a turbulent world: the Reparatory devotion of the Five First Saturdays and the Consecration of Russia to the Immaculate Heart of Mary.

APPENDIX E

FATIMA TIMELINE

The 100th anniversary of the 1917 Fatima miracle is approaching. The following timeline, modified for this book, is courtesy of *Fatima Network Essentials*.[665]

1915

Lucia dos Santos and three other young girls see an angel.

1916

Spring, Summer and Autumn: Three Portuguese shepherd children of Fatima — Lucia dos Santos and her two cousins, Francisco and Jacinta Marto — were visited three times by the Angel of Peace.

1917

May 13: Our Lady appears to the three children at the Cova da Iria and asks that they return for five more months in succession, on the 13th day, at the same hour.

June 13: Our Lady tells the children that God wants to establish in the world devotion to the Immaculate Heart of Mary. About 50 people come to the Cova da Iria to witness the apparition.

July 13: Our Lady shows the children a vision of hell and tells them that She will come back at a later date to ask for the consecration of Russia to Her Immaculate Heart and the Communion of Reparation on the First Saturdays. She tells the children the Secret (in three parts) and promises to prove Her appearances with a miracle on October13, 1917. About 5,000 people come to the Cova on July 13.

August 13: The children are kidnapped by Freemason Arthur Santos, the Mayor of Ourém, and miss their appointed meeting with Our Lady.[666] About 15,000 people come to the Cova and many witness supernatural phenomena indicating that Our Lady came nonetheless.

August 19: Our Lady visits the children in nearby Valinhos and again prophesizes the working of a miracle in October while telling the children to pray and make sacrifices for sinners.

September 13: Our Lady tells the children that in October, Our Lord will come, as well as Our Lady of Sorrows and Our Lady of Carmel. Also, Saint Joseph will appear with the Child Jesus in order to bless the world. About 30,000 people come to the Cova and again, many witness supernatural phenomena indicating Our Lady's presence.

October 13: Our Lady announces: "People must amend their lives and ask pardon for their sins. They must not offend Our Lord any more for He is already too much offended." She tells us to continue to pray the Rosary every day. Then the 70,000 people present witness the Miracle of the Sun at the Cova da Iria.

1925

December 10: Our Lady appears to Sister Lucy at Pontevedra in Spain to relate the specific requirements for the Communion of Reparation on the First Saturdays.

1929

June 13: In fulfillment of Her promise at Fatima on July 13, 1917, Our Lady of Fatima appears to Sister Lucy at Tuy, Spain in the visible presence of the Most Holy Trinity and asks for the consecration of Russia to Her Immaculate Heart.

1931

August: Jesus says to Sister Lucy: "Make it known to My ministers, given that they follow the example of the King of France in delaying the execution of My command, they will follow him into misfortune." Our

Lord gives to Sister Lucy in Rianjo, Spain this warning addressed to the Pope and bishops.

1937

March 19: Pope Pius XI promulgates his encyclical against atheistic Communism. He first explains that he has already condemned Communism in 1924, 1928, 1931, 1932 (twice) and 1933. But it is his solemn duty once more to raise his voice and remind the faithful yet again against the dangers of Communism. Among many other things, the Pope solemnly says: "Communism is intrinsically evil, and no one who would save Christian civilization may collaborate with it in any undertaking whatsoever."

Pope Pius XI's warning against Communism deepens when you realize that in 1884 Pope Leo XIII provided an almost identical warning about the Brotherhood of Death which the kingdom of Satan used to create Communism.[667]

1941

Sister Lucy reveals the first two parts of the Secret in her Memoirs, first on August 31st in her Third Memoir and then again on December 8 in her Fourth Memoir.

1942

October 31 and December 8: Pope Pius XII, acting alone, consecrates the world, but not Russia, to the Immaculate Heart of Mary. The requirement that the Pope act in partnership with bishops around the world is not met. Our Lord tells Sister Lucy that as a result World War II will be shortened but that world peace will not result from this consecration.

1943

October: After one month of prayer and reflection, the Bishop of Fatima, His Excellency José da Silva, gives Sister Lucy a formal, written order to write down the Third Secret. Sister Lucy tries to obey immediately, but for over two months is mysteriously unable to commit the Third Secret to paper.

1944

January 2: Our Lady appears to Sister Lucy and bids her to write down the Third Secret. Our Lady asks it to be revealed to the world not later than 1960. When later asked why the people had to wait for the Third Secret to be revealed in 1960, Sister Lucy states: "Because the Blessed Virgin wishes it so," and "It [the Third Secret] will be clearer then."

January 9: Sister Lucy commits both texts of the Third Secret to paper by this date.

June 17: The Third Secret is given by Sister Lucy herself to her confessor, Bishop da Silva, since she would not let anyone but a bishop bring it to the Bishop of Fatima. Sister Lucy's confessor bishop delivers the Third Secret to the Bishop of Fatima on this same day.

1949

January 3: A photograph of Bishop da Silva posing in front of the 20 to 25-lines of Third Secret text, which is enclosed in the bishop's own outer envelope, appears in *Life* magazine.

1950

October 30: At 4 p.m. Pope Piux XII sees the miracle of the sun from the Vatican Gardens. He is awestruck and sees the dancing sun again on October 31st, November 1st and November 8th. He sees the sun phenomenon a total of four times. Pius XII wrote, "I have seen the 'miracle of the sun,' this is the pure truth."[668]

1952

May: Our Lady appears to Sister Lucy saying: "Make it known to the Holy Father that I am always awaiting the Consecration of Russia to My Immaculate Heart. Without that Consecration, Russia will not be able to convert. Without that Consecration, the world cannot have peace."

July 7: Pope Pius XII consecrates Russia specifically, but he does not ask for the bishops to join him. As in 1942, the Pope is not joined by the Catholic bishops of the world and the Blessed Virgin's requirement is not satisfied.

August 29: As a result of the Blessed Virgin's request not being fully honored, the Madonna at Syracuse, Italy begins to weep and cries for four days. The weeping phenomenon, declared authentic by the Catholic Church, was supported by scientific proof that the tears were human.[669]

September 2: Austrian Jesuit Fr. Joseph Schweigl is sent by Pope Pius XII to Coimbra, Portugal to discuss the Third Secret with Sister Lucy. Fr. Schweigl later confides to one of his colleagues: "I cannot reveal anything of what I learned at Fatima concerning the Third Secret, but I can say that it has two parts: one concerns the Pope. The other, logically — although I must say nothing — would have to be the continuation of the words: In Portugal the dogma of the Faith will always be preserved." In Chapter 3 of this book, the first part concerning the Pope is named 3a and the second part is 3b.

1953

March 1: Stalin is in the final stages of launching an invasion of Europe and is suddenly struck by a cerebral hemorrhage.[670] He dies on March 5 as a result and the his plans to transform Europe are disrupted. Fatima faithful see the direct connection to Pope Pius XII's partial consecration and Our Lady's extraordinary promises.

1957

March: Bishop John Venancio holds up to a strong light the outer envelope of Bishop da Silva (photographed for *Life* magazine in 1949) containing an inner envelope of Sister Lucy, inside of which he sees the paper upon which is written the Third Secret. He carefully notes that the Secret is about 20 to 25 lines long and is written on a single sheet of paper with 3/4 centimeter margins on both sides. This 20 to 25 lines of text is the 3b part of the Third Secret.

April 16: The 20 to 25-lines of the Third Secret text, sealed with wax in the original envelope and the Bishop of Fatima's outer envelope, is received in the Vatican. The text is placed in a safe in the papal apartments (not in the Holy Office).

December 26: Fr. Fuentes, Postulator of the Cause for Beatification of Jacinta and Francisco Marto, interviews Sister Lucy. In an allusion to the contents of the Third Secret, she tells him of many nations disappearing from the face of the earth, she speaks about the crisis in the priesthood, and of many souls going to hell as a result of ignoring Our Lady's Fatima Message.

1958

Fr. Fuentes publishes the interview with Sister Lucy with the Imprimatur of the Bishop of Fatima. It is read widely and no one questions its authenticity.

October: The magazine *Paris-Match* publishes a photo of the wooden safe in Pope Pius XII's apartment in which was kept the 3b part of the Third Secret.

1959

July 2: Fr. Fuentes' interview with Sister Lucy is suddenly denounced as fraudulent in an anonymous report from the bishop's chancery office in Coimbra, Portugal. To this day, more than fifty years later, no official will take responsibility for this report.

August 17: Pope John XXIII reads the 20 to 25 lines of the 3b part of the Third Secret which was taken from the papal apartment and then has his personal secretary, Msgr. Loris Capovilla, write on the envelope: "I leave it to others to comment or decide."

1960

February 8: As the world anxiously awaits the full revelation of the Third Secret, an unnamed person, who is close to the Pope, authorizes the Press to quote him anonymously that the Third Secret will not be revealed in 1960 and "would probably remain, forever, under absolute seal."

Sister Lucy is officially forbidden to speak about the Third Secret and not allowed to receive any visitors except close relatives and people she has known for a long time. Her own confessor of many years returns from Brazil and is not allowed to see her. Due to a noticeable change in her physical appearance, Fatima researchers begin to question if an imposter has replaced Sister Lucy.[671]

Pope John XXIII reads the part 3a 62-line text of the Third Secret, contained in another sealed envelope. Unlike the first text, which he opened in 1959 but could not read without the aid of a translator because of its difficult Portuguese dialect, this text posed no difficulty for the Pope and he was able to comprehend it completely on his own reading.

<u>1961</u>

With the Blessed Virgin's order that the public be informed of the Third Secret in 1960 ignored, the Blessed Virgin appeared in Garabandal, Spain to four young schoolgirls. Fr. Malachi Martin confirms the Garabandal message contains parts of the Third Secret. The Garabandal message communicates that many cardinals, bishops, and priests are on the road to hell and dragging souls down into hell.

<u>1962</u>

October: Just prior to Vatican Council II, the Vatican Secretariat of State agrees with Moscow that the Council will not condemn Soviet Russia or Communism, in exchange for which two Russian Orthodox observers would attend the Council. This agreement launches the policy of Ostpolitik. This Vatican-Moscow Agreement, which is not allowed by traditional Catholic moral theology (see entry for 1937), nevertheless is followed and thus the Vatican Secretariat of State silences those bishops and priests in the Church who are anti-Communist at the Second Vatican Council and afterward.

1963

June 27: Less than a week after becoming pope, Paul VI reads the text of the 3b part of the Third Secret kept in the papal apartment after the Substitute Secretary of State telephones Msgr.

Capovilla, personal secretary to Pope John XXIII, to inquire as to where to find it. Capovilla testifies to this fact in his certified note of May 17, 1967. It is this text — the one which contains Our Lady's words — that is later identified by Cardinal Ottaviani as being 20 to 25-lines long.

1964

November 21: At the last day of the third session of the Second Vatican Council, Pope Paul VI consecrates the world to the Immaculate Heart of Mary with no mention of Russia, and the bishops look on but do not join in.

1965

March 27: Pope Paul VI reads the other text of the Third Secret — the part 3a that is 62-lines long. Cardinal Bertone claims that Paul VI read the Third Secret for the first time on this date. However, Archbishop Capovilla testified in his certified note of May 1967 that Paul VI read the Third Secret for the first time on June 27, 1963.

1966

The Bishop of Fatima commissions a learned Claretian priest, Fr. Joaquin Alonso, to establish a complete critical history of the revelations of Fatima. Ten years later, Fr. Alonso will complete his work, entitled *Fatima Texts and Critical Studies*.

1967

Sister Lucy's *Memoirs* are published, in which she reveals Our Lady's 1929 request for the Consecration of Russia.

May 13: Sister Lucy meets Pope Paul VI in Fatima and asks him to release the Third Secret, but he refuses.[672]

1973

October 13: The Blessed Virgin warned in Akita, Japan that there would be a worldwide chastisement for sins in which a great part of humanity would be killed and that those who survive would envy the dead. The former Philippine ambassador to the Vatican, Howard Dee, said that "Bishop Ito was certain Akita was an extension of Fatima, and Cardinal Ratzinger personally confirmed to me that these two messages, of Fatima and Akita, are essentially the same.

1975

After 10 years of studying the Fatima archives, Fr. Alonso declares, in public, that Fr. Fuentes' published 1957 interview of Sister Lucy was a true and accurate report of her statements concerning the content of the Message of Fatima.

Fr. Alonso's 24 volumes of 800 pages each are ready for publication. This monumental work on the Message of Fatima includes at least 5,396 documents. The presses are literally stopped by the new Bishop of Fatima, Monsignor do Amaral. Fr. Alonso's ten years of research are stopped from reaching the public. At least 20 of these 24 volumes are still under lock and key.

1978

February 27: Pope Paul VI approves the Congregation for the Doctrine of the Faith's Norms of the Congregation for Proceeding in Judging Alleged Apparitions and Revelations. These norms provide the criteria for evaluating such phenomenon and establish the local Ordinary as the competent authority to do so.

October 16: Pope John Paul II is elected Pope and reads a text of the Third Secret — the 20 to 25 line text that is kept in the papal apartment — within days of his election, according to a statement to *Associated Press* in May 2000 by his spokesman, Joaquin Navarro-Valls.

The statement by Navarro-Valls is contradicted by Msgr. Bertone when he claimed in June 2000 that the Pope first read the Third Secret on July 18, 1981.

<u>1981</u>

May 13: Pope John Paul II is shot and seriously wounded by an assassin.

June 7: The Pope consecrates the world, but not Russia, to the Immaculate Heart of Mary.

July 18: According to Cardinal Bertone, Pope John Paul II reads the Third Secret for the first time. The text he reads is the part 3a 62-line text that is kept in the Holy Office archives.

<u>1982</u>

March 21: Sister Lucy informs the Papal Nuncio of the requirements for a valid Consecration of Russia according to the request of Our Lady of Fatima. Sister Lucy's full message is not transmitted to the Pope by the Nuncio. Following the suggestion of Bishop Amaral of Fatima, the Nuncio fails to mention the requirement that the world's bishops participate in the Consecration.[673]

May 12: L'Osservatore Romano publishes an article by Fr. Umberto Maria Pasquale, S.D.B. (a well-known Salesian priest who has known Sister Lucy since 1939 and had received over 150 letters from her) reveals that Sister Lucy clearly and emphatically told him that Our Lady of Fatima never asked for the consecration of the world but only the consecration of Russia. Fr. Pasquale also publishes a photographically-reproduced copy of a handwritten note by Sister Lucy attesting to their conversation on this point.

May 13: Pope John Paul II consecrates the world, but not Russia, at Fatima. The bishops of the world do not participate.

<u>1983</u>

March 19: Sister Lucy meets with the Papal Nuncio and confirms that the Consecration of Russia was not done because Russia was not clearly the object of the consecration and the Catholic bishops of the world did not join in.

1984

March 25: Pope John Paul II, before 250,000 people in Rome, consecrates the world to the Immaculate Heart of Mary. Immediately after he pronounced the words of consecration, he departs from his prepared text and prays "Enlighten especially the peoples of which You Yourself are awaiting our consecration and confiding." The Pope thus publicly acknowledges that Our Lady of Fatima is still awaiting the Consecration of Russia.

March 26: The Pope's own newspaper, *L'Osservatore Romano*, reports the exact words spoken by the Holy Father on the 25th.

March 27: The Italian Catholic bishops' newspaper *Avvenire* reports that the Holy Father, on March 25 at 4:00 in the afternoon, three hours after he consecrated the world, prays at St. Peter's, asking Our Lady to bless "those peoples for whom You Yourself are awaiting our act of consecration and entrusting," and thus again the Pope acknowledges that he did not fulfill Our Lady's request for the Consecration of Russia.[674]

September 10: Bishop Alberto Cosme do Amaral, the Bishop of Fatima, declares during a question and answer session in the aula magna of the Technical University of Vienna, Austria: "Its [the Third Secret's] content concerns only our faith. To identify the Secret with catastrophic announcements or with a nuclear holocaust is to deform the meaning of the message. The loss of faith of a continent is worse than the annihilation of a nation; and it is true that faith is continually diminishing in Europe."

November 11: *Jesus* magazine publishes an interview with Cardinal Ratzinger. The interview is entitled "Here is Why the Faith is in Crisis," and is published with the Cardinal's explicit permission. Cardinal Ratzinger reveals that he has read the Third Secret and that the Secret refers to "dangers threatening the faith and the life of the Christian and therefore (the life) of the world." Cardinal Ratzinger says in the same interview that the Secret also refers to "the importance of the Novissimi [the Last Times]" and "the absolute importance of history." He says "the things contained in this 'Third Secret' correspond to what has been announced in Scripture and has been said again and again in many other Marian apparitions, first of all that of Fatima ..."

1985

September: In an interview in *Sol de Fatima* magazine, Sister Lucy affirms that the Consecration of Russia still has not been done because Russia was not the clear object of the 1984 consecration and the world's episcopate did not participate.

1987

July 20: Interviewed quickly outside her convent while voting, Sister Lucy confirms to journalist Enrico Romero that the Consecration of Russia has not been done.

1989

July: Fr. Messias Coelho reveals that Sister Lucy and others have received an anonymous "instruction" from unidentified persons in the Vatican stating that she (and they) must now say that the Consecration of Russia was accomplished on March 25, 1984.

August through November: Five computer-generated and typewritten notes and letters supposedly signed by Sister Lucy suddenly appear, contradicting her previous statements that the Consecration of Russia has not been done. These texts are quickly proven to be fakes and this fact is published worldwide.

1990

October 11: Sister Lucy's blood-sister, Carolina, reveals that Sister Lucy does not know how to type.

1991

May 13: Pope John Paul II visits Fatima and meets with Sister Lucy for thirty minutes. After the meeting, neither the Pope nor Sister Lucy make any announcement concerning the Consecration of Russia.

1992

October: The Fatima Center holds its Bishops Conference in Fatima and 65 bishops attend. The Rector of the Fatima Shrine, Msgr. Guerra, holds his own conference and there Frère Francois denounces the five fake letters produced in 1989 and accuses in public, before many witnesses, to their faces — namely Fr. Fox, Fr. Kondor, and Msgr. Guerra — that they are the authors of these fake, forged letters attributed to Sister Lucy. Not one of them denies his accusation.

1995

In a personal communication to Professor Baumgartner in Salzburg, Austria, Cardinal Mario Luigi Ciappi — the personal theologian of John Paul II (and of the four popes before him) — reveals that: "In the Third Secret it is foretold, among other things, that the great apostasy in the Church will begin at the top."

1998

Howard Dee, former Philippine ambassador to the Vatican, said in an interview with *Inside the Vatican* magazine that "Bishop Ito was certain Akita was an extension of Fatima, and Cardinal Ratzinger personally confirmed to me that these two messages, of Fatima and Akita, are essentially the same."

2000

May 13: At the beatification ceremony of Jacinta and Francisco Marto at Fatima, the Vatican Secretary of State, Cardinal Sodano, announces that the Third Secret of Fatima will be revealed.

June 26: At a press conference, Archbishop Bertone publishes the 62-line text which he claims is the entire Third Secret and claims it refers to the 1981 assassination attempt of John Paul II. The 62-line text describes a vision in which the Pope (a "Bishop dressed in White") is killed by a band of soldiers. This text, containing none of the elements described by Cardinal Ratzinger in his 1984 interview in Jesus magazine, is obviously incomplete. Also, Cardinal Bertone claims the Consecration of Russia is done and, as proof, offers a quote from one of the five fake letters of 1989.

October 8: Pope John Paul II consecrates the world, but not Russia, in an "entrustment" ceremony.

November 30: A Cardinal described as "one of the Pope's closest advisors" (Cardinal Tomko) admits to a Vatican magazine editor that he advised Pope John Paul II to not make mention of Russia in any consecration ceremony because it would offend the Russian Orthodox.

2001

May 16: Reflecting the growing skepticism of millions of Catholics, Mother Angelica states on her live television show on this date that she does not believe the Vatican has revealed the entirety of the Third Secret. "Mother Angelica Live" as a live program is taken off the air forever by December.

October 25: Cardinal Ratzinger admits to a "destabilizing [of] the internal equilibrium of the Roman Curia" due to reports (following the September 11th terrorist attack on New York and the invasion of Afghanistan) of a recent letter from Sister Lucy to the Pope concerning the Third Secret and dangers to the world and the person of the Pope.

November 17: Archbishop Bertone (later to become Cardinal Bertone, Vatican Secretary of State) travels from Rome to Coimbra to interview Sister Lucy about the Third Secret and claims the interview went on for two hours, but the communiqué later published by Bertone contains only 44 words alleged to be from the mouth of Sister Lucy concerning the matters of the Third Secret and the Consecration of Russia controversies.

December 20: L'Osservatore Romano publishes the secret "interview" of Sister Lucy, conducted by Archbishop Bertone on

November 17, 2001 at the convent in Coimbra. According to Bertone, Sister Lucy said that the consecration of the world in 1984 has been "accepted by heaven." but yet never even asks Sister Lucy if she wrote and signed the contested fake letters that Bertone relies upon to tell us that Sister Lucy said it was done. No transcript or other independent record of the "interview" is provided.

2005

February 13: Sister Lucy of Fatima dies less than two months short of her 98th birthday.

2006

November 22: Renowned Italian Catholic commentator and journalist Antonio Socci publishes his book, *The Fourth Secret of Fatima*, which accuses Cardinal Bertone of covering up the complete Third Secret. The book cites the testimony of Archbishop Loris F. Capovilla in July 2006, to Catholic researcher Solideo Paolini, that there are two different texts and two different envelopes pertaining to the Third Secret, that one of the envelopes and its contents — the "Capovilla envelope"[3b] — was kept in the papal apartment, not in the archives of the former Holy Office where the text of the vision [3a] was lodged, and that Paul VI read its contents on June 27, 1963, two years before the Bertone "official account" which claims that Pope Paul VI first read the text of the Third Secret on March 27, 1965. The "Capovilla envelope" and text have never been produced.

2007

May 10: Attempting to discredit Socci, Cardinal Bertone publishes his own book, *The Last Visionary of Fatima*, written in the form of an interview by a Vatican affairs reporter, Giuseppe De Carli, who poses no challenging questions but rather de facto avoids all of the issues, including Msgr. Capovilla's explosive testimony. In response, on May 12 Socci proclaims and explains publicly (in his weekly column in the Italian journal Libero) that his own book has been vindicated by the Cardinal's complete failure to answer it, which Socci calls a disturbing development as it means that there is indeed an ongoing cover-up on the part of the Vatican regarding the Third Secret.

May 31: Cardinal Bertone appears by remote live feed on the very popular Italian TV talk show Porta a Porta to again respond to Socci's book. During this telecast Bertone displays not only the text of the vision but also two separate sealed envelopes prepared by Sister Lucy, each bearing the explicit statement in Sister Lucy's own handwriting that "By express order of Our Lady, this envelope can be opened in 1960 only by the Cardinal Patriarch of Lisbon or the Bishop of Leiria." The two sealed envelopes, and other revelations by Cardinal Bertone during the telecast, further confirm the existence of two texts comprising the Third Secret in its entirety. Further, the "express order of Our Lady" noted on the envelopes flatly contradicts Cardinal Bertone's earlier repeated representations (only said after Sr. Lucy's death in 2005) that Sister Lucy "confessed" to him in private, unrecorded conversations that the Virgin has never given any such order.

June 2: Following the telecast, from which Socci has been excluded, Socci publishes his response in Libero. He declares that Bertone has not only failed to "give even one answer" to Socci's book, but "On the contrary, he did more: He offered the proof that I am right" and "that as a matter of fact the explosive part of the 'Third Secret of Fatima' exists yet is well hidden…."

September 21: Bertone stages a second television appearance for himself, this time on the *Telepace* network, to officially launch his own book which had been published in May and also to try yet again to discredit Socci's book for a third time. The press are invited to attend. Socci, as a journalist, appears at the telecast location to question Cardinal Bertone. He acts in a proper way but is forcibly removed from the premises by security guards. During the telecast Bertone once again avoids any discussion of the issues. Instead, he presents a heavily-edited videotape of an interview of Archbishop Capovilla conducted by Giuseppe De Carli, a partisan of Cardinal Bertone, in which the Archbishop not only fails to deny the testimony he gave to Paolini (whose name is never mentioned) about the "Capovilla envelope," but rather fully confirms its existence and location in the papal apartment, and the reading of its contents by Paul VI in 1963, not 1965 as the Bertone "official account" had claimed.

September 22: The Italian newspaper Il Giornale reports that before the guards removed Socci from the location of the telecast of September

21, he was able to play for the assembled journalists an audiotape of Capovilla's statements to Paolini during a meeting on June 21, 2007. On the tape Capovilla is heard to state: "Besides the four pages [of the vision of the bishop dressed in white] there was also something else, an attachment, yes." As the reporter from Il Giornale concludes, Capovilla's statement "would confirm the thesis of the existence of a second sheet with the interpretation of the Secret" — namely, the words of the Virgin following the "etc."

September 23: Socci again responds to Cardinal Bertone in his column in Libero. Socci again calmly demonstrates that Cardinal Bertone is hiding a major part of the Third Secret.

2008

January 25: Christopher A. Ferrara's book, *The Secret Still Hidden*, goes to press; 100,000 copies are printed. In this book, the author gives the history of the Third Secret up to that time. He proves beyond any reasonable doubt that there is a second text, still hidden by the Vatican bureaucrats, which contains the words of Our Lady which follow "In Portugal the dogma of the Faith will always be preserved etc." He demonstrates his proof using the facts and details provided by both Socci and Bertone. The Italian version of his book is sent to 12,000 Italian priests in June 2008. Cardinal Bertone is sent a copy of Ferrara's book by August 2008 and Bertone acknowledges receipt of the book but refuses to answer the substance of any of Ferrara's arguments.

2010

May 4: Vatican journalist Giuseppe De Carli, co-author with Cardinal Bertone of *The Last Visionary of Fatima* (re-issued in 2010 under the new title, *The Last Secret of Fatima*), and an apologist for Cardinal Bertone's now discredited explanations of the Third Secret, admits to the Fatima Challenge Conference before the TV cameras that ."..they could have tricked me."

May 11: Pope Benedict XVI, on his pilgrimage to Portugal in May, stunned the press and the Catholic world by saying that the Third Secret of Fatima tells us that "not only from the outside come the attacks against the Pope and the Church, but the sufferings of the Church come from right inside the Church, from the sin that resides inside the Church... we see this today really in a terrifying way: the greatest persecution against the Church doesn't come from its enemies outside, but starts from the sins within the Church."

May 13: Before 500,000 pilgrims, the Pope proclaimed (in reference to the Third Secret): "Whoever thinks that the prophetic mission of Fatima is concluded deceives himself."

July 13: Giuseppe De Carli dies on the 93rd anniversary of the imparting of the Third Secret by Our Lady of Fatima to the three shepherd children.

2011

May 11: Christopher Ferrara publishes the updated 2nd edition of the Italian version of *The Secret Still Hidden*. Using De Carli's statement from the year before and referring to the 2nd edition of Bertone's book, he further proves that Bertone is still hiding a major part of the Third Secret.

July – August: Christopher Ferrara's book, *The Secret Still Hidden*, receives an endorsement in the August-September issue of the prestigious *Inside the Vatican* magazine. There the editor Robert Moynihan relates a recent conversation with the late Archbishop Pietro Sambi, who died in July. Archbishop Sambi was Papal Nuncio to the United States and thus a key attaché of the Vatican Secretariat of State under Cardinal Bertone. The report of Moynihan, in part, goes as follows: "We [Sambi and Moynihan] were discussing the Third Secret of Fatima, the allegations that the Vatican has not published the entire text of the Third Secret as revealed to Sister Lucia, and the response of Cardinal Tarcisio Bertone, the Vatican Secretary of State, in a book where Bertone states that there is nothing more to be revealed. "Archbishop Sambi said, 'Excuse me.' He got up, went out of the room, and came back with a book. 'Here,' he said. 'Do you know this book? You should read it.' It was Christopher Ferrara's *The Secret Still Hidden*. 'Wait,' I said. 'You are the Pope's representative in the US, and you are urging me to read a book that questions what the Secretary of State wrote?' "Sambi replied: 'All I am saying as that there are interesting things worth reading in this book. And in the end, we are all after the truth, aren't we? The truth is the important thing...'"

2012

November 1: News services report Vladimr Putin has a serious medical problem. "[675] Putin is believed to ask Our Lady to intercede and help him. As his health improves he reads the book *The Devil's Final Battle* and becomes a Fatima believer.[676]

2013

February 28: Pope Benedict XVI resigned and retains his papal name rather than reverting to his birth name.

March 13: Cardinal Jorge Mario Bergoglio is elected as the first Jesuit to become Pope and chooses the name Francis.[677]

November 25: Vladimr Putin meets with Pope Francis. The Pope is reported as telling Putin "We will not discuss Fatima!"[678]

2014

September 13: Pope Francis warns 'Piecemeal' World War III has begun. Pope Francis noted that in a certain sense, World War III has already begun.[679]

2015

March 13: Pope Francis predicts a short papacy and announces an extraordinary Jubilee.[680]

April 29: David Dionisi travels from California to Massachusetts to meet with Father Nicholas Gruner to discuss the book you are now reading. Before the two men meet for the first time, Father Gruner, dies from a heart attack.

August 6-9: The publication of the book *Atomic Bomb Secrets* in Japan and documentary *The Secret of Nagasaki* (online at www.thesecretofnagasaki.com) helps people understand the direct connection between Akita, Fatima and the atomic bombs.

2016

April 8: Pope Francis issues "Amoris Laetitia" which is Latin for "The Joy of Love." In this apostolic exhortation, he communicates it is more important for people to not feel excluded than for people to go to hell.

November 20: The extraordinary Year of Mercy Jubilee ends.[681]

INDEX

Index

ENDNOTES

[1] A summary of the Vigilant Christian books is provided in Appendix B.
[2] Eric Arthur Blair (25 June 1903 - 21 January 1950) is better known by his name George Orwell.
[3] They have hated him that rebuketh in the gate: and have abhorred him that speaketh perfectly.
[4] Matthew 5: 10-12 – "Blessed are they that suffer persecution for justice' sake: for theirs is the kingdom of heaven. Blessed are ye when they shall revile you, and persecute you, and speak all that is evil against you, untruly, for my sake: Be glad and rejoice, for your reward is very great in heaven. For so they persecuted the prophets that were before you."
[5] Teach Peace Foundation 2009 photograph modified to include the All-Seeing Eye from a U.S. dollar bill as the capstone. This image is for illustrative purposes as the planned capstone is made with gold. Additional information is provided in Chapter 6.
[6] For additional evidence that the kingdom of Satan is real and has successfully deceived people to support evil, read *Atomic Bomb Secrets, Vigilant Christian I: The New World Order, Vigilant Christian II: Preventing an American Hiroshima, Vigilant Christian III: The Occult Religion of the 9/11 Attackers, Vigilant Christian IV: 9/11 - The Secret War, and Vigilant Christian V: Perfect Money Planning.*
[7] Pope Paul VI informed the world in two books he wrote and statements that the smoke of Satan had entered the Vatican. A specific example is June 29, 1972 during a homily given at a Mass for the solemnity of Saint Peter and Saint Paul he said: "From some fissure the smoke of Satan has entered the temple of God." Additional information is online at http://the-american-catholic.com/2014/10/19/pope-paul-vi-and-the-smoke-of-satan/.
[8] Fr. Paul Kramer (editor and compiler, *The Devil's Final Battle: Our Lady's Victory Edition* (Buffalo, New York: The Missionary Association), 2010 Second Edition.
[9] Sandro Magister and translated by Matthew Sherry, "Groundbreaking: The Last Warning to the Pope's Electors," *Chiesa*, 13 August 2013 and online at http://chiesa.espresso.repubblica.it/articolo/1350575?eng=y.
[10] Ibid.
[11] Ibid. The Augustinian Maltese Prosper Grech also said: "Moreover, let us not forget the warning of the prophets of ancient Israel not to seek alliances with Babylon or with Egypt, but to follow a pure policy 'ex fide' trusting solely in God and in his covenant. Courage! Christ relieves our minds when he exclaims: 'Have trust, I have overcome the world' (John 16:33)."
[12] John 3:1-8 – "And there was a man of the Pharisees, named Nicodemus, a ruler of the Jews. This man came to Jesus by night, and said to him: Rabbi,

we know that thou art come a teacher from God; for no man can do these signs which thou dost, unless God be with him. Jesus answered, and said to him: Amen, amen I say to thee, unless a man be born again, he cannot see the kingdom of God. Nicodemus saith to him: How can a man be born when he is old? can he enter a second time into his mother's womb, and be born again? Jesus answered: Amen, amen I say to thee, unless a man be born again of water and the Holy Ghost, he cannot enter into the kingdom of God. That which is born of the flesh, is flesh; and that which is born of the Spirit, is spirit. Wonder not, that I said to thee, you must be born again. The Spirit breatheth where he will; and thou hearest his voice, but thou knowest not whence he cometh, and whither he goeth: so is every one that is born of the Spirit."

[13] Matthew 6:9-13 – "Thus therefore shall you pray: Our Father who art in heaven, hallowed be thy name. Thy kingdom come. Thy will be done on earth as it is in heaven. Give us this day our supersubstantial bread. And forgive us our debts, as we also forgive our debtors. And lead us not into temptation. But deliver us from evil. Amen." Note the words "supersubstantial bread" in the Our Father prayer. In 2011, Catholics were informed "consubstantial" would be used in the Nicene Creed instead of saying "one in being with the Father."

[14] John De Marchi, *The Immaculate Heart: The True Story of Our Lady of Fatima* (New York: Farrar, Straus and Young, 1952). The photograph is opposite page 64 and the photographer is unknown. The book is online at www.ewtn.com/library/MARY/TSFATIMA.HTM.

[15] Exodus 12:1-14 provides the precedent of a final terrible plague that descends upon the people of Egypt. The firstborn sons were killed except for the faithful which mark the doorposts of their homes with the blood of an unblemished lamb. The Fatima message global cleansing is not limited to the firstborn sons.

[16] Revelation 12:11 – "And they overcame him by the blood of the Lamb, and by the word of the testimony, and they loved not their lives unto death."

[17] God used rain to destroy the Brotherhood of Death during the time of Noah.

[18] One of the three children that saw the Blessed Virgin was Francisco Marto (June 11, 1908 – April 4, 1919). This young boy lived a very holy life and still did not go directly to Heaven. The Blessed Virgin said: "Yes, he will go there, but he will have to recite the Rosary many times."

[19] Teach Peace Foundation 2009 photograph from inside the Dominus Flevit Church. Dominus Flevit was built in 1955 to commemorate the Lord's weeping over Jerusalem.

[20] The fourth station of the Cross is where Jesus sees his mother. In the context of modern times, this can be compared with the 1917 Fatima

message. We now appear to be approaching the tenth station of the Cross. The 14 Stations of the Cross provide are:
1. Christ condemned to death;
2. The cross is laid upon him;
3. His first fall;
4. He meets His Blessed Mother;
5. Simon of Cyrene is made to bear the cross;
6. Christ's face is wiped by Veronica;
7. His second fall;
8. He meets the women of Jerusalem;
9. His third fall;
10. He is stripped of His garments;
11. His crucifixion;
12. His death on the cross;
13. His body is taken down from the cross; and
14. Laid in the tomb.

[21] An example is the Mormon religion which was founded by Freemason Joseph Smith and not surprisingly teaches man can become god. Mormons are often some of the nicest and more loving people you will meet. This is also true of people who are Freemasons and other religions serving the kingdom of Satan. Joseph Smith is an example of a blind leader leading the blind into the pit. Mormons are sometimes deceived to believe they are Christians but are not because the religion denies one or more of the essential doctrines of Christianity. An example is the Mormon religion teaches there are multiple gods and God lives on a planet near the star Kolob. Many Mormon teachings are very transparent as coming from mystery religions. For example, the teaching that you can identify a false angel by offering to shake his hand is from Freemasonry. Shown in the picture is the Salt Lake Temple All-Seeing Eye.

You can find the Salt Lake City Temple All-Seeing Eye on the east and west center tower above the second window. Morman leaders will tell you it is the eye of the Great Jehovah and from Proverbs 15:3 ("the eyes of the Lord are in every place, beholding good and evil" but explanation of this "one eye" vs. "eyes" is a deception). If needed to convince you, you may be told the All-Seeing Eye is a reference to the dedicatory prayer of the Temple of Solomon found in 1 Kings 8:29.

[22] Revelation 18:14-17 – "And the fruits of the desire of thy soul are departed from thee, and all fat and goodly things are perished from thee, and they shall find them no more at all. The merchants of these things, who were made rich, shall stand afar off from her, for fear of her torments, weeping and mourning. And saying: Alas! alas! that great city, which was clothed with fine linen, and purple, and scarlet, and was gilt with gold, and precious stones, and pearls. For in one hour are so great riches come to nought; and every shipmaster, and all that sail into the lake, and mariners, and as many as work in the sea, stood afar off."

[23] Pope Leo XIII's name was Vincenzo Gioacchino Raffaele Luigi Pecci (2 March 1810 - 20 July 1903).

[24] This text is from the long version of Pope Leo XIII's prayer to St. Michael. The long version of Pope Leo XIII's St. Michael prayer is online at www.teachpeace.com/stmichaelprayer.htm.

[25] Ibid.

[26] Pope Leo XIII (*Humanum Genus*), 1884, 19. Additional information is online at www.teachpeace.com/humanum%20genus.htm.

[27] Ibid., 4.

[28] Ibid. Teach Peace Foundation picture of the booklet distributed by Freemasonry.

[29] Revelation 11:19 – "And the temple of God was opened in heaven: and the ark of his testament was seen in his temple, and there were lightnings, and voices, and an earthquake, and great hail." Revelation 12:1 – "And a great sign appeared in heaven: A woman clothed with the sun, and the moon under her feet, and on her head a crown of twelve stars:"

[30] Jeremiah 3:16-17 – "And when you shall be multiplied, and increase in the land in those days, saith the Lord, they shall say no more: The ark of the covenant of the Lord: neither shall it come upon the heart, neither shall they remember it, neither shall it be visited, neither shall that be done any more. At that time Jerusalem shall be called the thrown of the Lord: and all the nations shall be gathered together to it, in the name of the Lord to Jerusalem, and they shall not walk after the perversity of their most wicked heart."

[31] Teach Peace Foundation drawing of the Ark of the Covenant.

[32] The Ark of the Covenant is claimed to be in Axum, Ethiopia which is the original capital of the Kingdom of Aksum. Axum is one of the oldest

continuously inhabited places in Africa. The official position of the Ethiopian Orthodox Church is it keeps the Ark of the Covenant in a treasury known as The Chapel of the Tablet near the Church of Our Lady Mary of Zion. Replicas of the Axum Ark of the Covenant are kept in every Ethiopian Christian church. The following picture is a 2010 photograph by the author of The Chapel of the Tablet and of a covered Ark replica in Lalibela, Ethiopia.

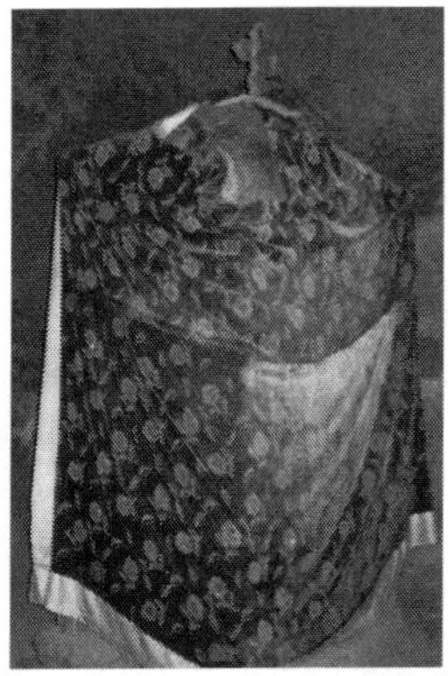

[33] Rabbi Abraham Stone, *Highlights of Moshiach: Based upon Talmudi, Midrashic and classical Rabbinic sources* (Brooklyn, New York: Sichos In English), 1991.

[34] Ibid., Rabbi Abraham Stone unknowingly supports Mary is the New Ark that comes down from heaven. He wrote: "Thus, it wasn't possible for the Ark to fit through the gates. At that time, King Solomon called out, "Raise your heads, O gates, and let the King of glory enter," alluding to the Holy Ark and the Tablets therein. In response to Solomon's plea, the gates uplifted themselves and permitted the Ark to enter. For this reason, the enemy forces did not destroy the gates but they sunk (intact) into the ground. In light of the above, it seems that the Holy Temple itself will come down from Heaven." The quoted text is online at www.sie.org/library/article_cdo/aid/2313097/jewish/Moshiach-Will-Build-The-Beis-Hamikdash-Holy-Temple.htm.

[35] Daniel 12:11-12 – "And from the time when the continual sacrifice shall be taken away, and the abomination unto desolation shall be set up, there shall be a thousand two hundred ninety days, Blessed is he that waiteth and cometh unto a thousand three hundred thirty-five days."

[36] The Brotherhood's Ark of Hope is to contain miniature granite versions of the Georgia Guidestones which are explained in Chapter 8. As background, in 1987 The World Commission on Environment and Development or "Brundtland Commission" published a new charter or "orders for a new world." In 1994, Brotherhood agents Maurice Strong (Secretary-General of

the Rio Summit) and Mikhail Gorbachev (former President of the Soviet Union), led the creation of the Earth Charter. Both men used organizations that they founded (Earth Council and Green Cross International respectively). In 1997, the Earth Charter Commission was formed to finalize the charter and obtain global consensus. Source: "Background History Of The Earth Charter Movement" online at www.earthcharterinaction.org/content/pages/History.html

[37] Teach Peace Foundation 2015 illustration based on a photograph courtesy of the Ark of Hope.org and online at www.arkofhope.org.

[38] Isaiah 57:8 – "And behind the door, and behind the post thou hast set up thy remembrance: for thou hast discovered thyself near me, and hast received an adulterer: thou hast enlarged thy bed, and made a covenant with them: thou hast loved their bed with open hand." The rebuilt Ark had counterfeit Ten Commandments.

[39] Deuteronomy 10:5 – "And returning from the mount, I came down, and put the tables into the ark, that I had made, and they are there till this present, as the Lord commanded me." The Ark of the Old Covenant contained the Word of God. John 1:1 – "In the beginning was the Word, and the Word was with God, and the Word was God." John 1:1 explains the Virgin Mary contained the Word made flesh.

[40] The miracle was performed at a wedding in the village of Cana. John 2:1-11 – "And the third day, there was a marriage in Cana of Galilee: and the mother of Jesus was there. And Jesus also was invited, and his disciples, to the marriage. And the wine failing, the mother of Jesus saith to him: They have no wine. And Jesus saith to her: Woman, what is that to me and to thee? my hour is not yet come. His mother saith to the waiters: Whatsoever he shall say to you, do ye. Now there were set there six waterpots of stone, according to the manner of the purifying of the Jews, containing two or three measures apiece. Jesus saith to them: Fill the waterpots with water. And they filled them up to the brim. And Jesus saith to them: Draw out now, and carry to the chief steward of the feast. And they carried it. And when the chief steward had tasted the water made wine, and knew not whence it was, but the waiters knew who had drawn the water; the chief steward calleth the bridegroom, And saith to him: Every man at first setteth forth good wine, and when men have well drunk, then that which is worse. But thou hast kept the good wine until now. This beginning of miracles did Jesus in Cana of Galilee; and manifested his glory, and his disciples believed in him."

[41] The reason the king would resist allowing this marriage is Abisag was King David's last wife and by marrying her Adonias could make a claim for the throne.

[42] 1 Kings 2:17-19 – "And he (Adonias) said: I pray thee speak to king Solomon (for he cannot deny thee any thing) to give me Abisag the

Sunamitess to wife. And Bethsabee said: Well, I will speak for thee to the king. Then Bethsabee came to king Solomon, to speak to him for Adonias: and the king arose to meet her, and bowed to her, and sat down upon his throne: and a throne was set for the king's mother, and she sat on his right hand."

[43] Ibid.

[44] 1 Samuel 5:1-5 – "And the Philistines took the ark of God, and carried it from the Stone of help into Azotus. And the Philistines took the ark of God, and brought it into the temple of Dagon, and set it by Dagon. And when the Azotians arose early the next day, behold Dagon lay upon his face on the ground before the ark of the Lord: and they took Dagon, and set him again in his place. And the next day again, when they rose in the morning, they found Dagon lying upon his face on the earth before the ark of the Lord: and the head of Dagon, and both the palms of his hands were cut off upon the threshold: And only the stump of Dagon remained in its place. For this cause neither the priests of Dagon, nor any that go into the temple tread on the threshold of Dagon in Azotus unto this day."

[45] *Defeating the Brotherhood of Death*, 2015 edition, provides more information about the Fatima miracle. Additional information about this book is in Appendix B.

[46] In 1915, Lucia dos Santos and three other young girls see an angel. In the Spring, Summer and Autumn of 1916, Lucia dos Santos, Francisco Marto and Jacinta Marto see the Angel of Peace.

[47] John De Marchi, *The Immaculate Heart: The True Story of Our Lady of Fatima* (New York: Farrar, Straus and Young, 1952), 284. De Marchi was an Italian Catholic priest and researcher. From 1943 to 1950 he conducted first-hand research with people who witnessed the October 13, 1917 miracle. The Blessed Virgin was seen by Lucia more than six times including a seventh time at Cova da Iria on June 18, 1921. This seventh apparition occurred on Lucia's last day in Aljustrel just prior to her leaving for the Vilar convent school.

[48]Ibid., 139. By the official government time it was well past one o'clock but by the visible sun time it was precisely noon.

[49] Joshua 10:13 – "And the sun and the moon stood still, till the people revenged themselves of their enemies. Is not this written in the book of the just? So the sun stood still in the midst of heaven, and hasted not to go down the space of one day."

[50] This is a October 13, 1917 photograph and the photographer is unknown.

[51] This is a 1917 photograph and the photographer is unknown.

[52] Pope Piux XII witnessed the miracle from the Vatican Gardens. On October 13, 1930 the Catholic Church officially acknowledge the miracle.

[53] Courtesy of the *Ilustração Portuguesa* newspaper October 29, 1917. This is a October 13, 1917 photograph in the and the photographer is unknown.
[54] The new devotion includes the daily Rosary to defeat evil. Faithful are instructed to say after each mystery of the Rosary: "O Jesus, forgive us our sins, save us from the fires of hell, lead all souls to heaven, especially those who have most need of your mercy." In addition, the faithful should for five first consecutive Saturdays: receive Holy Communion within 24 hours and Confession within 8 days (before or after), pray five decades of the Rosary, and spend 15 minutes in meditation on the mysteries of the Rosary. The above are to be offered up in reparation for sins and ingratitude against the Immaculate Heart of Our Lady. The devotion includes offering in reparation and consecration to the Immaculate Heart of Mary. Any formula may be used which expresses a sincere confiding of oneself without reserve.
[55] Ibid.
[56] Antonio Socci, *The Fourth Secret of Fatima* (Fitzwilliam, New Hampshire: Loreto Publications, 2006). He wrote in his introduction on page 4: "I had not expected the discovery of a colossal enigma, of a mystery that spans the history of the Church of the 20th century, something unutterable, something "chilling" that has literally terrorized different Popes who succeeded each other in mid-century, something that certainly regards the Church, but also the proximate future of us and of our brothers.
[57] On June 26, 2000, the Vatican released a part of the Third Secret that was revealed by the Blessed Virgin to the three shepherd children on July 13, 1917. The text that the Vatican released is as follows: "After the two parts which I have already explained, at the left of Our Lady and a little above, we saw an Angel with a flaming sword in his left hand; flashing, it gave out flames that looked as though they would set the world on fire; but they died out in contact with the splendour that Our Lady radiated towards him from her right hand: pointing to the earth with his right hand, the Angel cried out in a loud voice: 'Penance, Penance, Penance!'. And we saw in an immense light that is God: 'something similar to how people appear in a mirror when they pass in front of it' a Bishop dressed in White 'we had the impression that it was the Holy Father'. Other Bishops, Priests, men and women Religious going up a steep mountain, at the top of which there was a big Cross of rough-hewn trunks as of a cork-tree with the bark; before reaching there the Holy Father passed through a big city half in ruins and half trembling with halting step, afflicted with pain and sorrow, he prayed for the souls of the corpses he met on his way; having reached the top of the mountain, on his knees at the foot of the big Cross he was killed by a group of soldiers who fired bullets and arrows at him, and in the same way there died one after another the other Bishops, Priests, men and women Religious, and various lay people of different ranks and positions. Beneath the two

arms of the Cross there were two Angels, each with a crystal aspersorium in his hand, in which they gathered up the blood of the Martyrs and with it sprinkled the souls that were making their way to God."

[58] The first Secret: "She [Our Lady of Fatima] opened Her hands once more, as She had done during the two previous months. The rays of light seemed to penetrate the earth, and we saw as it were a sea of fire. Plunged in this fire were demons and souls [of the damned] in human form, like transparent burning embers, all blackened or burnished bronze, floating about in the conflagration, now raised into the air by the flames that issued from within themselves together with great clouds of smoke, now falling back on every side like sparks in huge fires, without weight or equilibrium, amid shrieks and groans of pain and despair, which horrified us and made us tremble with fear. (It must have been this sight which caused me to cry out, as people say they heard me). The demons could be distinguished [from the souls of the damned] by their terrifying and repellent likeness to frightful and unknown animals, black and transparent like burning coals. This vision lasted but an instant. How can we ever be grateful enough to our kind heavenly Mother, Who had already prepared us by promising, in the first apparition, to take us to Heaven. Otherwise, I think we would have died of fear and terror." The source is Sister Lucia's memoirs." Our Lady then explained to the children, "You have seen hell where the souls of poor sinners go."

[59] The second Secret: "To save them [poor sinners who are on the road to hell], God wishes to establish in the world devotion to My Immaculate Heart. If what I say to you is done, many souls will be saved and there will be peace. The war is going to end; but if people do not cease offending God, a worse war will break out during the reign of Pius XI. When you see a night illumined by an unknown light, know that this is the great sign given you by God that He is about to punish the world for its crimes, by means of war, famine, and persecutions against the Church and against the Holy Father. To prevent this, I shall come to ask for the consecration of Russia to My Immaculate Heart, and the Communion of Reparation on the First Saturdays. If My requests are heeded, Russia will be converted and there will be peace; if not, she will spread her errors throughout the world, causing wars and persecutions against the Church. The good will be martyred, the Holy Father will have much to suffer, various nations will be annihilated."

The conclusion to the Whole Secret of Fatima was also communicated with the second Secret. Our Lady said: "In the end, My Immaculate Heart will triumph. The Holy Father will consecrate Russia to Me, and she will be converted, and a period of peace will be granted to the world."

---

[60] Dom José Alves Correia da Silva (15 January 1872 - 4 December 1957) was a Portuguese priest from 1920 until his death. The photographer of this Bishop da Silva picture is unknown. On the envelope containing the Secret which is shown in this photograph Bishop da Silva wrote: "This envelope with its contents shall be entrusted to His Eminence Cardinal Manuel (Cerejeira), Patriarch of Lisbon after my death." Leiria, December 8, 1945 Jose, Bishop of Leiria.

[61] The June 2000 Congregation for the Doctrine of the Faith "The Message of Fatima" authored by the Secretary of the Congregation for the Doctrine of the Faith Cardinal Tarcisio Bertone is online at www.vatican.va/roman_curia/congregations/cfaith/documents/rc_con_cfaith_doc_20000626_message-fatima_en.html.

[62] Ibid.

[63] The 3a text shown to the public was on four sheets of paper. The text released by the Vatican in 2000 is not the 20 to 25 lines on one sheet of paper as observed by Bishop João Pereira Venâncio.

[64] Fr. Paul Kramer (editor and compiler), *The Devil's Final Battle: Our Lady's Victory Edition* (Terryville, Connecticut: The Missionary Association, 2010 Second Edition), 223-243. Contributors to the book are Andrew Cesanek, Mark Fellows, Christopher Ferrara, Fr. Nicholas Gruner, Fr. Gregory Hesse, Fr. Paul Kramer and John Vennari. Unlike the 3a, the 3b is signed by Sister Lucia, has margins of three quarters of a centimeter, explains the vision, is at most 25 lines of text, and the text contains the word of the Blessed Virgin.

[65] The 3b secret length is estimated at 20 to 25 lines of text. Third Secret is sometimes called the Fourth Secret due to the courageous work of author Antonio Socci. In 2006, Socci's book *The Fourth Secret of Fatima* was published and exposed the Vatican attempt to conceal the part of prophecy pertaining to the 21st century.

[66] While the author is careful to provide the most accurate understanding of the Fatima secret, it is important to remember that what is presented is a reconstruction and not the translation based on the secret in the possession of the Catholic Church. The text from the *Neues Europa* 1963 version helped researchers because people who read the secret confirmed messages that were in the Third Secret. The *Neues Europa* 1963 version incorrectly communicated the Fatima message only in the context of the 20th century. In 1963, this mistake was especially understandable because President John Kennedy, Great Britain's Prime Minister Harold MacMillan and the Soviet Premier Khrushchev were working to prevent nuclear war. The Fatima message helped break the ice between world leaders prompting Kennedy to publically desire peace and arms control (see www.teachpeace.com/JFK%20Commencement%20Address%20June%2010%201963.pdf). Kennedy said

in his address: "All this is not unrelated to world peace." The declassified previously Secret CIA Information Report on the Communist reaction to Kennedy's June 10, 1963 American University Commencement address is online at www.teachpeace.com/Khrushchev%20reaction%20to%20JFK%20speech%20June%201963.pdf. The men signed the Limited Test Ban Treaty on August 5, 1963. Regarding the value of the *Neues Europa* account, Cardinal Alfredo Ottaviani (29 October 1890 – 3 August 1979) thought it was close enough that it should be shared widely. Priest Messias Coelho said the *Neues Europa* 1963 version fundamentally corresponds to the accurate Fatima message: "Cardinals will be against Cardinals and bishops against bishops. Satan will put himself in their midst. In Rome, also, there will be big changes. What is rotten will fall, and what will fall must not be maintained. The Church will be darkened and the world plunged into confusion." In addition, the Blessed Virgin warned: "Millions and millions of men will lose their lives from one hour to the next, and those who remain living will envy those who are dead. There will be tribulation as far as the eye can see, and misery all over the earth and desolation in every country."
Matthew 13:39 – "And the enemy that sowed them, is the devil. But the harvest is the end of the world. And the reapers are the angels."

[67] Teach Peace Foundation 2015 illustration placing the compiled 3b text on a paper 4.4 inches x 6.8 inches or 11.25 cm x 17.25 cm. The size as shown is very close to the actual size as observed by Bishop João Pereira Venâncio. He measured the document on March 1, 1957 by holding Sister Lucia's envelope to the light. Both the text and size shown also complies with first-hand accounts of people who read the Third Secret.

[68] Earthquakes (Revelation 6:12 and Matthew 24:7), comets or meteors (Revelation 8:8), pandemics (Matthew 24:7), or wars and rumors of war involving Israel (Luke 21:20).
Revelation 6:12 – "And I saw, when he had opened the sixth seal, and behold there was a great earthquake, and the sun became black as sackcloth of hair: and the whole moon became as blood:"
Matthew 24:7 – "For nation shall rise against nation, and kingdom against kingdom; and there shall be pestilences, and famines, and earthquakes in places:"
Revelation 8:8 – "And the second angel sounded the trumpet: and as it were a great mountain, burning with fire, was cast into the sea, and the third part of the sea became blood:"
Luke 21:20 – "And when you shall see Jerusalem compassed about with an army; then know that the desolation thereof is at hand."
David J. Dionisi, *Vigilant Christian II: Preventing an American Hiroshima* (Davis, CA: Teach Peace Foundation, 2015). Other ways to annihilate

nations include electromagnetic pulse weapons, space-based weapons, weather modification weapons, biological weapons (Ebola, Bird Flu, etc.), mind control weapons, genetically modified food weapons, nuclear weapons, and chemicals including illegal drugs. Electromagnetic weapons are extremely likely to destroy online information exposing the Brotherhood of Death. This is one reason Teach Peace Foundation books are available at www.teachpeace.com as printed books. In addition, *Vigilant Christian V: Perfect Money Planning* explains the United States will be financially annihilated. The national debt in 2015 is over $18 trillion. Just ask yourself, how can each taxpayer pay their share, which is $154,000 and growing?

[69] In 1963 the Brotherhood of Death formed a 15-member special study group. The group wrote *The Report from Iron Mountain*. The resulting 1967 report recommends a fabricated extraterrestrial life threat. See Chapter 7 for additional information and *The Report from Iron Mountain* is available at www.teachpeace.com/Report_from_Iron_ Mountain.pdf.

[70] The three days of darkness over the whole earth have been announced by many people. Examples include Blessed Anna-Maria Taigi, Padre Pio, Elizabeth Canori-Mora, Rosa-Colomba Asdente, Palma d'Oria, Fr. Nectou, St. Hildegard, Pere Lamy, Marie Baourdi, Marie Martel, Marie-Julie Jahenny, and St. Columba.

[71] People who are outside or in some way see God's wrath are not expected to survive the three days of darkness.

[72] Tanguma was assisted by Cheryl Detwiler, Bill Meredith, John Ochsner, and Leticia Tanguma.

[73] Teach Peace Foundation 2010 photograph of the mural inside the Denver International Airport and online at http://images.flydenver.com/ keyword/conspiracy/. The full set of murals are explained in *Vigilant Christian II: Preventing an American Hiroshima*. The soldier is the Brotherhood of Death and uses the Muslim sword to destroy three buildings. The three buildings may represent the Twin Towers and Building 7 destroyed on September 11, 2001. More photos of the murals are online at www.vigilantchristian.org/denverairport.html.

[74] This is a 2014 photograph provided courtesy of Denver International Airport and online at http://images.flydenver.com/keyword/conspiracy/i-87P5Bb8/A.

[75] Luke 18:8 – "I say to you, that he will quickly revenge them. But yet the Son of man, when he cometh, shall he find, think you, faith on earth?"

[76] Matthew 24:24 – "For there shall arise false Christs and false prophets, and shall shew great signs and wonders, insomuch as to deceive (if possible) even the elect."

[77] The book, *Vigilant Christian IV: 9/11 - The Secret War* provides the comprehensive evidence that Osama bin Laden is not responsible and the Brotherhood of Death used the Mossad to implement the 9/11 terrorism.
[78] Michael Davies, *Liturgical Time Bombs In Vatican II: The Destruction of the Catholic Faith Through Changes in Catholic Worship* (Rockford, Illinois: Tan Books and Publishers, Inc., 2003). The *Missa Normativa* was imposed on Catholics by Pope Paul VI in 1969 with the *Novus Ordo Missae* or *New Order of Mass*. The mural communicates additional liturgical changes pave the way for Christians to forget Jesus.
[79] This is a 2014 Photograph provided courtesy of Denver International Airport and online at http://images.flydenver.com/keyword/conspiracy/i-2SWrB2V/A.
[80] The Georgia Guidestones, the counterfeit Ten Commandments, are explained in Chapter 8.
[81] Frère Michel de la Sainte Trinité, *The Whole Truth About Fatima, Volume III: The Third Secret* (Buffalo, New York: Immaculate Heart Publications, 1990), 710. Fr. Joseph Schweigl spoke with Sister Lucia on September 2, 1952. Additional information about Fr. Schweigl's comment is on page 31 in *The Devil's Final Battle* 2002 advance reading edition.
[82] Pope John Paul II (18 May 1920 - 2 April 2005) was born with the name Karol Józef Wojtyła. He made this statement in Fatima, Portugal on May 13, 2000. Pope John Paul II's statement at Fatima is explained on page 94 in *The Devil's Final Battle* 2002 advance reading edition as both a stunning papal authentication of Fatima as relevant for our time and the very fulfillment of Apocalypse 12:1 – "And a great sign appeared in heaven: A woman clothed with the sun, and the moon under her feet, and on her head a crown of twelve stars:"
[83] Cardinal Mario Luigi Ciappi (October 6, 1909 - April 23, 1996) was the personal papal theologian to Popes Pius XII, John XXIII, Paul VI, John Paul I and John Paul II. His quote is from the March 2002 issue of the journal *Catholic*.
[84] Fr. Malachi Martin's July 19, 1988 interview with Art Bell on the Coast to Coast AM radio show #223 is online at www.youtube.com/watch?v=gn--7GTffn8 and http://web.archive.org/web/20070416024836/http://www.paranetinfo.com/shows5.html. Fr. Martin explained the Third Secret, on one piece of paper, is awful and should be disclosed. At 1:05:07-26 he says: "I consider it [the Fatima revelation] to be the key event in the declining fortune of the Roman Catholic organization and the defining event for the near future of the Church in the next millennium, the third millennium."At 1:03:15-1:04:37 Fr. Martin says: "I have no authority. I have no revelation. No angel has tapped

me on the shoulder. I have had no private divine dream like St. Joseph or Joseph in the Old Testament had. I have no authority and I cannot arrogate to myself that authority because I may be putting my foot in my mouth. To put it in a mild fashion, I may be going ahead of the Lord and we are supposed to walk in the words of one Roman Saint five yards behind the Holy Ghost the Holy Spirit. Besides that there is the question of shock, scandal, of [said twice] frightening people and polarizing my human society to which I belong and which I am happy to belong as God made me to belong to it as a member of the human race. I cannot do that. Not, not just like that, I just can't. I wish I could, but in human calculation this will shock, this will jolt people up, this will fill the confessionals on Saturday evening. This will fill up the cathedrals and the basilicas and the churches with worshippers kneeling down striking their breasts."

[85] Ibid. At 59:57-1:00:22 Fr. Malachi Martin explains how he came to read the Third Secret. He died before finishing the book *Primacy: How the Institutional Roman Catholic Church Became a Creature of the New World Order*.

[86] Ibid. The sentence is read on July 19, 1998 by Art Bell at 1:46:40-43 and online at www.youtube.com/watch?v=gn--7GTffn8.

[87] Ibid. The text is confirmed by Fr. Martin Malachi at 1:46:54-1:47-18. He also observed: "Eventually the secret will be revealed and work its way out... The text is very dry and specific." Fr. Martin also said on July 19, 1998 regarding the 3b secret: "We are in apostasy to a large degree." In response to a question by a woman named Bonnie is there anything that we can do as individuals other than praying to avert what is coming in that Third Secret he responded: "We can't avert it now. It is coming, when is something else. It is coming for sure. We can mitigate it. We can mitigate it slightly, if you know what I mean. We can't avert it. It is too late. Pray, go to communion, say your Rosary, cultivate the Saints, stay in a state of grace, do good, visit the sick, visit those in prison, do corporal works of mercy, in other words Bonnie we know what to do exactly, if we want to do it." Another interview was on July 12, 1998, show #222 and is available online at https://www.youtube.com/watch?v=zhkSCjwdjm8. In this interview Fr. Martin says at 1:45:22-58: "It is a very exact description of what is now happening and apparently what is going to happen shortly but in cold hard terms. There is no exaggeration. There is no use of adjectives or adverbs or anything like that. It is a blanket statement, a very factual thing. Stated boldly with no adulteration, no flourishes, no purple patches. Yeah, it is a frightening document." At 1:56:47 Fr. Martin is asked "if the United States is specifically mentioned in the Third Secret. At 1:56:48-54 he replied: "No it is not mentioned specifically, but, something very relevant is mentioned."

[88] Fr. Fuentes interviewed Sister Lucia on December 26, 1957. Additional information about this interview is on page 31 in *The Devil's Final Battle* 2002 advance reading edition.
[89] Frère Michel de la Sainte Trinité, *The Whole Truth About Fatima, Volume III: The Third Secret* (Buffalo, New York: Immaculate Heart Publications, 1990), 675-676. Bishop Alberto Cosme do Amaral (October 12, 1916 - October 7, 2005) made this statement on September 10, 1984 during a question and answer session at the Technical University of Vienna, Austria.
[90] Cardinal Silvio Oddi (November 14, 1910 - June 29, 2001) testimony to Lucia Brunelli on March 17, 1990 and published in the journal *Il Sabato*.
[91] Fr. Joaquin Alonso (1913 - 1981) served for sixteen years as the official Fatima archivist.
[92] The July 6, 1973 message from the Blessed Virgin was: "My daughter, my novice, you have obeyed me well in abandoning all to follow me. Is the infirmity of your ears painful? Your deafness will be healed, be sure. Does the wound of your hand cause you to suffer? Pray in reparation for the sins of men. Each person in this community is my irreplaceable daughter. Do you say well the prayer of the Handmaids of the Eucharist? Then, let us pray it together. Most Sacred Heart of Jesus, truly present in Holy Eucharist, I consecrate my body and soul to be entirely one with Your Heart, being sacrificed at every instant on all the altars of the world and giving praise to the Father pleading for the coming of His Kingdom. Please receive this humble offering of myself. Use me as You will for the glory of the Father and the salvation of souls. Most holy Mother of God, never let me be separated from Your Divine Son. Please defend and protect me as Your Special Child. Amen. Pray very much for the Pope, Bishops, and Priests. Since your Baptism you have always prayed faithfully for them. Continue to pray very much...very much. Tell your superior all that passed today and obey him in everything that he will tell you. He has asked that you pray with fervor."
The August 3, 1973 message from the Blessed Virgin was: "My daughter, my novice, do you love the Lord? If you love the Lord, listen to what I have to say to you. It is very important...You will convey it to your superior. Many men in this world afflict the Lord. I desire souls to console Him to soften the anger of the Heavenly Father. I wish, with my Son, for souls who will repair by their suffering and their poverty for the sinners and ingrates. In order that the world might know His anger, the Heavenly Father is preparing to inflict a great chastisement on all mankind. With my Son I have intervened so many times to appease the wrath of the Father. I have prevented the coming of calamities by offering Him the sufferings of the Son on the Cross, His Precious Blood, and beloved souls who console Him

forming a cohort of victim souls. Prayer, penance and courageous sacrifices can soften the Father's anger. I desire this also from your community...that it love poverty, that it sanctify itself and pray in reparation for the ingratitude and outrages of so many men. Recite the prayer of the Handmaids of the Eucharist with awareness of its meaning; put it into practice; offer in reparation (whatever God may send) for sins. Let each one endeavor, according to capacity and position, to offer herself entirely to the Lord. Even in a secular institute prayer is necessary. Already souls who wish to pray are on the way to being gathered together. Without attaching to much attention to the form, be faithful and fervent in prayer to console the Master. Is what you think in your heart true? Are you truly decided to become the rejected stone? My novice, you who wish to belong without reserve to the Lord, to become the spouse worthy of the Spouse, make your vows knowing that you must be fastened to the Cross with three nails. These three nails are poverty, chastity, and obedience. Of the three, obedience is the foundation. In total abandon, let yourself be led by your superior. He will know how to understand you and to direct you."

[93] Teach Peace Foundation August 2, 2015 photograph of Sister Agnes Sasagawa.

[94] In the 1899 Douay-Rheims American Edition the text is "I will put enmities between thee and the woman, and thy seed and her seed: she shall crush thy head, and thou shalt lie in wait for her heel."

[95] For more information, *The Catholic Encyclopedia* online at www.newadvent.org/cathen/07674d.htm is recommended.

[96] *Inside the Vatican*, November 1998 (http://insidethevatican.com/). Bishop John Shojiro Ito (March 13, 1909 - March 14, 1993) was the bishop of Akita.

[97] The complete Akita message is available online at http://www.ewtn.com/library/MARY/AKITA.HTM.

[98] Ibid. April 22, 1984 – After eight years of investigations, Rev. John Shojiro Ito, Bishop of Niigata, Japan, recognized "the supernatural character of a series of mysterious events concerning the statue of the Holy Mother Mary and authorizes "throughout the entire diocese, the veneration of the Holy Mother of Akita, while awaiting that the Holy See publishes definitive judgment on this matter."

[99] Hosea 4:6 – "My people have been silent, because they had no knowledge: because thou hast rejected knowledge, I will reject thee, that thou shalt not do the office of priesthood to me: and thou hast forgotten the law of thy God, I also will forget thy children."

[100] OPEC was founded in Baghdad, Iraq in 1960 by Iran, Iraq, Kuwait, Saudi Arabia and Venezuela.

[101] Teach Peace Foundation photograph of the "House of the Temple" Order from Chaos stained glass window. This October 2014 photograph was shot inside the temple for the Supreme Council, 33°, Ancient & Accepted Scottish Rite of Freemasonry, Southern Jurisdiction in Washington D.C.
[102] Pope Leo XIII (*Humanum Genus*), 1884. Additional information is online at www.teachpeace.com/humanum%20genus.htm.
[103] Arcanum Arcanorum is Latin for secrets of secrets.
[104] Satanists teach there are 77 names for the Devil and at least this many names for the Devil's plan.
[105] Shekinah, pronounced "Shock-n-Awe," was the name of the Pentagon plan announced prior to the 2003 Iraq invasion. In the Brotherhood of Death religion, Shekinah is pronounced to summon Enoch or Metratron to deliver overwhelming demonic power.
[106] In this ritual it is common for the initiate to adopt a new name.
[107] The octopus image is a 2012 Teach Peace Foundation illustration.
[108] Antony C. Sutton, *America's Secret Establishment: An Introduction to the Order of Skull & Bones* (TrinDay LLC, 1983 and 2002 edition), 5, 22, 23 and 238. On page 5 Sutton observes Skull and Bones was "once known as the Brotherhood of Death." The Skull and Bones name is an external name that is deemed suitable for the general public. A name used internally and externally is "The Order." The name for internal use only is Brotherhood of Death. Sutton notes on pages 22-23 that other researchers called The Order the "Brotherhood of Death." On page 238 Sutton shows that the name "Brotherhood of Death" was used to criticize Skull and Bones in October 1873. The name Brotherhood of Death is also used at the inner circle level by other interlocking secret societies. For example Hitler's SS was also known as the "Brotherhood of Death."
[109] Teach Peace Foundation October 2014 photograph of the marble sphinx guard at the main entrance to the temple for the Supreme Council, 33°, Ancient & Accepted Scottish Rite of Freemasonry, Southern Jurisdiction in Washington D.C.
[110] Ian Johnson, *A Mosque in Munich* (New York, New York: Houghton Mifflin Harcourt Publishing Company), 2010, 109. Johnson wrote: "According to documents seized by the British at the start of World War II, the Brotherhood received significant funds from a German journalist affiliated with the German legation in Cairo. The Nazi money was used to establish the Brotherhood's quasi-military "Special Apparatus." Hitler's Brotherhood of Death relationship, which terminated in 1934, is explained in detail in *Vigilant Christian III: The Occult Religion of the 9/11 Attackers*.
[111] Ian Johnson, "Our Secret Connections with the Muslim Brotherhood," *New York Review of Books*, 10 March 2011 and online at

www.nybooks.com/articles/ archives/2011/mar/10/our-secret-connections-muslim-brotherhood/. In this article
Johnson writes: "By the end of the decade, the CIA was overtly backing Ramadan."

[112] The Brotherhood of Death goddess is Isis. ISIS/ISIL is officially attributed to the Jordanian Salafi Jihadist Abu Musab al-Zarqawi and his militant group Jama'at al-Tawhid wal-Jihad which was founded in 1999. Another name for ISIS is ISIL which is the Islamic State of Iraq and the Levant.

[113] Christof Lehmann, "U.S. Embassy in Ankara Headquarter for ISIS War on Iraq - Hariri Insider," *NSNBC International*, 22 June 2014 and online at http://nsnbc.me/2014/06/22/u-s-embassy-in-ankara-headquarter-for-isis-war-on-iraq-hariri-insider/.

[114] David D. Kirkpatrick with Ali Hamza contributing, "Suspicions Run Deep in Iraq That C.I.A. and the Islamic State are United," *The New York Times*, 20 September 2014 and online at www.nytimes.com/2014/09/21/world/middleeast/suspicions-run-deep-in-iraq-that-cia-and-the-islamic-state-are-united.html.

[115] Ibid.

[116] Ibid.

[117] "Baghdadi Mossad trained," *Gulf Daily News: The Voice of Bahrain*, 15 July 2014 and online at www.gulf-daily-news.com/NewsDetails.aspx?storyid=381153.

[118] "Why America is Not Normal," Aydinlik Daily, 27 February 2015 and online at www.aydinlikdaily.com/world/iraqi-mp-we-took-down-the-british-plane-carrying-arms-to-isis-h219.html.

[119] Ibid.

[120] David J. Dionisi, *Vigilant Christian II: Preventing an American Hiroshima*, 2004. In the 2015 edition al Qaeda and ISIS are explained in Chapter 4 - The Real Terrorists. ISIS is the name of the Brotherhood of Death's Egyptian goddess and also the abbreviation for the Islamic State of Iraq and Syria or Islamic State of Iraq and al-Sham. Another name is ISIL which is the Islamic State of Iraq and the Levant.

[121] Freemasonry claims at least four million members with an active presence in almost every country in the world. Nohea O. A. Peck explains Masonry formally started in Japan in 1866. *Masonry in Japan, The First One Hundred Years, 1866 - 1966* (Tokyo, Japan: The Voyagers' Press, 1969), inside front cover.

[122] Inquire Within is the pseudonym for Christina M. Stoddard. Her book, *The Trail of the Serpent* was first published in 1936. The quote from Jean-Emmanuel Le Counteulx de Canteleu's 1863 book *Les Sectes et Sociétés secrètes, politiques et religieuses, essai sur leur histoire depuis les temps les*

plus reculés jusqu'à la Révolution française, can be found on page 10 of Stoddard's book made available by Kessinger Publishing in Whitefish, MT. According to Le Couteulx de Canteleu, a confederation of philosophers formed in ancient Egypt. Classes of people existed with gods at the top (today's pharaohs or Brotherhood of Death leaders), priests, greater initiates, and lesser initiates. The majority of people, including the Hebrews, did not fit into these classes and were to be treated as animals.

[123] Freemasonry claims at least four million members with an active presence in almost every country in the world.

[124] Tubalcain, also spelled Tubal Cain, is the founder of the Gild of Smiths or Metal Workers.

[125]Sir John A. Cockburn, *Freemasonry; What, Whence, Why, Whither* (London, England: Masonic Record Limited, estimated at 1923), 47-48. The year the book was published was not printed in the book. Cockburn (23 August 1850 - 26 November 1929) was initiated into Freemasonry in 1876 and on page 7 he writes his knowledge is from "about forty-seven years in the Craft."

[126] The 2007 House Resolution 33 online at www.govtrack.us/congress/billtext.xpd?bill=hr110-33. The number 33 has special significance as Freemasonry consists of 33 degrees. Upon attaining the 33 degree followers believe they are illuminated by receiving secret information.

[127] Ibid.

[128] The Masonic Presidents of the United States is a permanent exhibit in the Masonic Library and Museum of Pennsylvania. The information in this exhibit is online at www.pagrandlodge.org/mlam/presidents/index.html. Lyndon Johnson was an Entered Apprentice and received his first degree on October 30, 1937. On a related note, Abraham Lincoln applied for membership in Tyrian Lodge, Springfield, Ill., shortly after his nomination for the presidency in 1860. He withdrew the application and advised the lodge that he would resubmit his application again when he returned from the presidency. After Lincoln was assassinated, the Tyrian Lodge adopted a resolution on April 17, 1865 to say "that the decision of President Lincoln to postpone his application for the honours of Freemasonry, lest his motives be misconstrued, is the highest degree honorable to his memory."

[129] Ronald Reagan was made an honorary member of the Imperial Council of the Shrine. He participated in numerous Masonic functions throughout his career. Thomas Jefferson, James Madison, Zachary Taylor, Franklin Pierce, and William Clinton appear in some Masonic lists, but publicly Masonic officials usually claim their membership status is uncertain. For example,

according to page 49 of the 1951 edition of the *Holy Bible, Masonic Edition*, Thomas Jefferson was a Mason.

[130] Courtesy of the Harry S. Truman Library in Independence, Missouri. Picture shows President Truman in his Masonic regalia and was taken on June 6, 1951 in Alexandria, Virginia (online at www.trumanlibrary.org/photographs/displayimage.php?pointer=3155&people=Truman%2C+Harry+S.%2C+1884-1972&listid=0).

[131] The St. John's Masonic Lodge Bible was almost used by George W. Bush, but inclement weather resulted in a decision to protect the Bible from rain. The Bible was used in 1921 to swear in Freemason Warren Harding. Elite Masons believe this Bible is extremely significant, and it is used for special ceremonies, including Washington's funeral in December, 1799, the dedication of the Washington Monument in 1885, the re-laying of the U.S. Capitol's cornerstone in 1959, and the christening of the aircraft carrier USS George Washington at Norfolk, Va., in 1992.

[132] The George Washington image is courtesy of the George Washington Masonic National Memorial Association. The image of President Washington is cropped, and the full image is online at www.gwmemorial.org/tour.php. The mural is on the George Washington Masonic Memorial Hall South Wall and depicts the 1793 Masonic cornerstone ceremony for the United States Capitol.

[133] John 18:20 – "Jesus answered him: I have spoken openly to the world: I have always taught in the synagogue, and in the temple, whither all the Jews resort; and in secret I have spoken nothing." Scripture references are available in over 30 versions of the Bible (see www.vigilantchristian.org/accessover30bibleversions.html). Throughout this book the Douay-Rheims 1899 American Edition is used unless otherwise noted.

[134] Walton Hannah, *Darkness Visible: A Revelation and Interpretation of Freemasonry* (London: Augustine Press, 1952), 99 and 101.

[135] Teach Peace Foundation photograph.

[136] Many gematria codes and calculators are online (see www.vigilantchristian.org/gematria.html).

[137] Orpheus was a mythical ancient Greek prophet and hero with superhuman capabilities. He was able to charm all living things and coax even trees into movement. Orpheus is a key figure in multiple mystery religions. In one mythical story he uses his divine music to retrieve his wife, Eurydice, from hell.

[138] Henry Cornelius Agrippa, *Three Books of Occult Philosophy* (Llewellyn Publication, republished in 1992). The original 1531 edition, in Latin, was published in Antwerp, Belgium. Agrippa explains the Rosicrucian

philosophy in the 16th century. The series includes the gematria key equating Jesus Christ with the numerical value of 1275.

[139] Teach Peace Foundation photograph.

[140] Ibid.

[141] Albert Pike (December 29, 1809 - April 2, 1891), *Morals and Dogma* (Charleston, South Carolina, 1871). The picture from *Morals and Dogma* is in the public domain as it was first published in the United States prior to 1923. The book was first published in 1871. The 2011 version is available to the general public and seeks to sidestep what has been previously revealed with changes and annotations by Arturo de Hoyos. Hoyos is the 33° Scottish Rite's Grand Archivist and Grand Historian.

[142] Teach Peace Foundation photograph.

[143] Official Records of the Rebellion, Series 1, Vol. 8, 99. The official records of the Union and Confederate Armies were prepared under the direction of Secretary of War Alexander Ramsey (September 8, 1815 - April 22, 1903) and published in 1880.

[144] Walter Lynwood Fleming identified Albert Pike as the chief judicial officer on page 19 in the 1905 update to the 1884 book *Klan, Ku Klux Klan: Its Origin, Growth and Disbandment.* This book is authoritative because the 1884 authors, Captain John C. Lester and D.L. Wilson, are two of the KKK founders. Pike's picture is shown on page 19 in the center of the pictures of the six former Confederate officers credited as the KKK founders.

[145] Susan Lawrence Davis, *Authentic History of the Ku Klux Klan 1865 - 1877* (New York, New York: American Library Service, 1924), 270-271 and 276-277. Davis published Pike's involvement as was confirmed by two Arkansas Klan organizers. In 1866 the Ku Klux Klan was founded in Polaski, Tennessee by six former Confederate officers. The first Imperial Wizard of the KKK was Freemason Nathan Bedford Forrest. Pike likely used the Maya serpent god name Kukulkan, which the Aztecs called Quetzalcoatl and Freemasons call Lucifer, to create the name Ku Klux Klan. Lower level members were told Ku Klux Klan was the Greek word Kuklos meaning circle.

[146] Eleven holds special magical power in Brotherhood of Death religion. In the Brotherhood religion, key human sacrifices often occur on the 11 day in the month (e.g., 9/11). For the Ku Klux Klan, the letter K is the eleventh number in the alphabet. Three times eleven is 33. In Christianity, the book of Daniel signals the return of the Antichrist who is the eleventh horn on the beast.

[147] The Albert Pike statue is in Judiciary Square at 3rd St NW & D St NW in Washington, D.C.

[148] Albert Pike, *Morals and Dogma* (Charleston, South Carolina, 1871). Teach Peace Foundation picture. An upgraded official reprint of the book was published in 2011. The 21st century edition of *Morals and Dogma* does not include the death penalty warning and is crafted as a version for the general public. Lucifer is explained as the good god in the 1871 edition. In the 1950 edition, see pages 102 and 321. A few sentences from page 321 follow. "Lucifer, the Son of the Morning! It is he who bears the Light...Doubt it not!"
[149] William Guy Carr, R.D., *Pawns in the Game* (Willowdale, Ontario, Canada: Federation of Christian Layman, 1954), xv.
[150] Albert Pike's *Magnum Opus or The Great Work of the Ancient and Accepted Scottish Rite of Freemasonry* first published around 1869 and on page 61 in the 2010 Kessinger Publishing edition.
[151] Ibid. Pike's quote that the secret cartel is to once again be a world power on pages 94 and 95 in *The Cause of World Unrest* (New York and London, G. P. Putnam's Sons The Knickerbocker Press, 1920). The five hundred years in Pike's quote is referring to the elimination of his secret society as a world power when the Knights Templar Grand Commander Jacques de Molay (also spelled Molai) was punished with the death penalty in 1314. Pike's quote is not pointing to the starting point of the secret society which started before 1314 but is communicating that a secret cartel has working for centuries to reclaim its influence as a world power.
[152] Albert Pike, *Morals and Dogma* (Charleston, South Carolina, 1871). The photo of Pike shows includes the 1891 date because the edition shown is the 1950 version. An upgraded official reprint of the book was published in 2011.
[153] J. S. M. Ward, *Freemasonry and the Ancient Gods* (London: Simpkin, Marshall, Hamilton, Kent & Co. Ltd., 1921 with a second edition in 1926).
[154] Ibid., iii.
[155] David Ovason, *The Secret Architecture of Our Nation's Capital* (New York, New York: Harper Collins, 1999), viii. Christian Fred Kleinknecht, Jr. (14 February 1924 - 1 December 2011) was a 33rd degree Sovereign Grand Commander of the Supreme or Mother Council of the World, Southern Jurisdiction, Washington, D.C.
[156] Ibid. Kleinknecht retired in 2003 and died in 2011.
[157] David Yallop, *In God's Name: An Investigation into the Murder of Pope John Paul I* (New York, New York: Carroll and Graf Publishers, 2007), 308 and 312. First published in 1984 by Jonathan Cape Ltd.
[158] John Daniel, *Scarlet and the Beast: A History of the War between English and French Freemasonry* (Tyler, Texas: JKI Publishing, 1995 Second Edition, Volume 3), 110. Calvi's death was initially announced as a suicide but changed to a murder after two coroner's inquests and an independent

investigation. A Masonic cable tow is a hangman's noose with a short rope that signifies the First Degree binding the candidate to all the brothers of Freemasonry. In the Brotherhood religion, the cable tow is an umbilical cord to Lucifer.

[159] Rupert Cornwell, *God's Banker: An Account of the Life and Death of Roberto Calvi* (London, England: Victor Gollancz Ltd., 1984).

[160] David Yallop, *In God's Name: An Investigation into the Murder of Pope John Paul I* (New York, New York: Carroll and Graf Publishers, 2007), 129, 137, 263, 275, and 295. Yallop notes Calvi moved money from Banco Ambrosiano into a Vatican account and then to Danca del Gottardo or Unio de Banquest Suisse (UBS) serving a gamut of secret contacts.

[161] John Daniel, *Scarlet and the Beast: A History of the War between English and French Freemasonry* (Tyler, Texas: JKI Publishing, 1995 Second Edition, Volume 3), 109.

[162] Ibid., pages 117-121.

[163] Ibid.

[164] Captain William Morgan, *Illustrations of Masonry by one of the Fraternity Who has devoted Thirty Years to the Subject* (Batavia, NY: self-published, 1827).

[165] Ibid.

[166] Charles Grandison Finney, *The Character and Claims of Freemasonry* (Cincinnati, Ohio: Western Tract and Book Society, 1869). He also writes in Chapter 1: "It is high time that the Church of Christ was awake to the character and tendency of Freemasonry... I know something about it, for I have been a Freemason myself."

[167] Charles Grandison Finney, *Memoirs of Rev. Charles G. Finney* (Hodder & Stoughton, 1876).

[168] Front cover of Captain William Morgan's *Illustrations of Masonry by one of the Fraternity Who has devoted Thirty Years to the Subject* (Batavia, NY: self-published, 1827).

[169] Charles Grandison Finney, *The Character and Claims of Freemasonry* (Cincinnati, Ohio: Western Tract and Book Society, 1869). Chapter 2 in Finney's book includes Valance's confession as recorded by Dr. John L. Emery in the summer of 1848.

[170] Ibid., 13-14.

[171] Ibid., 15.

[172] Ibid.

[173] Ibid., 16.

[174] Ibid., 12.

[175] Cardinal José Maria Caro Rodriguez, *The Mystery of Freemasonry Unveiled* (Santiago, Chile: Society of the Good Press, 1925, Second Edition), 155-166.
[176] Rev. Martin L. Wagner, *Freemasonry: An Interpretation*, 1912, 10.
[177] Millard Fillmore (January 7, 1800 - March 8, 1874) became the president from 1850 to 1853 after Zachary Taylor died.
[178] Ibid., 17.
[179] The Captain William Morgan monument image is a drawing made from a 19th century photograph.
[180] Cardinal José Maria Caro Rodriguez, *The Mystery of Freemasonry Unveiled* (Santiago, Chile: Society of the Good Press, 1925, Second Edition), 160-161.
[181] Ibid.
[182] Pope Pius IX (13 May 1792 - 7 February 1878), born Giovanni Maria Mastai-Ferretti, led the Catholic Church from 16 June 1846 until his death. He was the longest-reigning elected Pope in the history of the Catholic Church.
[183] P. A. Berthe, trans. Lady Herbert, *Garcia Moreno: President of Ecuador: 1821 - 1875* (London: Burns & Oates, 1889), viii.
[184] Ibid and the Catholic Encyclopedia online at www.newadvent.org/cathen/06379b.htm.
[185] Cardinal José Maria Caro Rodriguez, *The Mystery of Freemasonry Unveiled* (Santiago, Chile: Society of the Good Press, 1925, Second Edition), 160-161.
[186] Ibid. When informed of the death of García Moreno, Pope Pius IX ordered a solemn Mass of Requiem to be celebrated in the Church of Santa Maria in Trastevere.
[187] Teach Peace Foundation October 2014 photograph from inside the Supreme Council, 33°, Ancient & Accepted Scottish Rite of Freemasonry, Southern Jurisdiction in Washington D.C.
[188] Dr. Theodore Graebner, *Is Masonry a Religion?* (Saint Louis, Missouri: Concordia Publishing House, 1946), 18-19.
[189] Former Masons disclosed in multiple books that the Mystic Shrine and their activities were crafted to lead people to believe Freemasonry was a charitable organization. Revelations of large percentages of charitable funds being retained or allocated for non-charitable purposes put pressure on Shriners to make changes. In 2000, Mystic Shrine membership was no longer limited to elite Freemasons, which resulted in an increase in the number of Masons supporting charitable activities.
[190] Teach Peace Foundation drawing of Freemasonry levels. This 2012 drawing is based on a 1929 drawing by a Freemason named I. Bernard Edelstein.

[191] Albert Pike sent a letter on July 14, 1889 to the twenty-three Supreme Councils of Freemasonry confirming Lucifer as their god. Pike is the person Palladium Freemasons worship to this day as a man-god Sovereign Pontiff of Universal Freemasonry.
[192] A letter written by General Albert Pike entitled "Instructions" on July 14, 1889, as recorded by A. C. De La Rive in La Femme et l'Enfant dans la Franc-Maconnerie Universelle, page 588.
[193] The Masonic Service Association of North America provides membership statistics online at www.msana.com/msastats.asp. The number of members in the U.S. and Canada of 1,373,453 in 2010 was the lowest since the Masonic Service Association began compiling statistics in 1924.
[194] Manly P. Hall, *The Secret Destiny of America* (Los Angeles, CA: The Philosophical Research Society, Inc., 1944), 45-46 in the 1991 edition. Hall was a 33rd degree Mason and is one of the most highly regarded people in Freemasonry. He wrote: "Wise men, the ancients believed, were a separate race, and to be born into this race it was necessary to develop the mind to a state of enlightened intelligence….It is this larger and coming race that will some day inherit the earth."
[195] Manly P. Hall, *The Lost Keys of Freemasonry* (Richmond: Macoy Publishing and Masonic Supply Company, 1923), pages 50-51 in the 2006 Jeremy P. Tarcher/Penguin edition.
[196] Ibid.
[197] The Greek and Roman versions of Isis include Aphrodite, Athena, Diana and Venus. Osiris reappears as Mercury, Poseidon and Zeus.
[198] For example, the password for the Master Mason, or third degree, is Tubalcain. Tubalcain is found in Genesis. Genesis 4:22 – "And Zillah, she also bare Tubalcain, an instructor of every artificer in brass and iron: and the sister of Tubalcain was Naamah." In Freemasonry, Tubalcain is the first A. in M. or the first artificer in metals.
[199] Albert Pike, *The Holy Triad*, Washington, D.C., 1873. Pike's perspective on Satan as evil and Lucifer as good are further illustrated by his criticism of this secret word. Additional information on this unholy triad is provided in Walton Hannah's *Darkness Visible* on page 35.
[200] Egyptian trinity symbols are also applicable. Creator father names of Osiris and Ra, respectively accompany preserver mother names of Isis and Maat, and destroyer son names of Horus and Thoth.
[201] Walton Hannah, *Darkness Visible: A Revelation and Interpretation of Freemasonry* (London: Augustine Press, 1952), frontispiece. The title of the book *Darkness Visible* is highly appropriate as the purpose of Freemasonry is to conceal how evil is organized and worshipped. The scrambled and

unscrambled Holy Royal Arch altar-top images are Teach Peace Foundation illustrations of an authentic altar-top.
[202] Ibid.
[203] Ibid.
[204] Ibid., 181. Walton Hannah published the Royal Arch rituals. The explanations of the Masonic meanings comes from Freemasonry and specifically their "Address of the First Chair Mystical Lecture." Christian and Hebrew scholars often use "Yahweh" instead of Jehovah as a correct name for God.
[205] Ibid.
[206] Ibid., 182.
[207] Ibid.
[208] Ibid., 181.
[209] Ibid.
[210] Ibid., 182.
[211] Ibid.
[212] Statistics Fraternal Societies, 57th edition (Rochester, NY: Fraternal Monitor, 1951). Over six thousand Masonic Lodges existed under the jurisdiction of the English Grand Lodge.
[213] Walton Hannah, *Darkness Visible: A Revelation and Interpretation of Freemasonry* (London: Augustine Press, 1952). Hanna's book was well known in England because it followed his provocative 1951 article.
[214] The Knights Templar secret society practiced a mystery religion that managed to infiltrate the Catholic Church around 1129. King Philip IV of France rounded up Knights Templar members on October 13, 1307. Pope Clement V disbanded the Order in 1312.
Pike was the Grand Master of the Luciferian Order of the Palladium, also known as the Sovereign Council of Wisdom. This group is claimed to have started in Paris in 1737 but as Pike explained in a quote earlier in this chapter, the secret society is much older.
[215] One of the many pyramid or triangle shapes visible in the Washington, D.C. city design is highlighted in this Teach Peace Foundation drawing. The author's book, *Defeating the Brotherhood of Death*, explains Freemasons designed Washington, D.C. with many symbols hidden in plain sight.
[216] Charleston is 32.7 North and Baghdad is 33.1 North. In the occult religion of Freemasons and the Brotherhood, geographic location is important for harnessing the earth's energy.
[217] John Daniel, *Scarlet and the Beast: A History of the War between English and French Freemasonry* (Tyler, Texas: JKI Publishing, 1995 Second Edition, Volume 1 and page 331).
[218] William Guy Carr, R.D., *Pawns in the Game* (Willowdale, Ontario, Canada: Federation of Christian Layman, 1954), xv. Pike established three

New and Reformed Palladian Rite Supreme Councils. Pike led the Supreme Council in Charleston, South Carolina. Mazzini led the Supreme Council in Rome, Italy. Otto von Bismarck led the Supreme Council in Berlin, Germany. Henry Palmerston died in the early years of Palladism. Palmerston service to the Brotherhood included helping orchestrate British military interventions and establishing the basis of modern corporations. The Brotherhood needed corporate fronts to possess rights previously only assigned to humans in order to effectively shield inner circle Brotherhood families in the 20th and 21st century. One of Palmerston's major accomplishments for the Brotherhood was The Companies Act 1862.

[219] Giuseppe Mazzini (June 22, 1805 - March 10, 1872) helped create the Palladium-level.

[220] John Daniel, *Scarlet and the Beast: A History of the War between English and French Freemasonry* (Tyler, Texas: JKI Publishing, 1995 Second Edition, Volume 1 and page 331). Daniel explains the acronym M.A.F.I.A. is Italian for Mazzini autorizza furti, incendi, e attentati or Mazzini authorizes theft, arson, and kidnapping.

[221] Efforts to deny the letter's existence are claimed to have started on April 23, 1885.

[222] Cardinal José Maria Caro Rodriguez (June 23, 1866 - December 4, 1958), *The Mystery of Freemasonry Unveiled* (Santiago, Chile: Society of the Good Press, 1925, Second Edition), 19. Cardinal Rodriguez states a former Freemason who used the name Copin-Albancelli was one of several insiders who revealed Masonic secrets. Cardinal Rodriguez wrote that Copin-Albancelli "on the eve of ascending to another higher degree, withdrew also and devoted himself to revealing the danger which Masonry held for his country, France, and for Christian civilization."

[223] Ibid., 86, 118 and 119.

[224] Ibid. On page 118 Cardinal Rodriquez explained that Albert Pike's letter was in the British Museum Library. Proving Pike did write the letter by analyzing the original letter is difficult. Decades after Cardinal Rodriguez's identification of the location of the original letter, William Carr attempted to obtain the letter and was informed by the British Museum Library that there was no record of the letter. Carr raised the possibility that the Brotherhood had all evidence of the letter's existence at the British Museum Library erased after Cardinal Rodriguez's book was published in 1925. Carr wrote on page 39 in his book *Satan, Prince of this World* with an unusual footnote: "The Keeper of Manuscripts recently informed the author that this letter is NOT catalogued in the British Museum Library. It seems strange that a man of Cardinal Rodriguez's knowledge should have said that it WAS in 1925."

225 *The Cause of World Unrest* (New York and London, G. P. Putnam's Sons The Knickerbocker Press, 1920), 50-51. *The Cause of World Unrest* was written by an anonymous author and published by G. P. Putnam's Sons in 1920. Albert Pike is explained as authoring the 1871 letter to Mazzini with the help of ten Ancients of the Grand Lodge of the Supreme Orient of Charleston.
226 Pike's letter is explained in *Le Palladisme* on page 186 published by Falque in 1895.
227 Ibid., 20.
228 Hoaxers Dr. Karl Hacks and Leo Taxil helped Freemasonry by promoting false information that served to conceal Palladism. The hoax was revealed in 1897 by Taxil. Taxil's confession of orchestrating the hoax is online at www.teachpeace.com/leotaxilconfession.htm.
Edith Starr Miller was a secret society insider and wrote *Occult Theocracy* years after the 1897 hoax. She also supported the claim that Domenico Margiotta was a 33rd degree Freemason.
229 Teach Peace Foundation October 2014 photograph of Albert Pike inside the Albert Pike room in the temple for the Supreme Council, 33°, Ancient & Accepted Scottish Rite of Freemasonry, Southern Jurisdiction in Washington D.C.
230 Cardinal José Maria Caro Rodriguez, *The Mystery of Freemasonry Unveiled* (Santiago, Chile: Society of the Good Press, 1925, Second Edition), 118.
231 Ibid.
232 William Guy Carr, R.D., *Pawns in the Game* (Willowdale, Ontario, Canada: Federation of Christian Layman, 1954), xv.
233 Ibid.
234 Sir John A. Cockburn, *Freemasonry; What, Whence, Why, Whither* (London, England: Masonic Record Limited, 1923), 24.
235 Ibid., 24-25.
236 The Office of the Sacred Congregation for the Doctrine of the Faith, 26 November 1983 and online at www.vatican.va/roman_curia/congregations/cfaith/documents/rc_con_cfaith_doc_19831126_declaration-masonic_en.html. This declaration on Masonic Associations approved by Pope John Paul II states: "Therefore the Church's negative judgment in regard to Masonic association remains unchanged since their principles have always been considered irreconcilable with the doctrine of the Church and therefore membership in them remains forbidden. The faithful who enrol[l] in Masonic associations are in a state of grave sin and may not receive Holy Communion."
237 Rupert Cornwell, *God's Banker: An Account of the Life and Death of Roberto Calvi* (London, England: Victor Gollancz Ltd., 1984). The

Freemasonry is "Satan's synagogue" statement is also explained by Paul A. Fisher in *Behind the Lodge Door: Church, State and Freemasonry in America* on page 22 in the 1994 TAN Books and Publishers edition.

[238] Pope Leo XIII (*Humanum Genus*), 1884. Pope Leo XIII used St. Augustine's image of the two cities, the City of man and the City of God, to warn organized evil would incite revolutions to advance world government and attempt to destroy the Catholic Church via modernism.

[239] Pope Leo XIII based on a circa 1900 public domain photograph (unknown photographer).

[240] Pope Leo XIII (*Humanum Genus*), 1884. The Latin version is on page 3 and this English text is on page 19. The 1884 encyclical and Albert Pike's response are available online at www.teachpeace.com/humanum%20 genus.htm.

[241] Ibid.

[242] Ibid. Teach Peace Foundation 2015 photograph.

[243] Response by Albert Pike, "A Reply for The Ancient and Accepted Scottish Rite of Freemasonry to The Letter Human Genus of Pope Leo XIII," Grand Orient of Charleston, South Carolina, 1884, 3-4. Pike's complete response is online at www.teachpeace.com/humanum%20 genus.htm.

[244] *Ekklesia*, no. 48, 4 December 1933, Athens, Greece. Walton Hannah published it in *Darkness Visible: A Revelation and Interpretation of Freemasonry* (London: Augustine Press, 1952), 70-73. Words are not changed either for capitalization or American English. This means the *Ekklesia* text provided here will show the translation as provided by Fr. Krivoshein (e.g., masonic vs. Masonic as capitalized in the other sections of this book).

[245] The Lutheran Church-Missouri Synod (LCMS) is the second-largest Lutheran body in the United States after the Evangelical Lutheran Church in America. The Synod was founded in 1847 in Chicago by German-American immigrants.

[246] Walton Hannah, *Darkness Visible: A Revelation and Interpretation of Freemasonry* (London: Augustine Press, 1952), 76. Hannah notes a complete account of the American Lutheran condemnation of Freemasonry is provided in a series of two articles. "To Join or not to Join" which appeared in *The Lutheran Witness* (Concordia Publishing House, St. Louis, Missouri) on July 10 and 24, 1951, by Dr. Paul M. Bretscher, Chairman of the Commission on Fraternal Organizations.

[247] Dr. Theodore Graebner, *Is Masonry a Religion?* (Saint Louis, Missouri: Concordia Publishing House, 1946).

[248] The Catholic Church "Declaration on Masonic Associations" is online at www.teachpeace.com/library.htm and www.vatican.va/roman_curia/congregations/cfaith/documents/rc_con_cfaith_doc_19831126_declaration-masonic_en.html.
[249] Minutes of the Methodist Conference, 1927. Walton Hannah provides this and more information in *Darkness Visible* on page 75.
[250] Walton Hannah, *Darkness Visible: A Revelation and Interpretation of Freemasonry* (London: Augustine Press, 1952), 75.
[251] Pio of Pietrelcina, O.F.M. Cap. is best as Saint Padre Pio (May 25, 1887 - September 23, 1968). On June 16, 2002, he was canonized by Pope John Paul II.
[252] Some of his spiritual gifts include reading souls, prophecy, healing people, and the gift of conversions.
[253] The odour of sanctity is a specific scent that is often compared to flowers and emanates from the bodies of saints.
[254] Dr. Franco Adessa, *Who is Father Luigi Villa?* (Oconomowoc, WI: The Apostolate of Our Lady of Good Success), 2011 edition, 4. Dr. Adessa's book is online at http://padrepioandchiesaviva.com/uploads/Chi___don_Villa_OK_en.pdf.
[255] Cardinal Alfredo Ottaviani assigned the task of identifying Masonic infiltration in the Catholic Church to Fr. Villa.
[256] Ibid., 6. Dr. Adessa worked with Fr. Villa for more than twenty-years.
[257] Giovanni Battista Enrico Antonio Maria Montini (26 September 1897 - 6 August 1978).
[258] Fr. Luigi Villa Th.D., *Paul VI beatified?* (Oconomowoc, Wisconsin: The Apostolate of Our Lady of Good Success), 2009. Earlier editions were made available by other publishers.
[259] Bro. Charles Madden, O.F.M. Conv., *Freemasonry: Mankind's Hidden Enemy* (Rockford, Illinois: Tan Books and Publishers, Inc., 1995). Pages 1 and 10 in the 2005 Second Edition. He writes that the 1983 Code of Canon Law confirmed "membership in the Masons is forbidden to all Catholics and the membership is a serious sin which automatically denies Holy Communion to any Catholic who joins them."
[260] Ibid., 20.
[261] Isaiah 28:16 - "Therefore thus saith the Lord God, Behold, I lay in Zion for a foundation a stone, a tried stone, a precious corner stone, a sure foundation: he that believeth shall not make haste."
[262] Walton Hannah, *Darkness Visible: A Revelation and Interpretation of Freemasonry* (London: Augustine Press, 1952), 78.
[263] David Rockefeller, *Memoirs* (New York: Random House, 2002), 405.
[264] David Rockefeller, Sr. (June 12, 1915) is the current patriarch of the Rockefeller family and one of the most visible members of the New World

Order. He replaced his father, John D. Rockefeller, Jr., who also served the Brotherhood of Death.

[265] David Rockefeller, *Memoirs* (New York: Random House, 2002).

[266] A comprehensive list of insider and non-insider authors is available online at www.vigilantchristian.org/insiderdisclosure.html.

[267] Carroll Quigley (1910 - 1977) had a fatal heart attack on January 3, 1977. His obituary is online at www.teachpeace.com/carrollquigleyobituary.htm.

[268] John Emerich Edward Dalberg-Acton (January 10, 1834 - June 19, 1902) was an English Catholic historian often known as Lord Acton. He observed: "Power tends to corrupt, and absolute power corrupts absolutely. Great men are almost always bad men."

[269] Carroll Quigley, *Tragedy and Hope* (New York: The Macmillan Company, 1974 second printing), 950.

[270] Carroll Quigley, *The Anglo-American Establishment* (San Pedro, California: GSG Associates, written in 1949 but published posthumously in 1981), vii.

[271] Samuel L. Blumenfeld, "JFK Jr., Clinton and Quigley," *WND*, 29 July 1999 and online at www.wnd.com/1999/07/2807/. Also Scott McLemee's "The Quigley Cult" article published by *George Magazine* in December 1996.

[272] Bill Clinton's July 16, 1992 acceptance speech is online at www.teachpeace.com/billclintonthanksquigley.htm.

[273] Photo by the U.S. Army Signal Corps. Courtesy of the Harry S. Truman Library in Independence, Missouri. Picture taken on July 25, 1945. The Truman Library has this photo online at www.trumanlibrary.org/photographs/view.php?id=13342. Winston Leonard Spencer Churchill (30 November 1874 - 24 January 1965) became a Mason at Studholme Lodge 1591 on May 24, 1901. The 1941 book *A Picture of Life 1872 - 1940* by Charles Clive Bigham Mersey and published in London by John Murray explains Churchill's Masonic membership on page 188. Mersey wrote: "... that month I was initiated as a free mason at Studholme Lodge (1591). While waiting for the ceremony I walked round and round Golden Square with Winston Churchill, another candidate ..." Churchill passed the second degree on July 19, 1901 and the third Master Mason degree on March 5, 1902. Winston Churchill's secret society involvement is also confirmed by Freemasons. For an example read the article "Brother Winston: Churchill as a Freemason," *MQ Magazine*, Issue 3, October 2002. Online at www.mqmagazine.co.uk/issue-3/p-06.php.

[274] Joseph Stalin (December 6, 1878 - March 5, 1953) was born Iosif Vissarionovich Dzhugashvili (also known as Soso Djugashvili). Joseph Stalin's rise to power with Brotherhood of Death New York financial and

Masonic support is ignored in most historical accounts. Stalin was in Vienna in 1913 meeting with Freemasons and other Brotherhood of Death agents. At this same point in time and living close to Stalin were future Nazi leader Adolf Hitler, Yugoslav leader Marshal Tito, and Russian revolutionary Leon Trotsky. For more information read the April 17, 2013 *BBC* report "1913: When Hitler, Trotsky, Tito, Freud and Stalin all lived in the same place" online at www.bbc.co.uk/news/magazine-21859771. Stalin's organized crime involvement and Brotherhood of Death service is irrefutable although his Freemasonry membership is denied by official Masonic spokespeople. Freemasons make a tremendous effort to suppress memberships of people universally perceived as evil. The basis for the claim that Stalin was not a Freemason is often founded on the false notion that he did not believe in God and therefore he could not be a Freemason. While it is true that Freemasons must believe in a god, it is also true that in 1894 Joseph Djugashvili entered the seminary seeking to be a priest. Stalin in the years up to 1913 did believe in a god and throughout his life he faithfully served the god of Freemasonry.

[275] Edvard Radzinsky, *Stalin: The First In-depth Biography Based on Explosive New Documents from Russia's Secret Archives* (New York, New York: First Anchor Books, September 1997), 6, 232 and 237. Stalin's Brotherhood of Death "Order of Sword-Bearers" secret society followed rituals and practices similar to Freemasonry.

[276] Robert Weinberg, *Stalin's Forgotten Zion: Birobidzhan and the Making of a Soviet Jewish Homeland: An Illustrated History, 1928 - 1996* (Berkeley and Los Angeles, California: University of California Press, 1998). In 1934 Stalin established the Jewish Autonomous Region, the first Jewish State before the Jewish State. When Brotherhood of Death plans to create a homeland in Palestine became tangible in the 1930s, Stalin destroyed much of the framework of the nascent Jewish homeland with the purges of 1936 - 1938. The Brotherhood of Death purpose was to eliminate the claim that a viable Jewish homeland existed without seizing Palestinian land.

[277] Simon Sebag Montefiore, *Stalin: The Court of the Red Tsar* (New York, New York: Vintage Books, 2003), xix and 85. Montefiore observed on page xix: "I believe the placing of Stalin and his oligarchs in their idiosyncratic Bolshevik context as members of a military-religious 'order of sword-bearers' explains much of the inexplicable." On page 85 he wrote: "Stalin's 'order of the sword-bearers' resembled the Knights Templars, or even the theocracy of the Iranian Ayatollahs, more than any traditional secular movement...They regarded themselves as special 'noble-blooded' people."

[278] The Tsar's Secret Police were created in 1866 to stop Freemasons and other Brotherhood of Death "secret organizations" after a failed assassination attempt on Alexander II. The formal name was the Department

on Protecting the Order and Public Peace. A second assassination attempt failed and prompted the creation of the Department of State Police in 1880. On March 13, 1881, the Brotherhood of Death assassinated Alexander II. Three assassins from the Brotherhood of Death front Narodnaya Volya, which means the "People's Will," worked to murder Alexander II. The first assassin, Nikolai Rysakov, threw a bomb at Alexander II's carriage. While one person was killed and several people were injured, the carriage kept Alexander unharmed. The second assassin, Ignacy Hryniewiecki, threw a bomb at Alexander II after he stepped out of the carriage. Alexander II was killed. The third assassin, Ivan Emelyanov, was captured. He did not use the briefcase bomb he carried because Hryniewiecki's bomb accomplished their mission.

[279] Teach Peace illustration based on the Tsarist police mug shot photograph of Joseph Stalin in the 1911 - 1913 timeframe.

[280] Ibid. Stalin was arrested several times between 1906 and 1914. It is noteworthy that the occult dimension involving Stalin even includes a story that precedes his birth. Edvard Radzinsky wrote: "The Devil Amiran...Amiran was a Caucasian variant of Prometheus, but he was an evil Prometheus, a demon of destruction chained up somewhere on the summit of the Caucasus range. There was an ancient custom in Gori: once a year all the blacksmiths hammered on their anvils in the night so that this terrible spirit of destruction would not descend from his cliff. But the Blacksmiths hammered in vain" because Stalin was born on December 6, 1878. For more information read, Edvard Radzinsky, *Stalin: The First In-depth Biography Based on Explosive New Documents from Russia's Secret Archives* (New York, New York: First Anchor Books, September 1997), 20.

[281] Robert Payne, *The Rise and Fall of Stalin* (New York, New York: Simon and Schuster, 1965), 68. Payne met multiple top Brotherhood of Death leaders. In 1937 he met Adolf Hitler and during World War II he met key allied leaders while serving as a British Army Intelligence officer. The name Stalin is a combination of the Russian "stal" meaning steel and "Lenin." Source: Jewish Virtual Library and additional information is online at www.jewishvirtuallibrary.org/jsource/biography/stalin.html.

[282] The Masonic oath helps explain why on November 17, 1933, Freemason Roosevelt was the first United States president to formally recognize the Communist Soviet Union as a legitimate nation. Many people were surprised because the atrocities occurring under Stalin's totalitarian rule were well known.

[283] Even as soon as the late 1950s the Soviets wanted to distance Stalin's occult activities and direct links to Brotherhood of Death agents (e.g., Henry L. Stimson and Oscar Lange) from the Communist party. Stalin had

committed so many acts in the service of Satan, that in 1961 Nikita Khrushchev (April 15, 1894 - September 11, 1971) oversaw the removal of Stalin's body from Lenin's mausoleum. Khrushchev decreed on February 25, 1956: "The further retention in the mausoleum of the sarcophagus with the bier of J. V. Stalin shall be recognized as inappropriate since the serious violations by Stalin of Lenin's precepts, abuse of power, mass repressions against honorable Soviet people, and other activities in the period of the personality cult make it impossible to leave the bier with his body in the mausoleum of V. I. Lenin." Khrushchev's speech, now called "the Secret Speech" followed the end of the public session of the 20th Party Congress. The Brotherhood of Death had the speech, also called the report "On the Cult and Personality and Its Consequences," published in *The New York Times* on June 5, 1956. The "Top Secret" Soviet document was given to the *The New York Times* by the CIA which reported the transcript was obtained by Israel intelligence. The full text was published in the magazine Известия ЦК КПСС in March 1989. The catalyst for the speech was the Pospelov Commission which was authorized in 1955 to investigate the 1934 assassinations of leaders including delegates at the 17th Congress of the Communist Party of the Soviet Union. One example is Sergei Mironovich Kirov (March 27, 1886 - December 1, 1934), the most powerful Party leader next to Stalin, was assassinated. Noteworthy are the Brotherhood of Death 1934 actions involving Smedley Butler in the United States and Adolf Hitler in Germany. For more information, pages 42 and 43 in *Vigilant Christian III: The Occult Religion of the 9/11 Attackers* is recommended.

[284] Gary Allen and Larry Abraham, *None Dare Call It Conspiracy* (Cutchogue, New York: Buccaneer Books, 1972), 83 and 84. The Bolshevik Revolution was orchestrated by the Brotherhood of Death. Specifically, the historical record reveals the violence was funded by the Rothschilds, Rockefellers, Schiffs, Warburgs, Morgans, Harrimans, and Milners. On page 83 Allen and Abraham explain how Stalin was funded. "According to his grandson John, Jacob Schiff, long time associate of the Rothschilds, financed the Communist Revolution in Russia to the tune of $20 million. According to a report on file with the State Department, his firm, Kuhn Loeb and Co. bankrolled the first five year plan for Stalin. Schiff's partner and relative, Paul Warburg, engineered the establishment of the Federal Reserve System while on the Kuhn Loeb payroll, Schiff's descendants are active in the Council on Foreign Relations today." Allen and Abraham continued to explain Stalin's secret service to the Brotherhood of Death on page 84. "But obviously these men have no fear of international Communism. It is only logical to assume that if they financed it and do not fear it, it must be because they control it. Can there be any other explanation that makes sense? Remember that for over 150 years it has been standard operating

procedure of the Rothschilds and their allies to control both sides of every conflict. You must have an "enemy" if you are going to collect from the King. The East-West balance-of-power politics is used as one of the main excuses for the socialization of America. Although it was not their main purpose, by nationalization of Russia the Insiders bought themselves an enormous piece of real estate, complete with mineral rights, for somewhere between $30 and $40 million. Lord Alfred Milner, wealthy English man and front man for the Rothschilds, served as paymaster for the International bankers in Petrograd during the Bolshevik Revolution. Milner later headed secret society known as The Round Table which was dedicated to establishing a world government whereby a clique of super-rich financiers would control the world under the guise of Socialism. The American subsidiary of this conspiracy is called the Council on Foreign Relations and was started by, and is still controlled by Leftist international bankers."

[285] Additional information on the CFR is provided in *Vigilant Christian I: The New World Order* in Appendix C. The Council on Foreign Relations maintains a website at www.cfr.org.

[286] Carroll Quigley, *Tragedy and Hope* (New York, New York: The Macmillan Company, 1966), 951.

[287] John F. Kennedy confirmed in a letter in 1960 that he was at that time a member of and a "longtime subscriber" to the CFR journal, *Foreign Affairs*.

[288] The Council on Foreign Relations membership roster is available online at www.cfr.org/about/membership/roster.html.

[289] Michael Joseph Morell was the acting Director of the CIA for Barack Obama two times (July 1, 2011 to September 6, 2011 and November 9, 2012 to March 8, 2013).

[290] Obama's first CIA Director, Leon Panetta is an NWO secret society insider but not a CFR member. Panetta was replaced by CFR member David Petraeus.

[291] Donald Rumsfeld was counted twice because he served as Defense Secretary in two separate administrations.

[292] Neal Steven Wolin (born December 9, 1961) was the acting Secretary of the Treasury from May 18, 2009 to August 31, 2013).

[293] Peter Martin Phillips, *A Relative Advantage: Sociology of the San Francisco Bohemian Club, 1994,* Doctoral Dissertation (1994), 11 and online at http://library.sonoma.edu/regional/faculty/phillips/bohemianindex.php.

[294] Cremation of Care is a Luciferian ceremony using an owl statue to represent the god Moloch. A documentary called *Dark Secrets: Inside Bohemian Grove* by Alex Jones shows the Cremation of Care ritual. In the summer of 2000, Jones and a cameraman secretly videotaped the occult

ceremony. The religious dimension of the Brotherhood of Death is explained in *Vigilant Christian III: The Occult Religion of the 9/11 Attackers*.
[295] Teach Peace Foundation 2013 illustration based on a Cremation of Care ceremony photograph.
[296] John van der Zee, *The Greatest Men's Party on Earth: Inside the Bohemian Grove* (New York, New York: Harcourt Brace Jovanovich, 1974), 88. An example of an Old Guard president is Herbert Hoover. He was inducted into the Old Guard on March 19, 1953.
[297] Teach Peace Foundation 2013 illustration of the Brotherhood of Death Bohemian Grove owl symbol. Chapter 9 explains the owl symbol and can be found hidden in plain sight on many objects including the dollar bill and the U.S. Capitol.
[298] Teach Peace Foundation 2013 illustration based on a photograph of a Bohemian Grove sign.
[299] John van der Zee, *The Greatest Men's Party on Earth: Inside the Bohemian Grove* (New York, New York: Harcourt Brace Jovanovich, 1974), 111-126.
[300] The official Bilderberg Group website at http://bilderbergmeetings.org/meeting_2012.html. The public statement is: "Bilderberg takes its name from the hotel in Holland, where the first meeting took place in May 1954. That pioneering meeting grew out of the concern expressed by leading citizens on both sides of the Atlantic that Western Europe and North America were not working together as closely as they should on common problems of critical importance."
[301] Carroll Quigley, *Tragedy and Hope* (New York, New York: The Macmillan Company, 1966), 951.
[302] The Trilateral Commission membership list shows David Rockefeller as their founder and honorary chairman online at www.trilateral.org/.
[303] Anthony C. Sutton and Patrick M. Wood, *Trilaterals Over Washington, Volume I and II* (Scottsdale, AZ: The August Corporation, 1978 and 1981 respectively). The front cover of what has been the best work for over 30 years explaining the secret purpose of the Trilateral Commission is shown. The Brotherhood of Death attempted to use the chaos of the Great Depression to provide momentum for technocracy. Technocracy started in 1932 with its academic center at Columbia University. This alternative economic system is often now called a Carbon Currency system.
[304] Barry M. Goldwater, *With No Apologies: The Personal and Political Memoirs of United States Senator Barry M. Goldwater,* (New York, NY: William Morrow and Company, 1979), 128.
[305] Ibid., 284-285.
[306] Eduard Pestel and Mihajlo Mesarovic, "Regionalised [Regionalized] and Adaptive Model of the Global World System," 17 September 1973.

[307] Teach Peace Foundation drawing based on the Club of Rome Ten World Regions map.
[308] The Council on Foreign Relations regions are 1 (America, Canada and Mexico) and 2 (the European Union). The Trilateral Commission Pacific Asian Group regions are 3 (Japan), part of 4 (Australia, and New Zealand but not South Africa), 9 (South and Southeast Asia including India), and 10 (China including Mongolia).
[309] The 2014 Teach Peace Foundation illustration shows the inner circle and outer layers.
[310] David Rockefeller, *Memoirs* (New York: Random House, 2002), 405.
[311] Tidwell, Hall, and Gaddy, *Come Retribution: The Confederate Secret Service and the Assassination of Lincoln* (University Press of Mississippi Jackson, 1988), 26. August Belmont, Sr. (December 8, 1813 - November 24, 1890) service to the Brotherhood of Death is explained in *Vigilant Christian I: The New World Order.*
[312] Edward Mandell House (July 26, 1858 - March 28, 1938) was the son of a top Brotherhood of Death agent, Thomas William House, Senior.
[313] Walter Isaacson and Evan Thomas, *The Wise Men: Six Friends and the World They Made* (New York, New York: Simon & Schuster, 1986), 28. Stimson was the Secretary of War for William Howard Taft, Franklin Roosevelt and Harry Truman. He also served as Secretary of State for Herbert Hoover.
[314] David F. Schmitz, Henry L. Stimson: The First Wise Man (Wilmington, Delaware: Scholarly Resources, Inc., 2001), xv.
[315] David F. Schmitz, *Henry L. Stimson: The First Wise Man* (Wilmington, Delaware: Scholarly Resources, Inc., 2001), 173. On page 178 Stimson shines light that the atomic bomb was used to fit Japan into one of ten world regions. He wrote in his diary on April 25, 1945 that the key was "the proper use of this weapon." If it could be found, "we would have the opportunity to bring the world into a pattern in which the peace of the world and our civilization can be saved."
[316] Ibid. Transcript of a June 17, 1943 telephone conversation between Henry L. Stimson and Harry S. Truman. Truman in his *Memoirs*: *Year of Decisions* (New York, New York: Konechy & Konecky, 1955) offers slightly different phraseology with the same meaning on pages 10-11 in Volume 1. Truman wrote Stimson said: "I can't tell you what it is, but it is the greatest project in the history of the world. It is most top secret. Many of the people who are actually engaged in the work have no idea what it is, and we who do would appreciate your not going into those plants." Truman responded: "I'll take you at your word" and "I'll order the investigations into

---

those plants called off." Truman provides his account for the years 1946 - 1952 in Volume 2 titled *Memoirs: Years of Trial and Hope*.

[317] Ibid., Elting E. Morison, *Turmoil and Tradition* (Atheneum, 1964), 511.

[318] Ibid. James F. Byrnes wrote in *Speaking Frankly* (New York, New York: Harper & Brothers Publishers, 1947) his surprise the atomic bomb project remained secret. He wrote on page 259: "As a matter of fact, it was always amazing to me that the project did not become more generally known. It also was surprising that the Congress was willing to appropriate approximately two billion dollars without demanding more information on the use to which it was being put."

[319] Henry L. Stimson, *Henry L. Stimson Diaries* (New Haven, CT: Sterling Memorial Library, Yale University), 13 March 1944. Stimson also wrote Truman: "talks smoothly but he acts meanly."

[320] David F. Schmitz, *Henry L. Stimson: The First Wise Man* (Wilmington, Delaware: Scholarly Resources, Inc., 2001), 178. Truman in his *Memoirs*: *Year of Decisions* (NewYork, New York: Konechy & Konecky, 1955), 87 and 419. Stimson's statement reveals that he sent troops to fight the bloodiest battle of the Pacific, the invasion of Okinawa, for reasons other than military necessity. The massive loss of life at Okinawa served to establish the false notion the atomic bombs saved American lives.

[321] Ibid., 182. Stimson knew Nagasaki was of great religious significance to Christians and tried to conceal this fact with the cover story that he did not want to be the person responsible for destroying Kyoto due to its religious significance to the Japanese people. Stimson and the Brotherhood of Death plan was to have bad weather at Kokura be the reason Nagasaki was destroyed. Their plan was frustrated by good weather prompting General Leslie M. Groves to write: "At Kokura, they found that visual bombing was not possible, although the weather plane had reported that it should be."

[322] Martin Sherwin, *A World Destroyed: Destroyed: Hiroshima and Its Legacies* (Stanford University Press, August 11, 2003), 230. Truman in his *Memoirs*: *Year of Decisions* (NewYork, New York: Konechy & Konecky, 1955), 420-421 wrote that he learned of the target list from Stimson and approved the list. Truman literally rubber stamped what Stimson told him to do. Truman's memoir attempts to portray him as more powerful than Stimson and conceal the Brotherhood of Death objective to destroy Nagasaki using the only version of the atomic bomb proven to work. Neither Truman, Stimson, Baruch or any other Brotherhood of Death secret society member mentioned Nagasaki was of great religious significance to Japan's Christians. Truman's wrote: "Before the selected targets were approved as proper for military purposes, I personally went over them in detail with Stimson, Marshall, and Arnold, and we discussed the matter of timing and the final choice of the first target. General Spaatz, who commanded the

Strategic Air Forces, which would deliver the bomb on the target, was given some latitude as to when and on which of the four targets the bomb would be dropped. That was necessary because of weather and other operational considerations. In orders to instruct General Spaatz that the first bomb would be dropped as soon after August 3 as weather would permit. The order to General Carl Spaatz read as follows:

24 July 1945

To: General Carl Spaatz
Commanding General
United States Army Strategic Air Forces

1. The 509 Composite Group, 20th Air Force will deliver its first special bomb as soon as weather will permit visual bombing after about 3 August 1945 on one of the targets: Hiroshima, Kokura, Niigata and Nagasaki. To carry military and civilian scientific personnel from the War Department to observe and record the effects of the explosion of the bomb, additional aircraft will accompany the airplane carrying the bomb. The observing planes will stay several miles distant from the point of impact of the bomb.
2. Additional bombs will be delivered on the above targets as soon as made ready by the project staff. Further instructions will be issued concerning targets other than those listed above.
3. Dissemination of any and all information concerning the use of the weapon against Japan is reserved to the Secretary of War and the President of the United States. No communiqué on the subject or release of information will be issued by Commanders in the field without specific prior authority. Any news stories will be sent to the War Department for special clearance.
4. The foregoing directive is issued to you by direction and with the approval of the Secretary of War and the Chief of Staff, U.S.A. It is desired that you personally deliver one copy of this directive to General MacArthur and one copy to Admiral Nimitz for their information. /s/ Thos. T. Handy, General, GSC, Acting Chief of Staff.

[323] Bernard Baruch, *My Own Story* (New York, New York: Henry Holt and Company, 1957). Bernard Baruch's father, Simon Baruch, was a Brotherhood of Death spy during the American Civil War.

[324] Ibid., 107-108.

[325] Ibid. The inside information tip was from Arthur Housman and signaled the U.S. victory in the Spanish American War. Baruch was told on July 3, 1898 that Admiral Winfield Scott Schley (9 October 1839 - 2 October 1911) had destroyed the Spanish fleet at Santiago.

[326] Ibid., 108.

[327] W. L. White, *Bernard Baruch: Portrait of a Citizen* (New York, New York: Harcourt, Brace and Company, 1950), 47-48.
[328] Bernard Baruch, *The Public Years* (New York, New York: Holt, Rinehart and Winston, 1960), 91-109.
[329] Walter Isaacson and Evan Thomas, *The Wise Men: Six Friends and the World They Made* (New York, New York: Simon & Schuster, 1986), 28.
[330] Teach Peace Foundation 2013 illustration based on a World Wide Photos picture showing Winston Churchill, Bernard Baruch and Dwight Eisenhower meeting at Baruch's New York apartment in January 1952. The photograph of this illustration is between pages 146 and 147 in the 1960 memoir, *Baruch: The Public Years*.
[331] A. K. Chesterton, *The New Unhappy Lords: An Exposure of Power Politics* (London, England: The Candour Publishing Company, 1965). Page 35 in the August 2013 Fifth Edition.
[332] Ibid., 35. As President, Dwight Eisenhower attended the dedication of a New York park from land Baruch donated in 1939. The park, Baruch Playground, is at the corner of Baruch Place and Mangin Street in Manhattan. Eisenhower's Jewish heritage but rejection of Judaism combined with his participation in Bohemian Grove rituals helped contribute to his attainment of worldly power.
[333] Teach Peace Foundation 2013 illustration based on a the official 1967 White House portrait of Dwight Eisenhower by James Anthony Wills.
[334] A. K. Chesterton, *The New Unhappy Lords: An Exposure of Power Politics* (London, England: The Candour Publishing Company, 1965), page 36 in the 1970 third edition.
[335] Ibid.
[336] Samuel Prescott Bush (October 4, 1863 - February 8, 1948) was the father of Prescott Sheldon Bush (May 15, 1895 - October 8, 1972). In 1918, Samuel Prescott Bush was selected by Bernard Baruch to be the chief of the Ordnance, Small Arms, and Ammunition Section of the War Industries Board.
[337] Bernard Baruch, *The Public Years* (New York, New York: Holt, Rinehart and Winston, 1960), 357-382. On page 358 Baruch notes: "I have never forgotten the sense of awe I felt when I learned the meaning and implications of those gigantic and terrifying clouds which spread in evil splendor over Hiroshima and Nagasaki."
Bernard Baruch, *My Own Story* (New York, New York: Henry Holt and Company, 1957).
Baruch served the Brotherhood of Death after the atomic bombs were detonated. His memoirs explain his role controlling atomic energy as the first United States representative to the United Nations Atomic Energy Commission.

[338] David F. Schmitz, *Henry L. Stimson: The First Wise Man* (Wilmington, Delaware: Scholarly Resources, Inc., 2001), 168 for information about Hopkins service to Stimson. For Hopkins service to Baruch, The Harry L. Hopkins Papers: Series I - Correspondence, Box 1 and Folder 30, record of Bernard Baruch communications from September 27, 1937 to May 1, 1944. For Hopkins May 1945 meeting with Joseph Stalin and service to Brotherhood of Death, *From Major Jordan's Diaries* and pages 215 and 269-270. Major Jordan, not knowing Harry Hopkins worked for Bernard Baruch and the Brotherhood of Death wrote: "He was Administer of Lend-Lease. The law under which he operated was at no time submitted to any court for interpretation or test, and therefore it was he who "construed" the law, he who decided what we supplied Russia under Lend-Lease, and he himself tells us, addressing Marshal Stalin directly, that he construed the law liberally in sending non-military items to Stalin's aid."

[339] Major George Racey Jordan, *From Major Jordan's Diaries* (New York, New York: Harcourt, Brace and Company, January 1, 1952), 24-26 and 30-38. Harry Lloyd Hopkins was President Roosevelt's chief diplomatic advisor. He was the top U.S. official charged with dealing with Soviet officials during World War II. On page 269 Major Jordon explains Harry Hopkins directed the shipment of over $11 billion in lend-lease aid to the Soviet Union. Hopkins work providing Top Secret U.S. communication intelligence to the Soviet Union is explained in *Vigilant Christian II: Preventing an American Hiroshima.*

[340] Bernard Baruch, *The Public Years* (New York, New York: Holt, Rinehart and Winston, 1960), 388. On April 16, 1947 Bernard Baruch gave a speech given during the unveiling of his portrait in the South Carolina House of Representatives and described relations between the United States and the Soviet Union as a "Cold War." Throughout the Cold War relatively few people understood the Brotherhood of Death had financed the creation of the Soviet Union and played "capitalists" against "communists" to conceal their control of politicians, military leaders, media officials, corporations, and interlocking secret societies.

[341] Major George Racey Jordan, *From Major Jordan's Diaries* (New York, New York: Harcourt, Brace and Company, January 1, 1952), 5-6, 32-35, 38-39, 86, 96-122 and 235-237.

[342] The Select Committee to Investigate Tax-Exempt Foundations and Comparable Organizations was authorized by House Resolution 561 in the 82nd Congress to be an investigative committee of the United States House of Representatives between 1952 and 1954. The committee was led by Edward E. Cox and B. Carroll Reece. Known as the Cox or Reece Committee, Norman Dodd's official report is online at

www.teachpeace.com/Dodd-Report-to-the-Reece-Committee-on-Foundations-1954.pdf.
[343] "Norman Dodd Radio Interview," May 30, 1977, distributed by *American Opinion*, 395 Concord Avenue, Belmont, MA 02478. The location of the publishing operation changed to 770 N. Westhill Blvd, Appleton, WI 54914.
[344] "Norman Dodd Video Interview," 1982, distribution sponsored by Quantum Communications and online at www.youtube.com/watch?v=YUYCBfmIcH M&feature=related.
[345] Ibid.
[346] Ibid.
[347] "Brief History of the AHA," available online at http://historians.org/info/ahahistory.cfm.
[348] "Norman Dodd Radio Interview," May 30, 1977, distributed by *American Opinion* and located at 770 N. Westhill Blvd, Appleton, WI 54914.
[349] The Church Committee Reports were published in 1975 and 1976. The reports are provided online by the Assassination Archives and Research Center at www.aarclibrary.org/publib/contents/church/contents_church_reports.htm. The name of the committee comes from its chairman, Senator Frank Church (July 25, 1924 - April 7, 1984) of Idaho.
[350] The Church Committee of the Senate disclosed in 1976 that "well over a thousand books" had been produced or subsidized by the CIA. A few CIA sponsored books include *The New Class* by Milovan Djilas; *In Pursuit of World Order* by Richard N. Gardner; *The Yenan Way* by Eudocio Ravines; *The Anthill* by Suzanne Labin; *Why Viet Nam?* by Frank Trager; and *Terror in Vietnam* by Jay Mallin.
[351] A letter written by General Albert Pike entitled "Instructions" on July 14, 1889, as recorded by A. C. De La Rive in La Femme et l'Enfant dans la Franc-Maconnerie Universelle, page 588.
[352] Teach Peace Foundation October 2014 photograph of the Supreme Council, 33°, Ancient & Accepted Scottish Rite of Freemasonry, Southern Jurisdiction in Washington D.C. The photograph is modified and has the All-Seeing Eye from a U.S. dollar bill positioned as a capstone.
[353] Paul A. Fisher, *Behind the Lodge Door: Church, State and Freemasonry in America* (Bowie, MD: Shield Publishing, Inc., 1988), page 272 in the 1994 TAN Books and Publishers edition. Fisher wrote a Mason observed that the religious symbols painted upon the walls and tombs of ancient Egypt tend to make a Freemason "almost believe he was witnessing a scene at an initiation" due to the features common to Masonic lodges.
[354] Low-level Freemasons are taught the Masonic apron comes from the apron worn by operative Masons in the 5th to 15th centuries. Elite Freemasons are taught the apron predates ancient Egypt and originates with

Adam in the book of Genesis. For Freemasons, the apron symbolizes bondage to Lucifer.

[355] All the Abrahamic faiths and many other groups teach followers that they must use their wealth to help people. For Christians, following God's laws is the opposite of embracing the idea that the end justifies the means.

[356] Hanna Rosin, "Wiccan Controversy Tests Military Religious Tolerance," *Washington Post*, 8 June 1999, page A1. Online at www.washingtonpost.com/wp-srv/national/daily/june99/wicca08.htm. Fort Hood officials set aside a grassy campsite for occult worship and sanctioned the choice of high priestess to lead covens. In March 1999 the *Austin American-Statesman* published photos of the high priestess leaping over a fire.

[357] The Temple of Set was started in 1975 by Michael Aquino and other members of the Church of Satan.

[358] Satanism is often concealed with the media intentionally not reporting the satanic dimension of many crimes.

[359] "Royal Navy to Allow Devil Worship," *CNN.com*, 24 October 2004. Online at www.cnn.com/2004/WORLD/europe/10/24/uk.devilworship/index.html.

[360] Revelation 12:4 – "And his tail drew the third part of the stars of heaven, and cast them to the earth: and the dragon stood before the woman who was ready to be delivered; that, when she should be delivered, he might devour her son." In biblical imagery stars are symbols of angels. Lucifer's persuasion coerced a third of the angels to submit to him. Fallen angels are also called demons.

[361] Luke 10:18 states Jesus said, "And he said to them: I saw Satan like lightning falling from heaven."

[362] Isaiah 14:12 – "How art thou fallen from heaven, O Lucifer, who didst rise in the morning? how art thou fallen to the earth, that didst wound the nations?" To Luciferians, the Abrahamic God is Adonay. Adonay is represented by the black and Lucifer as the white in the black-and-white checkerboard pattern of Masonic floors.

[363] *The Holy Bible*, 2 Corinthians 11:13-15 – "For such false apostles are deceitful workmen, transforming themselves into the apostles of Christ. And no wonder: for Satan himself transformeth himself into an angel of light. Therefore it is no great thing if his ministers be transformed as the ministers of justice, whose end shall be according to their works."

[364] Illuminism is often associated with Adam Weishaupt (6 February 1748 - 18 November 1830). Weishaupt was a senior Brotherhood agent who infiltrated the Catholic Church and subsequently left to attack it via a secret society he helped create called the Bavarian Illuminati. The Illuminati was

founded on May 1, 1776 and is one of the historically documented Brotherhood front organizations.

[365] Two excellent books to learn more about Brotherhood of Death illegal drug operations is *The Politics of Heroin: CIA Complicity in the Global Drug Trade* by Alfred W. McCoy. The Brotherhood created CIA unsuccessfully attempted to suppress the 1972 edition of this book which was published by Harper and Row. The second book is *Dope, Inc.* This book with multiple authors (the U.S. Labor Party Investigating Team, Konstandinos Kalimtgis and David Goldman) was first published in 1978 by New Benjamin Franklin House Pub. Co. On a related note, Matthew 7:20 provides Jesus' advice for recognizing followers of Lucifer or Satan: "Wherefore by their fruits you shall know them."

[366] Sir John A. Cockburn, *Freemasonry; What, Whence, Why, Whither* (London, England: Masonic Record Limited, 1923, 7.

[367] Ibid., 12.

[368] Genesis 3:5 – "For God doth know that in the day ye eat thereof, then your eyes shall be opened, and ye shall be as gods, knowing good and evil."

[369] Alice A. Bailey, *Discipleship in the New Age Volume 2* (New York, New York: Lucis Trust, 1955). Bailey explains this eye is the Destroyer and first person of the occult Trinity. The Brotherhood, and sadly some well-intentioned religious organizations, seek to fool the public that the All-Seeing Eye is the "Eye of Providence" with God looking down on His creation. The All-Seeing Eye has a pejorative connotation of a person "looking down" and peeping through a keyhole in a door.

[370] Freemasons teach Osiris and Isis had a child who they named Horus which Masons call Hiram. The historical evidence of Egyptian writing and statues show Osiris, Isis, and Horus with a cobra often positioned in front of the forehead or "third eye." On a related note, the Mayan god Kukulkan and Aztec god Quetzalcoatl are both depicted as serpents.

[371] The female goddesses identified with Isis are Aphrodite, Astarte, Bellona, Ceres, Columbia, Cybele, Demeter, Diana, Juno, Minerva, Proserpine, and Venus.

[372] The All-Seeing Eye on the U.S. dollar bill was approved by Freemason President Franklin Delano Roosevelt in 1935 because for Masons the symbol is the eye of Lucifer. The Great Seal on the back of the current U.S. dollar bill was originally designed in 1782.

[373] For an explanation of the symbolism of the 2012 Olympic ceremonies and why these ceremonies were blatantly All-Seeing Eye occult rituals, go to www.vigilantchristian.org/2012olympics.html.

[374] Teach Peace Foundation photograph of the All-Seeing Eye on a U.S. dollar bill. The text on the U.S. dollar bill All-Seeing Eye "Annuit Coeptis" meaning "God favors our undertakings" has a dual meaning. Pronunciation

is more important than spelling in the Brotherhood of Death belief system. Displacing the letter "n" in "Annuit" produces Anunit and the meaning "Lucifer favors our work." This translation is supported by the Roman poet Virgil who wrote a Latin epic poem between 29 and 19 BC about Aeneas, a Trojan who became the ancestor of the Romans. The poem, the *Aeneid* states in book IX and line 625 "Iuppiter omnipotens, audacibus adnue coeptis." This prayer by Ascanius, translates to "Jupiter Almighty, favor bold undertakings." Throughout the *Aeneid*, gods are constantly influencing people to change the world.

[375] The Great Pyramid of Giza is also called the Pyramid of Khufu or the Pyramid of Cheops and is currently estimated to be built around 2,560 B.C.

[376] Dr. Zahi Hawass (born May 28, 1947), "News from the Pyramids," *Dr. Zahi Hawass Press Release*, December 1999. He wrote: "I discovered in Abu Sir, limestone blocks in which a scene shows the workman dragging a capstone, and [it] is written in hieroglyphics that it was encased in gold (electrum)." Electrum consists of primarily gold and silver but can have traces of other metals. Electrum would be superior to gold for a capstone because it is harder and much more durable. For more information about Dr. Zahi Hawass and the significance of the missing capstone, see *Vigilant Christian III: The Occult Religion of the 9/11 Attackers* and www.drhawass.com/about-zahi-hawass.

[377] Ibid., and his 1999 writings on "The Gold Pyramidion to Cap Khufu's Pyramid."

[378] Teach Peace Foundation 2013 illustration.

[379] Written and directed by Christian J. Pinto, *Riddles in Stone - Secret Mysteries of America's Beginnings Volume II: Secret Architecture of Washington, D.C.*, (Lexington, South Carolina: Antiquities Research Films, 2007), 33 minutes and 53 seconds to 34 minutes and 10 seconds. Pinto along with Executive Producer David E. Bay and a team of experts created a highly educational documentary which can be obtained at www.antiquitiesresearch.com.

[380] An example of an alternative Egyptian trinity is Ra (the father), Maat (the mother), and Thoth (the son). The religion of the Brotherhood teaches the Egyptian trinity is a descendent of the Babylonian trinity with Nimrod (the father), Semiramis (the mother), and Tammuz (the son).

[381] Sir John A. Cockburn, *Freemasonry; What, Whence, Why, Whither* (London, England: Masonic Record Limited, 1923), 39.

[382] Stephen Knight, *The Brotherhood* (Briarcliff Manor, NY: Stein and Day Publishers, 1984), 15.

[383] The Christian calendar counts the years before Christ (B.C.) and after the birth of Christ or Anno Domini (A.D.).

[384] Walton Hannah, *Darkness Visible: A Revelation and Interpretation of Freemasonry* (London: Augustine Press, 1952), 81. A.L. is also explained as based on Archbishop James Ussher (4 January 1581 - 21 March 1656) who concluded the world was completed by God on Saturday, October 9, 4004 BC and the first day of Creation being Sunday, October 2, 4004 BC.
[385] Variations within Freemasonry showing the equivalent of 2013 A.D.:, 5773 A.M. Scottish Rite Year of the World, 2543 A.I. Royal Arch Masonry Year of the Discovery, and 895 A.O. Knights Templar Year of the Order.
[386] William R. Denslow, *Transactions of the Missouri Lodge of Research, Freemasonry and the American Indian* (Missouri: 1956, Volume No. 13), 104-105. Brant was known as Thayendanega or "he places two bets" and this name is incorrectly spelled as Thayeadanegee on the certificate.
[387] Ibid., 102.
[388] Ibid., 103. The story of Indian Chief Joseph Brant taught by Freemasons is that at the Battle of the Cedars on May 20, 1776, a wounded Continental soldier named John McKinstry was about to be killed. He was captured during the battle thirty miles north of Montreal. McKinstry was about to be burned alive when he made "the great mystic appeal to a Mason in the hour of danger." Indian Chief Brant recognized the Masonic sign and honored his Masonic blood oath by immediately coming to McKinstry's aid. Brant personally escorted McKinstry to Quebec where he was safely placed in the hands of the British, who allowed him to return home.
[389] Richard Eugene Shields, Jr., *Befriend and Relieve Every Brother: Freemasonry During Wartime* (Monroe, North Carolina: The Carolina Trader, 1994), 2. Shields also reports the stories of how Joseph Brant saved the lives of Freemasons Lieutenant Boyd and Johnathan Maynard. In Appendix B of his book he includes a wartime certificate carried by Freemasons to remind enemy Freemasons of the oath to protect and aid brother Freemasons in distress.
[390] Manly P. Hall, *The Secret Destiny of America* (Los Angeles, CA: The Philosophical Research Society, Inc.), 108. Freemasons and Brotherhood leaders believe Atlantis really existed. Atlantis is a legendary island that Plato claimed existed west of Gibraltar and was destroyed with at least part of the civilization sunk beneath the sea.
[391] Ibid.
[392] Ibid., 119.
[393] Ferdinand II of Aragon (10 March 1452 - 23 January 1516) and Isabella I (April 22, 1451 - November 26, 1504, reigned 1474 - 1504) laid the foundation for the political unification of Spain under their grandson, Charles V, Holy Roman Emperor. Ferdinand II was given the honorary title of "the Catholic" on Dec. 2, 1496 by Pope Alexander VI.

---

[394] Seraphim G. Canoutas, *Christopher Columbus: A Greek Nobleman: A Disquisition Concerning The Origin and Early Life of the Great Discoverer and a Refutation of the Charges Against Him Which Have Appeared in Certain Recent Publications* (New York: St. Marks Printing, 1943). Spyros Cateras, *Christopher Columbus was a Greek and his real name was Nikolaos Ypshilantis, from the Greek island Chios* (1937). Manly P. Hall explains the importance of Catera's book in *The Secret Destiny of America* on page 83.

[395] The Atlantic occult meaning is the ocean to reach the New Atlantis and a site deemed a key center of the world outside the city of Atlanta and marked by the Georgia Guidestones, which is explained in Chapter 8. Perhaps the oldest mention of "Atlantic" is *The Histories of Herodotus* around 450 BC.

[396] William T. Still, *New World Order: The Ancient Plan of Secret Societies* (Lafayette, Louisiana: Huntington House Publishers, 1990), 45. Still notes that in an 1895 edition of the Theosophical Society magazine called *Lucifer*, author James Pryse explained the occult meaning of America is Amaruca, which means "Land of the Plumed Serpent." The Maya god Kukulkan and Aztec god Quetzalcoatl are both depicted as serpents.

[397] Ibid., 46.

[398] Ibid., 45.

[399] Ibid., 46.

[400] Steven Elkins of the National Science Foundation finding is reported in the June 14, 2012 article "Discovered: Honduras' Mythical City of Gold?" published by *The Week*. The article is online at http://theweek.com/article/index/229179/discovered-honduras-mythical-city-of-gold.

[401] Dr. Theodore Graebner, *Is Masonry a Religion?* (Saint Louis, Missouri: Concordia Publishing House, 1946), 62.

[402] God created angels and people in His image, which includes having a free will. The battle for souls may seem shocking but is less so when you realize this "war" between the devil and God has been ongoing throughout human history. In Genesis 3:1-3 the battle for souls is shown with "Now the serpent was more subtle than any of the beasts of the earth which the Lord God had made. And he said to the woman: Why hath God commanded you, that you should not eat of every tree of paradise? And the woman answered him, saying: Of the fruit of the trees that are in paradise we do eat: But of the fruit of the tree which is in the midst of paradise, God hath commanded us that we should not eat; and that we should not touch it, lest perhaps we die." In Revelation 20:9-10 the fate of the devil is explained with "And there came down fire from God out of heaven, and devoured them; and the devil, who seduced them, was cast into the pool of fire and brimstone, where both

the beast and the false prophet shall be tormented day and night for ever and ever."

[403] Fritz Springmeier, *Bloodlines of the Illuminati* (Pentracks Publications, 2007 3rd Edition). On the first page of Springmeier's book he explains the top 13 families in the Brotherhood seek to mock the 13 tribes of Israel. For more information about why there are 13 tribes, not 12, and many other details about the religion of the Brotherhood, read *Vigilant Christian III: The Occult Religion of the 9/11 Attackers*.

[404] Ibid. Springmeier also notes many other surnames used including Van Duyn, Alling (Allen), Boels, Brendel, Bullinger, Graeber, Hayes, Krupp, McDonald, Robertson, and Solveys.

[405] John Coleman, *The Conspirators' Hierarchy: The Committee of 300* (Las Vegas, Nevada: World International Review, 2010).

[406] Carroll Quigley, *Tragedy and Hope* (New York, New York: The Macmillan Company, 1966), 51-52.

[407] The twelve Olympians are: Zeus, Poseidon, Hades, Hestia, Hera, Ares, Athena, Apollo, Aphrodite, Hermes, Artemis, and Hephaestus.

[408] Genesis 10:8-10 – "Now Chus begot Nemrod: he began to be mighty on the earth. And he was a stout hunter before the Lord. Hence came a proverb: Even as Nemrod the stout hunter before the Lord. And the beginning of his kingdom was Babylon, and Arach, and Achad, and Chalanne in the land of Sennaar." The phrase "mighty hunter before the LORD" means "in opposition to" or to rebel against God. Nimrod is one of the names used by the Brotherhood for Satan.

[409] Fritz Springmeier, *Bloodlines of the Illuminati* (Pentracks Publications, 2007 3rd Edition), 5.

[410] Walter Rathenau (September 29, 1867 - June 24, 1922) in the December 24, 1912 *Vienna Free Press* wrote: "Three hundred men, each of whom knows all the others, govern the fate of the European continent, and they elect their successors from their entourage." He was the Foreign Minister of Germany during the Weimar Republic and assassinated for opposing the Brotherhood front of Zionism. His murder was a human sacrifice for Lucifer signified by taking place on the summer solstice.

[411] Fritz Springmeier, *Bloodlines of the Illuminati* (Pentracks Publications, 2007, 3rd Edition), 412.

[412] Ibid., 19.

[413] Ibid., 18.

[414] Ibid.

[415] Teach Peace Foundation 2009 photo showing Israel's Supreme Court in the background.

[416] Sir John A. Cockburn, *Freemasonry; What, Whence, Why, Whither* (London, England: Masonic Record Limited, 1923, 41. It is noteworthy that Cockburn writes Sun God and not Sun god.
[417] Ibid.
[418] Shira Schoenberg, "The Sanhedrin," *Jewish Virtual Library*, 2012 and online at www.jewishvirtuallibrary.org/jsource/Judaism/Sanhedrin.html. She wrote the Great Sanhedrin was destroyed when the Temple was destroyed. Tannaitic sources describe the Great Sanhedrin as a religious assembly of 71 sages who met in the Chamber of Hewn Stones in the Temple in Jerusalem. The Great Sanhedrin met daily during the daytime, and did not meet on the Sabbath, festivals or festival eves. It was the final authority on Jewish law and any scholar who went against its decisions was put to death as a zaken mamre (rebellious elder). The Sanhedrin was led by a president called the nasi (lit. "prince") and a vice president called the av bet din (lit. "father of the court"). The other 69 sages sat in a semicircle facing the leaders.
[419] In biblical Hebrew the Ten Commandments are transliterated as Asereth ha-D'bharîm meaning the ten verses, ten sayings or ten matters.
[420] Jack Bernstein, *The Life of an American Jew in Racist, Marxist Israel* (Newport Beach, California: Noontide Press, 1984), 6-7. Bernstein writes on page 17, "Anyone who has read the Bible with an open mind knows that God gave special favors to the Jews of that time. But that was in the form of covenants, which had conditions: God demanded that the Jews obey His word. Time after time the Jews broke the covenants. They rejected God and turned to adoring mammon. It doesn't take a biblical scholar to realize that long ago even the real Jews lost the right of being God's chosen people."
[421] Ibid., 5.
[422] Shlomo Sand, *The Invention of the Jewish People* (London: Verso, 2009), 214. The Jerusalem Talmud predates its counterpart, the Babylonian Talmud or Talmud Bavli, by about 200 years.
[423] Michael Hoffman, *Judaism Discovered* (Coeur d'Alene, Idaho: Independent History and Research, 2008), 891.
The Encyclopedia Judaica (1978), vol. 6, 378.
[424] Shlomo Sand, *The Invention of the Jewish People* (London: Verso, 2009), 215, 221 and 225.
[425] Ibid., King Bulan reigned some time between the mid-700s and the mid-800s.
[426] Ibid.
[427] Ibid., 228.
[428] Teach Peace Foundation 2015 illustration of the Khazar Seal and intended to closely match an actual relic found. This symbol has its origins in the mystery religion of ancient Babylon.

[429] Ibid. The Khazar presence along the Volga River, the longest river in Europe and a great artery between Russian and Central Asia, was substantial.
[430] Ibid., 217.
[431] Ibid., 218. Sand's concluded there was no doubt the sacred tongue and written language of the Khazars was Hebrew.
[432] Shlomo Sand, *The Invention of the Jewish People* (London: Verso, 2009), 224.
[433] Dr. John Coleman, *The Tavistock Institute of Human Relations: Shaping the Moral, Spiritual, Cultural, Political and Economic Decline of the United States of America* (Las Vegas, Nevada: World Intelligence Review, Inc.), 2006, 3.
[434] Shlomo Sand, *The Invention of the Jewish People* (London: Verso, 2009), The Star of David has been the symbol of Judaism since the 17th century. In Central Europe the symbol was used on some Jewish flags as early as the 14th century.
[435] Abraham Harkavy, *The Jews and the Languages of the Slavs*, 1867, 1.
[436] Norman Golb and Omeljan Pritsak wrote *Khazarian Hebrew Documents of the Tenth Century* (Cornell University, 1982).
[437] Peter Golden, *The Q'azars: Their History and Language as Reflected in the Islamic, Byzantine, Caucausian, Hebrew and Old Russian Sources* (New York, New York: Columbia University, 1970).
Peter Golden, *Khazar Studies: An Historico-Philological Inquiry into the Origins of the Khazars* (Budapest: Akademiai Kiado, 1980).
[438] Revelation 7: 8 - "Of the tribe of Zabulon were sealed twelve thousand. Of the tribe of Joseph were sealed twelve thousand. Of the tribe of Benjamin were sealed twelve thousand."
[439] Shlomo Sand, *The Invention of the Jewish People* (London: Verso, 2009), 238.
[440] Arthur Koestler, *The Thirteenth Tribe* (New York, New York: Random House, 1976), 17.
[441] Ibid.
[442] Ibid., 16 and the introduction of the second edition of *Khazaria: The History of a Jewish Kingdom in Europe* by A.N. Poliak published in 1951. Shlomo Sand observed Poliak's great sin was asserting categorically that the great bulk of Eastern European Jewry originated from the Khazar Empire.
[443] Shlomo Sand, *The Invention of the Jewish People* (London: Verso, 2009), 235.
[444] Ibid., 235-236.
[445] Ibid., 242.
[446] Ibid., 236.

[447] Jack Bernstein, *The Life of an American Jew in Racist, Marxist Israel* (Newport Beach, California: Noontide Press, 1984), 5.
[448] Jonathan Lis, "Top Israeli Intellectuals to State: Probe Rabbi's Alleged Link to Rabin Assassination," *Haaretz*, 13 February 2011 (see www.haaretz.com/news/national/top-israeli-intellectuals-to-state-probe-rabbi-s-alleged-link-to-rabin-assassination-1.343215?).
[449] Yolande Knell, "King's Torah Splits Israel's Religious and Secular Jews," *BBC News*, 19 July 2011 and online at www.bbc.co.uk/news/world-middle-east-14168618.
[450] Jack Bernstein, *The Life of an American Jew in Racist, Marxist Israel* (Newport Beach, California: Noontide Press, 1984), 1. Bernstein's death a few years after publishing his 1984 book is suspected to be the result of a Mossad assassination. Bernstein wrote that Zionists first ignore the charges but if the information reaches too many people they will ridicule the information followed by character assassination (e.g., falsely claim a person is a Holocaust denier) and if necessary murder. Bernstein explained true Jews are persecuted by one-world government imposters. Bernstein, an Ashkenazi Jew was not reporting that Ashkenazi Jews were of the synagogue of Satan. He was reporting that a group of Brotherhood insiders posing as Ashkenazi Jews were actively persecuting Jews.
[451] Nicholas II (18 May 1868 - 17 July 1918) public domain photograph courtesy of Boissonnas & Eggler in St. Petersburg circa 1909.
[452] Teach Peace Foundation 2009 photograph. Murmansk is the largest city in the world north of the Arctic Circle.
[453] The photographer of this 1918 picture is unknown. The Murmansk Military Museum has a collection of photographs showing the U.S. military deployed in Russia.
[454] Gary Allen and Larry Abraham, *None Dare Call It Conspiracy* (Cutchogue, New York: Buccaneer Books, 1972). On a related note on page 83 Allen and Abraham explain how Stalin was funded. "According to a report on file with the State Department, his firm, Kuhn Loeb and Co. bankrolled the first five year plan for Stalin. Schiff's partner and relative, Paul Warburg, engineered the establishment of the Federal Reserve System while on the Kuhn Loeb payroll, Schiff's descendants are active in the Council on Foreign Relations today." Allen and Abraham continued to explain Stalin's secret service to the Brotherhood of Death on page 84. "But obviously these men have no fear of international Communism. It is only logical to assume that if they financed it and do not fear it, it must be because they control it. Can there be any other explanation that makes sense?"

---

[455] Colonel Edward Mandell House (July 26, 1858 – March 28, 1938) was a Brotherhood of Death Wiseman.
[456] Ibid.
[457] W. Cleon Skousen, *The Naked Capitalist* (Salt Lake City, Utah: Reviewer), 1970 7th edition, 40.
[458] Ibid.
[459] Ibid., 41. The original source for the $20 million Jacob Schiff statement is the February 3, 1949 *New York Journal-American.* On a related note, Jacob Schiff's son, also named Jacob Schiff, explained his father's anti-Czarist activities in a book. The book Jacob Schiff wrote about his father is *His Life and Letters* (London: Cyrus Adler, 1929).
[460] Jacob Henry Schiff (born Jakob Heinrich Schiff; January 10, 1847 - September 25, 1920) served the Brotherhood of Death as a war profiteer. He made blood money from World War I, the Japanese military efforts against Tsarist Russia and the creation of Communist Russia. He also helped create Zionism as it is known today and was the director of multiple corporations (e.g., Equitable Life Assurance Society, National City Bank of New York, Wells Fargo & Company, and the Union Pacific Railroad).
[461] As part of the war against Christianity, Lenin allowed abortions and homosexuality activity. Hazard, John N., "Unity and Diversity in Socialist Law," *Law and Contemporary Problems* 30 (2): 1965, 277, 279. John Hazard was a professor of Public Law at Columbia University. Openly homosexual people were allowed to serve in Lenin's government. During Lenin's rule homosexual activity remained illegal in former territories of the Russian Empire. Anthony Sutton expands on the secret society creation of the Soviet Union in his book *Western Technology and Soviet Economic Development 1917-1930* (Hoover Institute: Stanford University, 1968).
[462] Arsene de Goulevitch, *Czarism and the Revolution* (Hawthorne, California: Omni Publications), 1962.
[463] Ibid., 224-225. In 1918, he served in the Russian White (North Western) Army. On page 225 he quotes General A. Nechvolodov, from the French Intelligence Service and author of *The Emperor Nicholas II and the Jews* (Paris, France: E. Cheron), 1924, 98. Nechvolodov wrote: "Twelve million dollars are reported to have been donated by Schiff to the Russian revolutionaries in the years preceding the war, while other sources confirm and amplify this fact."
[464] Rev. E. Cahill, S.J., *Freemasonry and the Anti-Christian Movement* (Dublin: M.H. Gill and Son Ltd., 1929),101. Pope Gregory XVI requested Cardinal Cretineau-Joly publish the *Permanent Instruction of the Alta Vendita* in his work, *L'Eglise en face de la Revolution.* Pope Pius IX approved of the publication.
[465] Ibid., 102.

---

[466] Ibid., 101.
[467] Three prime examples of people falsely attacked are Catholic priests Malachi Brendan Martin (July 23, 1921 – July 27, 1999), Nicholas Nightingale Gruner (born May 4, 1942) and Paul Leonard Kramer. All three men have been falsely attacked which only makes sense because the truth they speak is a direct threat to defeating the kingdom of Satan. A specific example is provided by Catholic priest Gruner who explains on YouTube why allegations he is suspended as a priest are false. To hear and see this information, the online address is www.youtube.com/watch?v=1Xh4-6muhoA.
[468] Gordon Dwight Mohr also known as Jack Mohr (January 1, 1916 – July 17, 2003) was a World War II and Korean War hero. He courageously spoke the truth and wrote: *A Study in Anti-Gentilism*, *The Hidden Power Behind Freemasonry*, *The Undeclared War!*, *Communist Terror in Peaceful Heaven*, and *Woe Unto Ye Fundamentalists!*
[469] February 1996 statement by Colonel Jack Mohr to Pastor Peter Peters in Little Rock, Arkansas and online at https://www.youtube.com/watch?v=EA78AXMsObE (starting at 1:13:22).
[470] Ibid and starting at 1:23:53).
[471] Ibid .
[472] Isser Harel was born Isser Halperin in 1912 and died on February 18, 2003.
[473] The book *Vigilant Christian IV: 9/11 - The Secret War* provides the evidence that the Brotherhood of Death is responsible for 9/11 and how the Mossad executed the violence and orchestrated the Osama bin Laden deception.
Christopher Bollyn explained in a September 27, 2014 presentation that in 1979 Isser Harel said to Mike Evans, a Zionist Christian minister from Texas: "that Arab terrorism will come to the United States and when it does it will bomb your tallest building in New York City because it is a fertility symbol." He explains this information at 11:09-11:37 in his presentation which is online at www.youtube.com/watch?v=sw4UDcm Oqp4.
[474] *The Report from Iron Mountain*, Dial Press, 1967 is online at www.teachpeace.com/Report_from_Iron_Mountain.pdf.
[475] The Brotherhood of Death alien threat may be manifested as both a fabricated extraterrestrial life threat and an immigration threat.
[476] "Hoax of Horror? A Book That Shook White House," *U.S. News & World Report*, 20 November 1967.
[477] Herschel McLandress, "News of War and Peace You're Not Ready For," *The Washington Post*, 26 November 1967, 5. John Kenneth Galbraith (1908 - 2006) used the pen name Herschel McLandress.

[478] "Touché Professor," *The Times*, 12 February 1968, 8 and see http://en.wikipedia.org/wiki/The_Report_from_Iron_Mountain for more information on the three Galbraith confirmations. A journalist from the Cambridge newspaper *Varsity* tape recorded his question "Are you aware of the identity of the author of [*The*] *Report from Iron Mountain*?" Galbraith responded, "I was in general a member of the conspiracy, but I was not the author. I have always assumed that it was the man who wrote the foreword - Mr. Lewin."

[479] Ibid. William F. Buckley had full Brotherhood of Death credentials including Yale University's Skull and Bones secret society membership. In 1951, Buckley joined the CIA and served in Mexico City as a political action specialist and with Special Activities Division under E. Howard Hunt. Dean Rusk was a Rockefeller Foundation trustee from 1950 to 1961 and in 1952 became president of this Brotherhood of Death foundation.

[480] Herschel McLandress, "News of War and Peace You're Not Ready For," *The Washington Post*, 26 November 1967, 5.

The claim that *The Report from Iron Mountain* is a hoax was made on March 19, 1972 when Leonard Lewin professed authorship of the report as a work of fiction. The hoax claim then led to other media manipulation efforts including getting the book listed in the *Guinness Book of World Records* as the "Most Successful Literary Hoax." The fact that the report is genuine is further strengthened by the accuracy of called for events that materialized after the report was published.

[481] 2 Thessalonians 2:1-11.

[482] John 8:32.

[483] In addition to the National Defense Authorization Act, H. R. 347 was signed into law on March 9, 2012 and is online at www.gpo.gov/fdsys/pkg/BILLS-112hr347enr/pdf/BILLS-112hr347enr.pdf. Free speech or protest of any type is potentially a federal offense with a penalty up to 10 years in federal prison. The government need only claim the protest occurred in the presence of elites brandishing Secret Service protection or was at a special event designated a National Special Security Event.

[484] The Bill of Rights was already on its last legs because the October 17, 2006 Military Commissions Act authorized the seizing of an American citizen without charge and holding people indefinitely. On May 9, 2007, Homeland Security Presidential Directive 20 and National Security Presidential Directive 51 enabled a president to take over both Congress and the Judiciary by simply declaring an emergency. A successful argument can be made that the Bill of Rights partially died as far back as World War II due to Presidential emergency decrees.

[485] "Investigation of Financial and Monetary Conditions in the United States Under House Resolutions Nos. 429 and 504," February 28, 1913, pages 1-258. The official finding by Congress and supporting documentation is online at www.teachpeace.com/Money%20Trust%20Investigation.htm. The transcript of the Money Trust hearings was published in three volumes. The transcript is available on the Teach Peace Foundation website with the original 29 parts. An index, a table of interlocking directorates, and the majority/minority report of the committee provide concrete evidence that the Money Trust was real. The Report of the Committee Appointed Pursuant to House Resolutions 429 and 504 to Investigate the Concentration of Control of Money and Credit is recommended reading for anyone doubting the Money Trust was publicly exposed.

[486] The dynastic banking families lost their renewal of the 1791 First Bank of the United States, their renewal of the 1816 Second Bank of the United States, and attempts to control the U.S. monetary supply after the Civil War. The Money Trust survived and created the Federal Reserve System which they still own via ownership in U.S. member banks.

[487] After the Civil War the international bank cartel that created the Federal Reserve System was commonly called the Money Trust. The Money Trust Investigation findings are online at www.teachpeace.com/Money%20Trust%20Investigation.htm.

[488] Investigation of Financial and Monetary Conditions in the United States Under House Resolutions Nos. 429 and 504, February 28, 1913. The Money Trust Investigation, 1912, subcommittee was convened by the Chairman Arsene P. Pujo of the House Banking and Currency Committee. The report is online at www.teachpeace.com/Money%20Trust%20Investigation.htm.

[489] The Federal Reserve System was created on December 23, 1913 with the enactment of the Federal Reserve Act.

[490] Teach Peace Foundation 2015 picture.

[491] Charles August Lindbergh (January 20, 1859 - May 24, 1924) served in the US Congress from Minnesota's 6th congressional district from 1907 to 1917. The quote is from a statement made on December 22, 1913. His knowledge of the Money Trust was extensive in part because his father, Ola Mansson, was an insider serving as the secretary (1847-1858) to King Carl XV of Sweden, a bank officer, and a prominent member of the Farmer's Estate of the Swedish Parliament. Ola Mansson immigrated to the U.S. and changed his name to August Lindbergh.

[492] Ibid. A more detailed version is available in *Vigilant Christian V: Perfect Money Planning.*

[493] Tyler E. Bagwell, *Images of America: The Jekyll Island Club*, (Charleston, SC: Arcadia Publishing, 1998), pages 18, 19. Bagwell was the historian for the Jekyll Island Museum.
G. Edward Griffin, *The Creature from Jekyll Island: A Second Look at the Federal Reserve*, American Media, 24th printing 2009 May edition, pp 5, 6. On May 3, 1931 the *New York Times* published that "One-sixth of the total wealth of the world was represented by members of the Jekyll Island Club."
[494] The New World Order's tactic in the early twentieth century was to use the preferred disabling term "paranoid." The public is now conditioned by the New World Order to associate the disabling label "conspiracy theorist" with unbalanced or paranoid. The messenger is attacked instead of the message even after Jekyll Island participant memoirs were published.
[495] JPMorgan Chase & Co. (JPMC) provided information online at www.jpmorganchase.com on 22 October 2009.
[496] In 1963 the Nobel Laureate economist Milton Friedman (July 31, 1912 - November 16, 2006) explained in his book the *Monetary History of the United States* that the Federal Reserve System caused the Great Depression.
[497] The *Commodity Futures Modernization Act of 2000*, HR. 4541 (www.govtrack.us/congress/bill.xpd?bill=h106-4541) and S. 3283 (www.govtrack.us/congress/bill.xpd?bill=s106-3283&tab=summary) in the 106th Congress was eventually passed as part of the *Consolidated Appropriations Act of 2001*. The legislation became law when signed by President Bill Clinton on December 21, 2000 (online at www.govtrack.us/congress/bill.xpd?bill=h106-4577).
[498] Only Congress, was "To coin Money, regulate the Value thereof, and of foreign Coin, and fix the Standard of Weights and Measures."
[499] Manly P. Hall, *The Secret Destiny of America* (Los Angeles, CA: The Philosophical Research Society, Inc.), 77.
[500] *The Georgia Guidestones*, published by Elberton Granite Finishing Co., Inc. and printed by *The Sun*, Hartwell, Georgia, March 1981. The book is online at www.wired.com/images/multimedia/magazine/1705/Wired_May_2009_Georgia_Guidestones.pdf. Randall Sullivan wrote an article on the subject for *Wired Magazine* on 20 April 2009 titled, "American Stonehenge: Monumental Instructions for the Post-Apocalypse." See www.wired.com/science/discoveries/magazine/17-05/ff_guidestones?currentPage=all.
[501] Raymond Wiley and KT Prime, *The Georgia Giudestones: America's Most Mysterious Monument* (New York, New York: The Disinformation Company, 2011), 103.
[502] Teach Peace Foundation 2012 photograph at the Philomatheo Lodge #25.

[503] Ibid., 34. The obituary for Jodi Minogue is online at www.unicorntrad.org/members/galadriel_memorial.html. She died on February 8, 2006 and was 49 years old.
[504] In Buddhism, sandalwood scent is believed to bring to life one's desires. John Minogue is an occult high priest and warlock. He uses the name Lord Athanor and is the founder of the pagan Grove of the Unicorn.
[505] Clay Ouzts, "Georgia Guidestones," *The New Georgia Encyclopedia*, 16 March 2009 online at www.georgiaencyclopedia.org/nge/Article.jsp?id=h-3163. From the north a person travels through Hart or "Heart" county to reach the Georgia Guidestones. A plaque explaining the Cherokee center of the world is in Hartwell, Georgia.
[506] The North Star changes. The current North Star is Polaris. Some five thousand and five hundred years from now the North Star is Alpha Cephei.
[507] Equinox occurs about March 21st and September 22nd. Equinox is the time when the sun crosses the plane of the earth's equator, making night and day of approximately equal length all over the earth. The solstice also occurs twice a year. Solstice is when the sun is at its greatest distance from the equator. In the Northern Hemisphere the longest day of the year is about June 21 and the shortest day of the year is about December 21.
[508] Georgia Guidestones picture shot by the author in July 2012.
[509] Moving clockwise around the monument from due north, the languages are English, Spanish, Swahili, Hindi, Hebrew, Arabic, Chinese, and Russian.
[510] Raymond Wiley and KT Prime, *The Georgia Giudestones: America's Most Mysterious Monument* (New York, New York: The Disinformation Company, 2011), 10.
[511] The term Antichrist, also known as the Dajjal in Islam, refers to one who fulfills Biblical prophecies for Christians and Hadith prophecies for Muslims. The word Antichrist is in John's epistles five times. A different name is used 33 times in Revelation. In Revelation he is called 'the Beast from the Abyss.' Other names for the Antichrist in the Bible include lawless one, son of perdition, man of sin, and the destroyer. The actual name of the Antichrist is provided in Revelation 9:11. "And they had a king over them, which is the angel of the bottomless pit, whose name in the Hebrew tongue is Abaddon, but in the Greek tongue hath his name Apollyon." The name of Satan's powerful tool is Apollo. This is likely why in the ancient Greek and Roman religion and modern Greco-Roman Neopaganism Apollo is worshipped. This Apollo is understood to be a god bringing deadly plague and performing great signs at the Oracle in Delphi. Both Christianity and Islam teach the Antichrist is defeated by Jesus.
[512] *The Georgia Guidestones*, published by Elberton Granite Finishing Co., Inc. and printed by *The Sun*, Hartwell, Georgia, March 1981, 6. The

pseudonym R. C. Christian was likely chosen to conceal the anti-Christian purpose of the monument. Mr. Christian is quoted by Fendley and Martin as saying, "My name is not Christian; I only use that name because I am a follower of the teachings of Jesus Christ" even though in John 18:20 Jesus taught transparency and did nothing in secret. "Mr. Christian" is insulting all the Abrahamic faiths with the Guidestones top commandment mandating that billions people alive today should be eliminated.

[513] *The Georgia Guidestones*, published by Elberton Granite Finishing Co., Inc. and printed by *The Sun*, Hartwell, Georgia, March 1981, page 31. The sun and the pyramid are powerful occult symbols in Freemasonry. *The Georgia Guidestones* book is interestingly made by *The Sun* printing company in Hartwell, Georgia and the granite is from Pyramid Quarry.

[514] The secret society connection of everyone directly connected to R. C. Christian is commonly ignored in works attempting to explain the Georgia Guidestones as good.

[515] Raymond Wiley and KT Prime, *The Georgia Giudestones: America's Most Mysterious Monument* (New York, New York: The Disinformation Company, 2011), 7. Wayne Mullinex, Hudson Cone, and other men connected to R. C. Christian and Freemasonry are documented as participating in the 1982 recovery of a buried granite statue in Elberton named Dutchy.

[516] Matt Smith, "Waiting for the end of the world: Georgia's 30-year stone mystery," *CNN*, 22 March 2010 and online at http://www.cnn.com/2010/US/03/22/georgia.mystery.monument/?hpt=C2. In 2010 the son of R. C. Christian notified Wyatt Martin that his father died.

[517] Woodrow Wilson, *The New Freedom*, Tutis Digital Publishing Private Limited, 2008, page 46. Tutis Digital Publishing Private Limited is a division of Corah Hub Online Services Private Limited which is a subsidiary of Vishal Information Technologies Limited in Mumbai, India. The online version of the book is at www.gutenberg.org/etext/14811.

[518] Aaron Russo was an American who worked passionately to expose the New World Order. He produced the films *America: Freedom to Fascism, Trading Places*, and *Mad as Hell*. He was a friend of Nick Rockefeller who in 2000 attempted to recruit Russo into the New World Order. Russo refused and began publicly declaring that Rockefeller warned him about 9/11 eleven months in advance.

Alex Jones, "Nick Rockefeller Revealed Elite Agenda to Aaron Russo During Friendship," *Jones Report*, 21 February 2007 and online at www.jonesreport.com/articles/210207_rockefeller_friendship.html. For more information see the 2006 Alex Jones documentary, *Reflections and Warnings: An Interview with Aaron Russo*.

[519] Teach Peace Foundation July 2012 Georgia Guidestones photograph.

---

[520] Deuteronomy 27:15 – " Cursed be the man that maketh a graven and molten thing, the abomination of the Lord, the work of the hands of artificers, and shall put it in a secret place: and all the people shall answer and say: Amen." Ecclesiastes 12:14 – "And all things that are done, God will bring into judgment for every error, whether it be good or evil."
[521] *The Georgia Guidestones*, published by Elberton Granite Finishing Co., Inc. and printed by *The Sun*, Hartwell, Georgia, March 1981, 27-36.
[522] Satan and his agents seek to kill life. God and his followers protect life. John 10:10 – "The thief cometh not, but for to steal, and to kill, and to destroy. I am come that they may have life, and may have it more abundantly." The first Georgia Guidestones commandment rejects God's authority and calls for global mass murder.
[523] Satan and his agents support abortion, eugenics, and the intention to corrupt and destroy God's creation. God has made people in his image. The second Georgia Guidestones commandment also rejects God and violates the commandment "You shall not kill."
[524] The story of Nimrod in the Bible reminds people that God's distribution of power has helped safeguard humanity from global totalitarian enslavement.
[525] In the planned post-apocalyptic future, the Abrahamic religions and nationalism will be falsely blamed for the global carnage. The New World Order elite seek to claim reason was not tempered allowing radical religious beliefs to disrupt global governance and ultimately result in global war.
[526] To readers in the early 21st century directive five usually appears as a good commandment. However, after a global Hiroshima, the surviving elite are communicating to survivors that the laws and courts are fair. This is a massive distortion when laws and courts violate God's laws. We have begun to see this in the 20th and 21st century with "fair laws and courts" that allow for murder, torture, economic exploitation, and inappropriate intervention in presidential elections.
[527] The concept of nations in the context of a one-world government is different. The commandment is referring to the ten nations or regions created under the one-world government. Following World War III, each region may have a population comparable to New York City in the early 21st century. Imagine a planet where a population significantly less than 500 million people are distributed in many cities with major global cities being Jerusalem, London, Berlin, Brussels, Paris, Cape Town, Sydney, Tokyo, Hong Kong, and Singapore. This Georgia Guidestones commandment violates "I am the Lord your God" by making the supreme authority a one world court that is not based on God's laws.

[528] Throughout history officials with integrity have helped keep the agents for the New World Order at bay. By eliminating the U.S. Constitution and other laws that safeguard God given rights and the officials calling for them, totalitarian rule is easier to maintain. Proverbs 29:2 – "When just men increase, the people shall rejoice: when the wicked shall bear rule, the people shall mourn."

[529] In the New World Order, personal rights including getting married, being a parent, and educating children are eliminated. The advocates for a world government seek to highly regulate marriage and the right to have a child. This Georgia Guidestones commandment violates coveting what belongs to neighbors. In the New World Order, property is seized by region controllers in service to the world government.

[530] Lucifer is taught as synonymous with "harmony" and the "infinite force" in the planned post-apocalyptic future. People and ideas determined ugly by the Brotherhood elite are eliminated. A central Luciferian teaching is truth, beauty and love require following your heart.

[531] God made people as blessed, superior to plants and animals, and nature is for the benefit of people. Genesis 1:28-30 – "And God blessed them, saying: Increase and multiply, and fill the earth, and subdue it, and rule over the fishes of the sea, and the fowls of the air, and all living creatures that move upon the earth. And God said: Behold I have given you every herb bearing seed upon the earth, and all trees that have in themselves seed of their own kind, to be your meat: And to all beasts of the earth, and to every fowl of the air, and to all that move upon the earth, and wherein there is life, that they may have to feed upon. And it was so done."
Reverend (Thomas) Robert Malthus (13 February 1766 - 23 December 1834) was a British cleric and New World Order scholar. His perspective that people are a cancer on the earth is explained by Malthus in his 1798 *An Essay on the Principle of Population*. Bertrand Arthur William Russell, (18 May 1872 - 2 February 1970), is another Brotherhood of Death scholar who preached population reduction is necessary.

[532] The Georgia Guidestones appear to have a special connection to "Towers of Babel" ranging from the One World Building scheduled for completion in 2013 to the 2010 Burj Khalifa in the United Arab Emirates. For example, Van Smith has calculated a correlation between the height of the Burj Khalifa, 2,717 feet, and the sum of the proportion of the major stones, Gnomon stone, and capstone.

[533] Photograph is courtesy of the National Park Service and online at www.nps.gov/wamo/learn/historyculture/index.htm.

[534] David Ovason, *The Secret Architecture of Our Nation's Capital* (New York, New York: Harper Collins, 1999), 10.

[535] The incomplete, broken, or open pentagram is believed in the Brotherhood religion to summon Satan. On a related note, Johann Wolfgang von Goethe (28 August 1749 - 22 March 1832) wrote in *Faust* that Mephistopheles or Satan is summoned with a pentagram that is "just a little open."

[536] The Washington Monument was 555 feet but is slowly sinking. The height in 2015 is 554 feet and 7 11/32 inches. Upon the public announcement of the rule of the Antichrist, it is expected that the Brotherhood will likely introduce a renovated capstone to restore the height to 555 feet.

[537] The Bible explains that 666 is the number or name of the wild beast with seven heads and ten horns. This beast has worldwide reach and is a gross failure in God's sight. For more information read Revelation 13:1-18.

[538] William Newton, *The Rejected Stone: Washington, Monument and Man*, 17 May 2011 and online at http://blogofthecourtier.com/2011/05/17/the-rejected-stone-washington-monument-and-man/.

[539] The National Parks Service provides additional information about the Washington Monument at www.nps.gov/wamo/learn/historyculture /index.htm.

[540] P.H. McLaughlin is shown setting the capstone on the Washington Monument. This 1884 illustration for *Harper's Weekly* is in the public domain because its first publication occurred prior to January 1, 1923. The Library of Congress digitial ID is cph.3b44599.

[541] Teach Peace Foundation 2010 photograph of the northern stelae field in Axum. The Great Stelae is ornamented with two false doors at the base and windows on all sides.

[542] The Imperator [H. Spencer Lewis], "The First Rosicrucians in America: Some interesting facts which some persons like to deny," *The Rosicrucian Digest*, November 1938. *The New Atlantis* describes the implementation of Rosicrucian ideals.

[543] Francis Bacon (22 January 1561 - 9 April 1626) is the author of *The New Atlantis,* which was published in 1627 by his literary executor.

[544] The pseudonym may have also been selected to mock the Catholic Church.

[545] William Tindall, *Standard History of the City of Washington from a Study of the Original Sources* (Knoxville, Tennessee: H. W. Crew and Co., 1914), 18. The book is available online at http://archive.org/stream/standardhistoryo00tind#page/18/mode/2up.

[546] Annapolis, Maryland State Archives. The manuscript is *Liber AA* for 1664 (formerly *Liber 6*), at folios 318-321, and is dated June 5, 1663. The text is on folio 319. Tindall's presentation of the title language in *Standard*

History of the City of Washington from a Study of the Original Sources has minor variations. He writes it reads: "Layd out for Francis Pope of this Province Gentleman a parcel of land in Charles County called Rome lying on the East side of the Anacostian River beginning at a marked oak standing by the riverside, the bounded tree of Captain Robert Troop and running north by the river for breadth the length 200 perches to a bounded oak standing at the mouth of a bay or inlet called Tiber." The center of Washington, D.C. or "Rome" is on the east side of the Potomac and west side of the Anacostia River.

547 The Imperator [H. Spencer Lewis], "The First Rosicrucians in America: Some interesting facts which some persons like to deny," *The Rosicrucian Digest*, November 1938.

548 Ibid. *The New Atlantis* is evidence in support of H. Spencer Lewis' statement the Bacon originated the plan to introduce Rosicrucianism in America.

549 Johann Jacob Zimmerman or Jakob Zimmerman (25 November 1642 and also evidence for 1644 - 1693). Zimmerman was born in the Duchy of Wurtenburg and was the founder of the "Company of Mystics." He was dismissed from his church ministry for putting Jakob Böhme or Jacob Boehme above Peter and Paul.

550 The Hatcher Families Genealogy Association provides detailed information on the Zimmerman family online at http://hatcherfamilyassn.com/getperson.php?personID=I490&tree=MILLER etal.

551 Ibid. The ship is called *Sara Maria* by Rosicrucians and is also known as the *Santa Maria.*

552 Ibid. The ship brought Maria Margaretha Schaal Zimmerman and her 4 children to the U.S.

553 Ibid.

554 John Clagett Proctor, *Proctor's Washington and Environs*: 1928 - 1949, (self published, 1949), 305. Frederick Calvert granted a tract of 88 acres to Henry Funk in 1754. Zimmerman's son or grandson may have used the pseudonym Jacob Funk. Jacob was the first name of Jacob Christopher Zimmerman (14 May 1683 - 1759) and Jacob Zimmerman (1710 - between 15 December 1789 and 15 March 1796). Evidence to confirm if a pseudonym was used or the identity of the buyer is inconclusive.

555 David Ovason, *The Secret Architecture of Our Nation's Capital* (New York, New York: Harper Collins, 1999), 1.

556 Modern Rosicrucians claim Thomas Jefferson was a member of their order.

---

[557] William Tindall, *Standard History of the City of Washington from a Study of the Original Sources* (Knoxville, Tennessee: H. W. Crew and Co., 1914), 21.

[558] William Tindall, *Standard History of the City of Washington from a Study of the Original Sources* (Knoxville, Tennessee: H. W. Crew and Co., 1914), 115. Tindall explains: "The Commissioners served for nearly two years without salary until March 4, 1793, when on the recommendation of the President it was resolved that they be allowed one thousand dollars per year each." On page 194 he notes that a few years later the salary was raised to $1,600 per year.

[559] William R. Denslow, *10,000 Famous Freemasons* [a four volume series with a Foreword by President Harry S. Truman, the Past Grand Master of the Grand Lodge of Missouri, (Richmond, Virginia: Macoy Publishing and Masonic Supply Co., Inc., 1957), Volume I, 184. Daniel Carroll participated in Masonic rituals including the U.S. Capitol dedication ceremony. Freemason Denslow worked in the Missouri Lodge of Research.
F. L. Brockett, Past Master of Lodge No. 22, *The Lodge of Washington* (Alexandria, Virginia: G. H. Ramey and Son, Publishers, 1899). Daniel Carroll was made a Freemason on May 8, 1781 at the Maryland Lodge No. 16.
Sister Mary Virginia Geiger, *Daniel Carroll, A Framer of the Constitution* (Washington, D.C.: Catholic University of America, 1943).

[560] Two important Washington, D.C. architects responsible for creating occult architecture are Elliott Woods and James Hoban. Both are recognized as members by Freemasonry.

[561] Courtesy of Library of Congress Geography and Map Division. Plan of the city intended for the permanent seat of the government of [the] United States : projected agreeable to the direction of the President of the United States, in pursuance of an act of Congress passed the sixteenth day of July, MDCCXC, "establishing the permanent seat on the bank of the Potomac": [Washington D.C.] / by Pierre or Peter Charles L'Enfant. Available online at www.loc.gov/item/91684074 and see www.loc.gov/search/?q=Plan+of+the+city+of+Washington.

[562]David Ovason, *The Secret Architecture of Our Nation's Capital* (New York, New York: Harper Collins, 1999), 10 and 430. Ovason includes corn symbols and Mercury symbols to calculate the number of Virgoan images in Washington, D.C.

[563] Courtesy of Library of Congress Geography and Map Division in Washington, D.C. Plan of the city of Washington / Thackara & Vallance sc., 1792. Available online at www.loc.gov/item/88694159 and see http://lccn.loc.gov/88694159.

---

[564] The decipher was made by the author. Placing it over a map of Washington, D.C., with a light beneath the map, is recommended. The 2012 Washington, D.C. Office of Zoning D. C. online map enables people to easily find other occult symbols. See http://maps.dcoz.dc.gov/#. Effective April 13, 2012, the Official Zoning Map is drawn and maintained on the Geographic Information System in the Office of Zoning pursuant to D.C. Zoning Commission ("Commission") Order No. 11-20. For more information go to www.dcoz.dc.gov.
[565] Courtesy of the D.C. Zoning Commission and online at http://maps.dcoz.dc.gov/#. Effective April 13, 2012, the Official Zoning Map is drawn and maintained on the Geographic Information System in the Washington D.C. Office of Zoning. For more information go to www.dcoz.dc.gov.
[566] Ibid. For more information go to www.dcoz.dc.gov and to see all three symbols traced go to www.vigilantchristian.org/washingtondcsymbols.html.
[567] Ibid.
[568] Ibid.
[569] Manly Palmer Hall (1901 - 1990) is acknowledged as being named a 33rd degree Freemason in 1973. This information is on the back cover of his book, *The Lost Keys of Freemasonry*.
Manly Palmer Hall, *The Secret Teachings of All Ages: An Encyclopedic Outline of Masonic, Hermetic, Qabalistic and Rosicrucian Symbolical Philosophy* (Radford, Virginia: A and D Publishing, 2007), 286. The first edition was published in 1928.
[570] James W. Maertens, Ph.D., "The Symbolism of the Pentagram," *Lake Harriet Lodge No. 277 of Minnesota*, 2012 and online at www.lakeharrietlodge.org/lhl277/MainMenu/Home/MasonicEducation/TheSymbolismofthePentagram/tabid/413/Default.aspx.
[571] Helena Petrovna Blavatsky, *Isis Unveiled, Volume I: Science* (New York, New York: Trow's Printing and Bookbinding Company, 1877).
[572] Ibid., xxxiii. Blavatsky's taught anti-Christian doctrine in the service of Satan.
[573] Ibid., 287.
[574] James W. Maertens, Ph.D., "The Symbolism of the Pentagram," *Lake Harriet Lodge No. 277 of Minnesota*, 2012 and online at www.lakeharrietlodge.org/lhl277/MainMenu/Home/MasonicEducation/TheSymbolismofthePentagram/tabid/413/Default.aspx.
[575] The five points of Masonic "fellowship" are help members, pray for members, deal heart-to-heart with members, listen to brothers attentively, and speak kindly to members with good advice.
[576] David Ovason, *The Secret Architecture of Our Nation's Capital* (New York, New York: Harper Collins, 1999), 257.

[577] Ibid., 255.
[578] Astronomy foundation charts are maps of the stars and planets.
[579] Pythagoras (c. 570 B.C. - c. 495 B.C.) was born on the island of Samos in Greece. He is the founder of the Order of Pythagoras, a secret society promoting Babylonian, Egyptian, and Greek mystery religion teachings.
[580] Teach Peace Foundation 2012 photograph.
[581] Albert Pike, *Morals and Dogma* (Charleston, South Carolina, 1871), page 850 in the 1950 edition.
[582] Ibid., 851. Pike expands on the explanation with "the Heavens and the Sun have always been regarded as male; as the generators that fructify the Earth and cause it to produce."
[583] Freemasons wearing jewelry and clothing with the square and compass are wearing the symbol for an unholy trinity.
[584] Courtesy of Library of Congress Geography and Map Division in Washington, D.C. The monumental and commercial center of the national capital and the surrounding residential neighborhoods: three dimensional map of central Washington / prepared by Joseph Passonneau & Partners; drawn by Vitaly Gevorkian and David Akopian in 1996. Available online at http://hdl.loc.gov/loc.gmd/g3851a.pm001119.
[585] Teach Peace Foundation 2012 illustration.
[586] Ibid.
[587] Wes Cook, Editor, *Did You Know? Vignettes in Masonry from the Royal Arch Mason Magazine* (Missouri Lodge of Research, 1965), 132.
[588] Ibid.
[589] Ibid., 38.
[590] Dr. Cathy Burns, *Masonic and Occult Symbols Illustrated* (Mt. Carmel, Pennsylvania: Sharing, 1998), 38.
[591] David Ovason, *The Secret Architecture of Our Nation's Capital* (New York, New York: Harper Collins, 1999), viii.
[592] Albert Pike, *Morals and Dogma* (Charleston, South Carolina, 1871), pages 14-15 in the 1950 edition. In Freemasonry a pentagram symbol has a different meaning than a Blazing or Flaming Star, which also includes a five-pointed star shape.
[593] Ibid.
[594] Ibid., 5. Sirius is the brightest star in the night sky. The name is derived from the ancient Greek language meaning "glowing" or "scorcher." Sirius appears to the unassisted eye as one star but is actually two stars, Sirius A and Sirius B.
[595] Pythagoras is credited with this theorem that in any right triangle the area of the square, whose side is the hypotenuse, is equal to the sum of the area of the squares whose sides are the two legs.

[596] Colin F. W. Dyer, *Symbolism in Craft Freemasonry* (Hersham, England: Lewis Masonic, 1976) 34.
[597] Freemasons believe Noah's Flood occurred and Enoch is the source of the Pythagorean equation. The claim is two pillars at Mt. Moriah, called Jachin and Boaz, were created by Enoch. Under these pillars Enoch buried nine hidden vaults stacked on top of each other. The Jachin and Boaz pillars marked the location for the buried vaults. Noah's flood buried the pillars and Pythagoras found one and Hermes found the other. The occult knowledge of the mystery schools is claimed to be derived from these two pillars and the buried vaults.
[598] W. Bro. Ronald Paul NG (an elite Freemason), "Pythagoras," *Lodge Star in the East No. 1600* (GLNF), 19 October 2007 and online at www.freemasons-freemasonry.com/freemasonry_pythagoras.html.
[599] Colin F. W. Dyer, *Symbolism in Craft Freemasonry* (Hersham, England: Lewis Masonic, 1976) 34.
[600] Teach Peace Foundation 2012 drawing.
[601] Christian J. Pinto, *Riddles in Stone - Secret Mysteries of America's Beginnings Volume II: Secret Architecture of Washington, D.C.*, (Lexington, South Carolina: Antiquities Research Films, 2007). Pinto along with Executive Producer David E. Bay and a team of experts created a highly educational documentary which explains many occult symbols in Washington, D.C.
[602] Teach Peace Foundation 2012 drawing.
[603] An example of an incomplete symbol is the inverted pentagram and number 5 shown which is above the White House. The part of the city design that remains to be completed is shown in the diagram with a dotted line.
[604] Said in South Africa in 1966 and engraved on his gravesite memorial at Arlington Cemetery.
[605] Matthew 5:8 explains that a clean or immaculate heart can see God. Faithful devoted to the Blessed Virgin seek to have a clean or immaculate heart.
[606] Saint Anthony of Padua (1195 - 1231). "So simple and resounding was his teaching of the Catholic Faith, so that the most unlettered and innocent might understand it, that he was made a Doctor of the Church by Pope Pius XII in 1946. His great protection against their lies and deceits in the matter of Christian doctrine was to utter, simply and innocently, the Holy Name of Mary. Source: *Catholic Online* at www.catholic.org/saints/saint.php?saint_id=24.
[607] Luke 18:31-33 – "Then Jesus took unto him the twelve, and said to them: Behold, we go up to Jerusalem, and all things shall be accomplished which were written by the prophets concerning the Son of man. For he shall be

delivered to the Gentiles, and shall be mocked, and scourged, and spit upon: And after they have scourged him, they will put him to death; and the third day he shall rise again." Zechariah 9:9 and Zechariah 13:1 are examples of predictions describing Jesus. Zechariah 9:9 – "Rejoice greatly, O daughter of Sion, shout for joy, O daughter of Jerusalem: BEHOLD THY KING will come to thee, the just and saviour: he is poor, and riding upon an ass, and upon a colt the foal of an ass." Zechariah 13:1 – "In that day there shall be a fountain open to the house of David, and to the inhabitants of Jerusalem: for the washing of the sinner, and of the unclean woman."

[608] Daniel 9:27 – "And he shall confirm the covenant with many, in one week: and in the half of the week the victim and the sacrifice shall fall: and there shall be in the temple the abomination of desolation: and the desolation shall continue even to the consummation, and to the end." Also Daniel 11:31 – "And arms shall stand on his part, and they shall defile the sanctuary of strength, and shall take away the continual sacrifice, and they shall place there the abomination unto desolation."

[609] Arnaldo Pomodoro (born 23 June 1926) is an Italian sculptor of occult objects. Additional Pomodoro spheres are at the Indianapolis Christian Theological Seminary, San Francisco's de Young Museum, the Dublin, Ireland Trinity College, the University of California at Berkeley and additional locations explained in *Vigilant Christian III: The Occult Religion of the 9/11 Attackers*.

[610] Arnaldo Pomodoro, November 19, 1999 and recorded in *Sphere Within a Sphere* by the Greater Des Moines Public Art Foundation.

[611] Ibid.

[612] Teach Peace Foundation photograph of the Vatican's "Sphere Within Sphere."

[613] Clark Bentson, "Pope's Exorcist Says the Devil Is In the Vatican," *ABC News*, 11 March 2010.

[614] Luke 21:17-22 – "And you shall be hated by all men for my name's sake. But a hair of your head shall not perish. In your patience you shall possess your souls. And when you shall see Jerusalem compassed about with an army; then know that the desolation thereof is at hand. Then let those who are in Judea, flee to the mountains; and those who are in the midst thereof, depart out: and those who are in the countries, not enter into it. For these are the days of vengeance, that all things may be fulfilled, that are written."

[615] Mark 13:14-16 "And when you shall see the abomination of desolation, standing where it ought not: he that readeth let him understand: then let them that are in Judea, flee unto the mountains: And let him that is on the housetop, not go down into the house, nor enter therein to take any thing out

of the house: And let him that shall be in the field, not turn back to take up his garment."

[616] Matthew 24:15. In Matthew 24:21-35 Jesus also says: "For there shall be then great tribulation, such as hath not been from the beginning of the world until now, neither shall be. And unless those days had been shortened, no flesh should be saved: but for the sake of the elect those days shall be shortened. Then if any man shall say to you: Lo here is Christ, or there, do not believe him. For there shall arise false Christs and false prophets, and shall shew great signs and wonders, insomuch as to deceive (if possible) even the elect. Behold I have told it to you, beforehand."

[617] Teach Peace Foundation 2009 photograph of the Dome of the Rock.

[618] King Antiochus or Antiochus III (c. 241 – 187 BC) was the 6th ruler of the Seleucid Empire. Ancient statues of Zeus show he was represented as a strong man with a beard. The Vatican Sistine Museum has a statue of Zeus and the Sala Rotonda is shaped like a miniature Pantheon.

The sacrificial imperial porphyry granite bowl from the Pantheon in the Vatican Sala Rotonda. Porphyry is from Greek and means "purple." The rock was the hardest known in antiquity. Teach Peace Foundation 2013 photograph.

[619] 1 Maccabees 1:57-58 – "On the fifteenth day of the month Casleu, in the hundred and forty-fifth year, king Antiochus set up the abominable idol of desolation upon the altar of God, and they built altars throughout all the cities of Juda round about: And they burnt incense, and sacrificed at the doors of the houses, and in the streets." This Antiochus or minor Anti-christ abomination of desolation was subsequently destroyed. 1 Maccabees 6:7 – "And that they had thrown down the abomination which he had set up upon

the altar in Jerusalem, and that they had compassed about the sanctuary with high walls as before, and Bethsura also his city."

620 Antiochus III the Great coin photograph. It is noteworthy that some false gods now in the Vatican Museum were once in the Pantheon. An example is Zeus. The statue of his son Hercules is in the Vatican Sala Rotonda. The Fatima prophecy of apostasy in the Vatican could mean Rome is the New Jerusalem or a staging ground for unholy relics that are one day transferred to help create the abomination of desolation in Jerusalem. The statues of the gods that were in the Pantheon were commissioned by Marcus Agrippa between 27 BC - 14 AD.

Helen's porphyry sarcophagus in the Vatican Museum is protected by Egyptian guards.

Teach Peace Foundation 2013 photographs in the Sala a Croce Greca of the Pio-Clementine area, immediately outside the Sala Rotonda room. Shown is the sarcophagus of Flavia Iulia Helena Augusta. Helena (c. 250 - c. 329) was the consort of the Roman emperor Constantius Chlorus and the mother of the emperor Constantine the Great. Helena is an important figure in the history of Christianity. Her role in transferring attention from the eastern region to the western section of Jerusalem as the place of the crucifixion, is cherished by the enemies of Christianity (read Vigilant Christian III: The Occult Religion of the 9/11 Attackers for more information). Helena's porphyry sarcophagus depicts a military triumph scene with slaves being crushed by the boot of their conquerors.

621 Exodus 25:31-40 – "Thou shalt make also a candlestick of beaten work of the finest gold, the shaft thereof, and the branches, the cups, and the bowls, and the lilies going forth from it. Six branches shall come out of the sides, three out of the one side, and three out of the other. Three cups as it were nuts to every branch, and a bowl withal, and a lily; and three cups, likewise of the fashion of nuts in the other branch, and a bowl withal, and a lily. Such

shall be the work of the six branches, that are to come out from the shaft: And in the candlestick itself shall be four cups in the manner of a nut, and at every one, bowls and lilies. Bowls under two branches in three places, which together make six coming forth out of one shaft. And both the bowls and the branches shall be of the same beaten work of the purest gold. Thou shalt make also seven lamps, and shalt set them upon the candlestick, to give light over against. The snuffers also and where the snuffings shall be put out, shall be made of the purest gold. The whole weight of the candlestick with all the furniture thereof shall be a talent of the purest gold.".

[622] The temple six oil lampstand menorah is different than the Hanukkah nine candle menorah. The temple golden lampstand originates with Moses. Hanukkah took place much later and about 170 years before Jesus was born. Hanukkah is to remember God's supernatural intervention resulting in the Jewish victory over the army of Antiochus. Hanukkah also serves to remember God's miracle of the temple lights burning for eight days with a supply of oil for one day.

[623] Teach Peace Foundation 2009 photograph showing David Dionisi standing in front of the golden menorah to be installed in the temple Holy Place. Oddly, the text on the sign that millions of people read when visiting Jerusalem has English errors. A photo below helps show where "Sanctury, is" should be "Sanctuary, it."

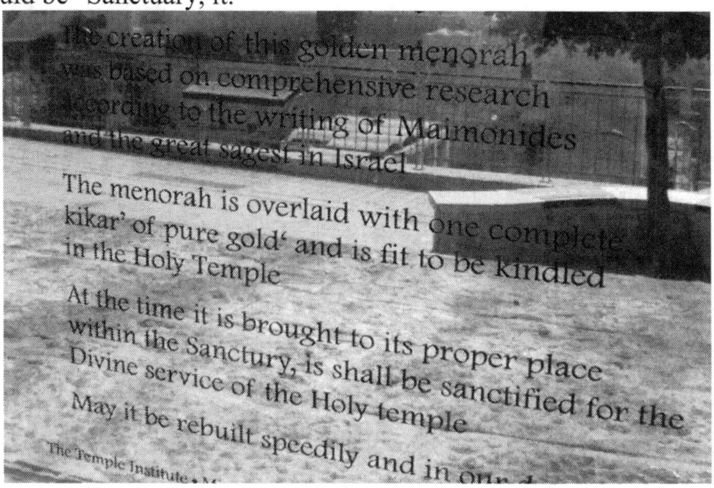

For easier reading the text is provided. "The creation of this golden menorah was based on comprehensive research according to the writings of Maimonides and the great sagest in Israel. This menorah is overlaid with one complete kikar of pure gold and is fit to be kindled in the Holy Temple. At the time it is brought to its proper place within the Sanctury, it shall be sanctified for the Divine service of the Holy temple. May it be rebuilt speedily and in our days."

[624] Daniel 2:36-45 – "This is the dream: we will also tell the interpretation thereof before thee, O king. Thou art a king of kings: and the God of heaven hath given thee a kingdom, and strength, and power, and glory: And all places wherein the children of men, and the beasts of the field do dwell: he hath also given the birds of the air into thy hand, and hath put all things under thy power: thou therefore art the head of gold. And after thee shall rise up another kingdom, inferior to thee, of silver: and another third kingdom of brass, which shall rule over all the world. And the fourth kingdom shall be as iron. As iron breaketh into pieces, and subdueth all things, so shall that break and destroy all these. And whereas thou sawest the feet, and the toes, part of potter's clay, and part of iron: the kingdom shall be divided, but yet it shall take its origin from the iron, according as thou sawest the iron mixed with the miry clay. And as the toes of the feet were part of iron, and part of clay, the kingdom shall be partly strong, and partly broken. And whereas thou sawest the iron mixed with miry clay, they shall be mingled indeed together with the seed of man, but they shall not stick fast one to another, as iron cannot be mixed with clay. But in the days of those kingdoms the God of heaven will set up a kingdom that shall never be destroyed, and his kingdom shall not be delivered up to another people, and it shall break in pieces, and shall consume all these kingdoms, and itself shall stand for ever. According as thou sawest that the stone was cut out of the mountain without hands, and broke in pieces, the clay, and the iron, and the brass, and the silver, and the gold, the great God hath shewn the king what shall come to pass hereafter, and the dream is true, and the interpretation thereof is faithful."

[625] "Pope Francis Predicts Short Papacy, Announces Jubilee Year Of Mercy," *Associated Press*, 13 March 2015 and online at www.huffingtonpost.com/2015/03/13/pope-francis-short-papacy-pizza_n_6864994.htmlPope Francis said he did not expect to be the Pope for many years. He said: "I have the sensation that my pontificate will be brief: Four or five years."

[626] December 8, 2015 is the feast of the Immaculate Conception and the Holy Year of Mercy Jubilee ends on November 20, 2016 which is the feast of Christ the King. More information about the Holy Year of Mercy is online at http://ncronline.org/news/vatican/francis-announces-new-global-jubilee-holy-year-mercy.

[627] This interpretation views the Jubilee cannot resume without the Sanhedrin which ceased with the destruction of the second temple in 70 AD. The Christian understanding is the Sanhedrin ceased to be the leadership of

God's law on earth before or upon the birth of Jesus. As a result, the Sanhedrin was not needed for the Jubilee law to resume.
[628] If the Jubilee were honored, all debts would be eliminated. Leviticus 25:8-17 – "Thou shalt also number to thee seven weeks of years, that is to say, seven times seven, which together make forty-nine years: And thou shalt sound the trumpet in the seventh month, the tenth day of the month, in the time of the expiation in all your land. And thou shalt sanctify the fiftieth year, and shalt proclaim remission to all the inhabitants of thy land: for it is the year of jubilee. Every man shall return to his possession, and every one shall go back to his former family: Because it is the jubilee and the fiftieth year. You shall not sow, nor reap the things that grow in the field of their own accord, neither shall you gather the first fruits of the vines, Because of the sanctification of the jubilee: but as they grow you shall presently eat them. In the year of the jubilee all shall return to their possessions. When thou shalt sell any thing to thy neighbour, or shalt buy of him; grieve not thy brother: but thou shalt buy of him according to the number of years from the jubilee. And he shall sell to thee according to the computation of the fruits. The more years remain after the jubilee, the more shall the price increase: and the less time is counted, so much the less shall the purchase cost. For he shall sell to thee the time of the fruits. Do not afflict your countrymen, but let every one fear his God: because I am the Lord your God." The Jubilee was to be observed after seven cycles of seven years and the 50th was a time of celebration. During the Jubilee both the land and the people had rest.
[629] Matthew 24:29 and Joel 2:10 also explain the moon will be darkened. Matthew 24:29 – "And immediately after the tribulation of those days, the sun shall be darkened and the moon shall not give her light, and the stars shall fall from heaven, and the powers of heaven shall be moved:" Joel 2:10 – "At their presence the earth hath trembled, the heavens are moved: the sun and moon are darkened, and the stars have withdrawn their shining."
[630] Teach Peace Foundation 2012 drawing.
[631] Corrections will be online at www.teachpeace.com/corrections.htm.
[632] Additional details about the new edition book offer are online at www.teachpeace.com/neweditionoffer.htm.
[633] Ezekiel 18:13 – "That giveth upon usury, and that taketh an increase: shall such a one live? he shall not live. Seeing he hath done all these detestable things, he shall surely die, his blood shall be upon him." Ezekiel 18:17 – "That hath turned away his hand from injuring the poor, hath not taken usury and increase, but hath executed my judgments, and hath walked in my commandments: this man shall not die for the iniquity of his father, but living he shall live."
[634] Exodus 22:25 – "If thou lend money to any of my people that is poor, that dwelleth with thee, thou shalt not be hard upon them as an extortioner, nor

oppress them with usuries." Leviticus 25:36-37 – "Take not usury of him nor more than thou gavest: fear thy God, that thy brother may live with thee. Thou shalt not give him thy money upon usury, nor exact of him any increase of fruits." Deuteronomy 23:19-20 – "Thou shalt not lend to thy brother money to usury, nor corn, nor any other thing: But to the stranger. To thy brother thou shalt lend that which he wanteth, without usury: that the Lord thy God may bless thee in all thy works in the land, which thou shalt go in to possess."

[635] Part of the answer lies in the fact that loans for business purposes seeking to make a profit were treated differently than loans for basic needs such as food, clothing, and going to school. Matthew 25:27 – "Thou oughtest therefore to have committed my money to the bankers, and at my coming I should have received my own with usury." The parable is not advocating Christians should charge interest or compromise by doing business with thieves but is about donating to help promote God's word.

[636] Isaiah 61:1-2 – "The spirit of the Lord is upon me, because the Lord hath anointed me: he hath sent me to preach to the meek, to heal the contrite of heart, and to preach a release to the captives, and deliverance to them that are shut up. To proclaim the acceptable year of the Lord, and the day of vengeance of our God: to comfort all that mourn:"

[637] Matthew 6:12 – "And forgive us our debts, as we also forgive our debtors."

[638] Luke 16:9 – "And I say to you: Make unto you friends of the mammon of iniquity; that when you shall fail, they may receive you into everlasting dwellings."

[639] Leviticus 25:10 – "And thou shalt sanctify the fiftieth year, and shalt proclaim remission to all the inhabitants of thy land: for it is the year of jubilee. Every man shall return to his possession, and every one shall go back to his former family:"

[640] Luke 6:27 – "But I say to you that hear: Love your enemies, do good to them that hate you." Mark 11:25 – "And when you shall stand to pray, forgive, if you have aught against any man; that your Father also, who is in heaven, may forgive you your sins." Exodus 13:5 – " If thou see the ass of him that hateth thee lie underneath his burden, thou shalt not pass by, but shalt lift him up with him." Acts 7:59 – " And falling on his knees, he cried with a loud voice, saying: Lord, lay not this sin to their charge. And when he had said this, he fell asleep in the Lord. And Saul was consenting to his death." Ephesians 4:32 – " And be ye kind one to another; merciful, forgiving one another, even as God hath forgiven you in Christ."

[641] Matthew 15:14 – "And if the blind lead the blind, both will fall into the pit."

---

[642] Jesus did not know the exact time or hour because Satan and demons are able to read the thoughts of humans. Since Jesus was fully human and fully God, Jesus did not possess all the knowledge of His Father.
[643] Matthew 24:36 – "But of that day and hour no one knoweth, not the angels of heaven, but the Father alone." Mark 13:32 – "But of that day or hour no man knoweth, neither the angels in heaven, nor the Son, but the Father."
[644] *Akita and the Fatima Secret* is a 2015 Teach Peace Foundation film and available online at www.teachpeace.com.
[645] The tradition of Holy Years started in 1300 under the reign of Pope Boniface VIII. Since then, the Catholic Church has celebrated 26 jubilees. Of those, only three have been "extraordinary." On April 6, 2016 multiple reports surfaced of a May 2014 event Pope Francis understood to be prophetic (e.g., "Rome Reports" online at www.romereports.com/2016/04/06/.vatileaks-2-vallejo-balda-s-accomplice-denies-having-leaked-documents and Angus MacKinnon, Vatican City (AFP) online at www.yahoo.com/news/did-not-sex-priest-vatican-leaks-trial-told-194848548.html).
[646] John L. Allen Jr., "Apocalyptic beliefs may explain why Francis is a pope in a hurry," Crux, January 25, 2015 and online at www.cruxnow.com/church/2015/01/25/apocalyptic-beliefs-may-explain-why-francis-is-a-pope-in-a-hurry/.
[647] AFP and other news services reported on August 18, 2014 that Pope Francis said he expects to only live two or three more years (see www.yahoo.com/news/god-two-three-more-years-says-pope-001955943.html).
[648] Catholic Online, "Pope Francis: World War III has begun - Third Secret of Fatima gives warning," November 19, 2015 and online at www.catholic.org/news/hf/faith/story.php?id=65403.
William Tindall, Standard History of the City of Washington from a Study of the Original Sources (Knoxville, Tennessee: H. W. Crew and Co., 1914, 18).
[649] Every time totalitarian rule has been attempted throughout history, it has failed. Examples include Lenin, Stalin, Hitler, and Mao. More distant examples are Nimrod, Nebuchadnezzar, Genghis Khan, Alexander the Great, the Caesars, Ivan the Terrible, Charlemagne, and Napoleon.
[650] The Council of Europe was created on May 5, 1949 when the Treaty of London was signed by ten European countries. Strasbourg was selected as the headquarters. The European Union was conceived by the Brotherhood in secret at a chateau near Brussels. The European Union was officially created by the 1957 Treaty of Rome. In 2012 the Brotherhood awarded the European Union the Nobel Peace Prize. For more information read the article by

Balazs Korany and Victoria Klesty, "European Union wins Nobel Peace Prize," published by *Reuters* on October 12, 2012.
[651] Teach Peace Foundation drawing.
[652] Ibid. The poster drawing has stars pointing down which symbolized a world ruled by Satan.
[653] The photograph is courtesy of France-based AS.Architecture-Studio agency which designed the European Parliament.
[654] Elisabeth Kübler-Ross, *On Death and Dying: What the dying have to teach to doctors, nurses, clergy, and their own families* (New York, New York: Scribner, 1969). The five stages of grief in the Kübler-Ross model are emotional stages experienced when faced with a major change. Kübler-Ross was influenced by her work with terminally ill patients and as a result focused on the impending death or death of a person. The model is not meant to be a complete list of emotions but a framework to understand how some people process new information.
[655] For purposes of comparison to the Contemporary English Version of Corinthians 13:1-8, the Douay-Rheims 1899 version follows: "If I speak with the tongues of men, and of angels, and have not charity, I am become as sounding brass, or a tinkling cymbal. And if I should have prophecy and should know all mysteries, and all knowledge, and if I should have all faith, so that I could remove mountains, and have not charity, I am nothing. And if I should distribute all my goods to feed the poor, and if I should deliver my body to be burned, and have not charity, it profiteth me nothing. Charity is patient, is kind: charity envieth not, dealeth not perversely; is not puffed up; Is not ambitious, seeketh not her own, is not provoked to anger, thinketh no evil; Rejoiceth not in iniquity, but rejoiceth with the truth; Beareth all things, believeth all things, hopeth all things, endureth all things. Charity never falleth away: whether prophecies shall be made void, or tongues shall cease, or knowledge shall be destroyed."
[656] Changes starting in the 1960s, using Vatican II as the authority, started to have people turn their backs to Christ. Time bombs were placed in the liturgy and some Church leaders increasingly made compromises with the Brotherhood of Death.
[657] Fr. Martin Malachi recommended saying: "O creature of God, in the name of the God who created you, and in the name of Jesus who saved me, I exercise you." At 42:05-28 this statement is online at www.youtube.com/watch?v=XlOMNHG6zVE
[658]Malachi Martin is one person who read the secret in 1960 and disclosed the Fatima message warned of a third world war and something even worse (e.g., most Catholics were going to hell). Martin was the personal secretary to Cardinal Bea knew John XXIII well. While traveling together in a car the

Pope gave Martin the one page secret which he immediately read. While Martin never broke his secrecy oath, he did confirm yes or no if presented with part or all of the Fatima message.

[659]William Guy Carr, R.D., *Pawns in the Game* (Willowdale, Ontario, Canada: Federation of Christian Layman, 1954), xv.

[660] Ibid.

[661] The original excerpt is "During world war two" and this was changed to "During World War Two" so as to not distract the reader.

[662] Ibid.

[663] "How Old is Your Church" is compiled courtesy of the *Eternal Word Television Network* or *EWTN*. The Most Holy Family Monastery in Fillmore, New York also provides a version of this information.

[664] The Fatima timeline is online at www.fatima.org/f4b/complete_fatima_ timeline.pdf. Modifications are made and provide additional developments.

[665] The Fatima timeline is online at www.fatima.org/f4b/complete_fatima_ timeline.pdf. Modifications are made and provide additional developments.

[666] John De Marchi, *The Immaculate Heart: The True Story of Our Lady of Fatima* (New York: Farrar, Straus and Young, 1952), 87.

[667] For more information about Pope Leo XIII's 1884 encyclical titled Humanum Genus, read Chapter 2.

[668] Antonio Gaspari, "Pius XII Saw "Miracle of the Sun," *ZENIT*, 4 November 2008 and online at www.zenit.org/en/articles/pius-xii-saw-miracle-of-the-sun.

[669] Saverio Gaeta, *The Madonna is Among Us. Here is the Proof* or *La Madonna e tra noi. Ecco le prove* (Milan, Italy: Piemme: 2003), volume II, 247.

[670] Stalin's end of carnage is a blessing and a reminder that if we live by the sword we die by the sword. Matthew 26:52 – "Then Jesus saith to him: Put up again thy sword into its place: for all that take the sword shall perish with the sword." Stalin killed many people and may have been assassinated by a Brotherhood of Death member. The 2004 book by Jonathan Brent and Vladimir Naumovr, *Stalin's Last Crime: The Plot Against the Jewish Doctors, 1948–1953* (HarperCollins), explains Stalin was poisoned. Specifically, Beria, with the complicity of Khrushchev, slipped warfarin into Stalin's wine either on evening of February 28th or after midnight on March 1, 1953.

[671] The evidence for an imposter Sister Lucia is overwhelming and a DNA test should be conducted. Intelligence officers are familiar with the deception of inserting a double or an imposter. Given the Fatima message threat to the kingdom of Satan, inserting an imposter and keeping the real Sister Lucia alive only as long as necessary is a possibility. People who are quick to dismiss this possibility are reminded that when a person is

imprisoned, they can speak with family and send letters for decades because they are carefully managed. This person can make carefully controlled appearances while the imposter simultaneously serves the Brotherhood. This hard to imagine scenario of two people with the same identity would explain why Sister Lucia's physical appearance differed, why she was gagged by Vatican officials, and why she was carefully managed until the day she died. On April 5, 2006, Fatima researcher Marian Horvat, Ph.D. published the article "Two Sister Lucys of Fatima?" He analyzed photographs of Sister Lucia and the evidence that he provides is not easily dismissed. Photographs showing the change in appearance are shown below.

Sister Lucia before being isolated   Sister Lucia after isolation

The teeth and U shape of Sister Lucia smiling before her appearance changed is shown on the left. On the right is the Sister Lucia the Vatican kept isolated. The Servants of the Holy Family had a company that shows age progression produce what Sister Lucia should have looked like in her senior years. The result is the image on the below left.

More information is available from The Servants of the Holy Family and online at www.servi.org/Sister_Lucy_Experiment.
[672] Concerns about Sister Lucia's appearance changing lessened after she asked Pope Paul VI to release the Secret. If she was an imposter, then her request to the Pope might have designed to silence concerns that she was an imposter.
[673] Sister Lucia's actions serve to suppress concerns that she is not the real Lucia.
[674] The same remarks were reported in L'Osservatore Romano on March 26-27, on page 6 (Italian edition).
[675] Adam Taylor, "Everyone In Moscow Is Starting To Freak Out About Vladimir Putin's Health," *Business Insider*, 1 November 2012 and online at www.businessinsider.com/putin-health-problems-2012-11.
[676] Fr. Paul Kramer (editor and compiler), *The Devil's Final Battle: Our Lady's Victory Edition* (Terryville, Connecticut: The Missionary Association, 2010 Second Edition).
[677] Caleb Bell with assistance from Alessandro Speciale, "Why the first Jesuit pope is a big deal," Religion News Service, 20 March 2013 and online at www.pcusa.org/news/2013/3/20/why-first-jesuit-pope-big-deal/. The article highlights that "Jesuits are bound by oath not to seek higher office in the Roman Catholic Church, and now one of them has been elected to its highest office: Bishop of Rome, Vicar of Christ, Pontifex Maximus."
[678] A video showing the quoted statement is titled "Putin requests the Consecration of Russia!" and is online at www.youtube.com/watch?v=-QmRyAJfJBg. The article "Putin and Pope Francis's first meeting focuses on Christians' plight in Mideast" by *RT* provides more information and is online at http://rt.com/news/putin-pope-christians-east-274/. The Associated Press related article " Putin shows faith in visit to Vatican" is online at www.bostonglobe.com/news/world/2013/11/26/putin-shows-faith-visit-vatican/dUSbTki3nQi7jtNxyn2jtJ/story.html.

[679] On September 13, 2014 the *BBC* reported "Pope Francis warns on piecemeal World War III." Pope Francis made this warning at Italy's World War I Redipuglia memorial altar. This article is online at www.bbc.com/news/world-europe-29190890.
John Vennari, "Pope Francis Warns 'Piecemeal' World War III Has Begun," *Fatima Network Essentials*, 17 September 2014 and online at www.fatima.org/news/newsviews/newsviews091714.asp.

[680] "Pope Francis Predicts Short Papacy, Announces Jubilee Year Of Mercy," *Associated Press*, 13 March 2015 and online at www.huffingtonpost.com/2015/03/13/pope-francis-short-papacy-pizza_n_6864994.html. Pope Francis said he did not expect to be the Pope for many years. He said: "I have the sensation that my pontificate will be brief: Four or five years."

[681] "Pope Francis Predicts Short Papacy, Announces Jubilee Year Of Mercy," *Associated Press*, 13 March 2015 and online at www.huffingtonpost.com/2015/03/13/pope-francis-short-papacy-pizza_n_6864994.html. Pope Francis said he did not expect to be the Pope for many years. He said: "I have the sensation that my pontificate will be brief: Four or five years."